NEW STUDIES IN BIBLICAL THEOLOGY 59

FROM PRISONER
TO PRINCE

NEW STUDIES IN BIBLICAL THEOLOGY 59

Series editor: D. A. Carson

FROM PRISONER TO PRINCE

The Joseph story in biblical theology

Samuel Emadi

APOLLOS

Academic

An imprint of InterVarsity Press
Downers Grove, Illinois

APOLLOS (an imprint of Inter-Varsity Press, England)
36 Causton Street, London SW1P 4ST, England
Website: www.ivpbooks.com
Email: ivp@ivpbooks.com

InterVarsity Press, USA
P.O. Box 1400, Downers Grove, IL 60515, USA
Website: www.ivpress.com
Email: email@ivpress.com

Inter-Varsity Press, England, publishes Christian books that are true to the Bible and that
communicate the gospel, develop discipleship and strengthen the church for its mission in the world.

IVP originated within the Inter-Varsity Fellowship, now the Universities and Colleges Christian
Fellowship, a student movement connecting Christian Unions in universities and colleges
throughout Great Britain, and a member movement of the International Fellowship of Evangelical
Students. That historic association is maintained, and all senior IVP staff and committee members
subscribe to the UCCF Basis of Faith. Website: www.uccf.org.uk.

InterVarsity Press®, USA, is the book-publishing division of InterVarsity Christian Fellowship/USA®
and a member movement of the International Fellowship of Evangelical Students.
Website: www.intervarsity.org.

Unless otherwise indicated, Scripture quotations are taken from the ESV Bible (The Holy Bible,
English Standard Version, Anglicized edition), copyright c 2001 by Crossway, a publishing ministry
of Good News Publishers. Used by permission. All rights reserved.

First published 2022

Set in 10/13.25pt Minion Pro and Gill Sans Nova
Typeset in Great Britain by CRB Associates, Potterhanworth, Lincolnshire
Printed and bound in Great Britain by Ashford Colour Press Ltd, Gosport, Hampshire

Printed on paper from sustainable sources.

UK ISBN: 978-1-78974-393-7 (print)
UK ISBN: 978-1-78974-394-4 (digital)

US ISBN: 978-1-5140-0546-0 (print)
US ISBN: 978-1-5140-0547-7 (digital)

British Library Cataloguing-in-Publication Data
A catalogue record for this book is available from the British Library.

Library of Congress Cataloging-in-Publication Data
A catalog record for this book is available from the Library of Congress.

Contents

Series preface   vii
Author's preface   ix
Abbreviations   xiii

1 Introduction   **1**
Thesis   4
Joseph in canonical context in pre-modern Christian literature   5
Modern scholarship on Joseph's significance in Genesis   7
The use of the Joseph narrative in later Scripture   11
Joseph as a type of Christ in modern scholarship   13
Preview of the argument   16

2 Biblical theology and typology   **19**
Defining biblical theology   19
Defining typology   20

3 The Joseph story in Genesis' *tôlĕdôt* structure   **31**
Function of the *tôlĕdôt* formula: tracing God's promise
    through each generation   33
The *tôlĕdôt* structure and the story of Joseph   36

4 Joseph and covenant: kingship   **39**
Introducing Joseph and Genesis 37 – 50   39
Joseph in biblical-theological perspective   43
Royal seed: primeval types and promises   44
Royal seed: Abrahamic types and promises   47
Joseph: Abraham's royal seed   51
Joseph and Judah: present and future royal seed   57

5 Joseph and covenant: seed   **65**
The 'seed' theme in Genesis   65
Preservation and proliferation   67
Seed conflict and sibling rivalry   78

6 Joseph and covenant: land and blessing 83

The land theme in Genesis 83

The Promised Land in the story of Joseph 84

Blessing in Genesis 88

Blessing in the Joseph story 89

Other possibly significant biblical-theological features
of the Joseph story 93

Suffering, glory and the promise-keeping God:
synthesizing the major themes of the Joseph story 95

Implications for a canonical understanding
of the Joseph narrative 99

7 Joseph in the Old Testament 101

Joseph and the exodus 101

Joseph in Psalm 105 103

Joseph and Daniel 108

The exalted Jew in a foreign court 115

Implications for a canonical understanding
of the Joseph narrative 120

8 Joseph in the New Testament 121

Joseph in Acts 7 121

Joseph in Hebrews 11 137

Allusions to the Joseph story in the parable of the tenants 139

Implications for a canonical understanding
of the Joseph narrative 145

9 Conclusion 147

Bibliography 150

Index of authors 179

Index of Scripture references 000

Series preface

New Studies in Biblical Theology is a series of monographs that address
key issues in the discipline of biblical theology. Contributions to the
series focus on one or more of three areas: (1) the nature and status
of biblical theology, including its relations with other disciplines (e.g.
historical theology, exegesis, systematic theology, historical criticism,
narrative theology); (2) the articulation and exposition of the structure
of thought of a particular biblical writer or corpus; and (3) the delinea-
tion of a biblical theme across all or part of the biblical corpora.

Above all, these monographs are creative attempts to help thinking
Christians understand their Bibles better. The series aims simultaneously to instruct and to edify, to interact with the current literature
and to point the way ahead. In God's universe, mind and heart should
not be divorced: in this series we will try not to separate what God has
joined together. While the notes interact with the best of scholarly literature, the text is uncluttered with untransliterated Greek and Hebrew,
and tries to avoid too much technical jargon. The volumes are written
within the framework of confessional evangelicalism, but there is always
an attempt at thoughtful engagement with the sweep of the relevant
literature.

In the convoluted annals of debates over the nature – indeed, over the
very existence – of typology, no biblical figure has generated more con-
troversy than Joseph. Until the onset of the more sceptical forms of 'higher
criticism' about two hundred years ago, most pastors and theologians
believed that Joseph prefigured the Messiah in some way or other. Today
it is much more common to dismiss such claims. Attempts to defend the
more traditional view have, by and large, not proved very convincing. So
this book by Dr Sam Emadi meets a great need. Immensely readable
despite its voluminous notes, Emadi's study carefully works through the
role of Joseph within Genesis, then his role within the Old Testament
canon, before exploring the subtle but undeniable appeal to the Joseph
narrative taken up by several New Testament writers. Dr Emadi's case
is cautious, understated, but interlocking and cumulative, and, finally,

convincing. This book is destined to generate both scholarly discussion and better biblical-theological sermons.

D. A. Carson
Trinity Evangelical Divinity School

Author's preface

Opportunities for formal gratitude to those who have cared for and loved us so well are regrettably infrequent. All the good in my life is a result of God's grace and kindness, and God has mediated much of that grace and kindness through his people. I am deeply aware of the countless resources that others have invested in me – a debt I can never repay.

This book is an edited version of the dissertation I wrote as a doctoral student at the Southern Baptist Theological Seminary. I owe an enormous debt of gratitude to the faculty there – particularly professors Tom Schreiner, Peter Gentry, Steve Wellum and Jim Hamilton. Tom Schreiner represents everything I aspire to be. His careful exegesis and theological acumen are surpassed only by his godliness and unrelenting joy. Peter Gentry instilled in me a deep love for the original languages and is a model of a true biblical scholar. I hope, for the rest of my life, to follow Dr Gentry's example and 'bury myself in a lexicon and arise in the presence of God'.

During my time at SBTS, I had more classes with Steve Wellum than with any other professor. Dr Wellum's rigorous theological method will forever shape the way I read Scripture and do theology. Finally, I am tremendously grateful for my friend, mentor and *Bible Talk* podcast co-host Jim Hamilton. Jim encouraged me every step of the way during this 'ambitious' project. His careful feedback, criticisms and corrections have proved invaluable. His love for Scripture and for the glory of God is infectious and his passion for personal holiness is evident.

Jack Brannen carefully read every word of this book multiple times and provided invaluable suggestions on style and structure. This book would not be nearly as interesting or as readable without Jack's keen editorial eye and incessant demand for clarity. If any sentence in this book is poorly written, it is likely due to the fact that I ignored Jack's suggestions to my own detriment.

Jon Pentecost has been a true friend and brother in the Lord. His commitment to local church health and congregational living ignites in my heart a deep desire to love the bride of Christ more each day.

Bobby Jamieson's theological and personal influence on me during the last decade has been incalculable. I have learned a great deal about theology, discipleship and academic faithfulness from Bobby. He steeled my resolve against theological liberalism when I most needed it. I will be forever grateful for his friendship. David Schrock taught me how to walk faithfully through trials, all the while modelling how to be a true pastor-theologian. Aubrey Sequeira, Matt Smethurst, Jamie Southcombe, Nick Dorsey, Ryan Troglin, Jon Swan, Colin Smothers and Matt Tyler have made my life and ministry a delight. I do not deserve such godly, faithful friends. I have benefited from them far more than they will ever benefit from me.

I cannot express enough gratitude to my dear friends and mentors at 9Marks. Jonathan Leeman, a man who truly fears God, has loved and discipled me in every conversation I have had with him over the last five years. I aspire to live up to his example of faithfulness to Christ and love for the local church. Alex Duke's infectious joy, love for the church and relentless happiness in the good of others spurs me on to reflect Christ's love better. Ryan Townsend has been the greatest, most generous boss. Ryan understands how to wield authority for the good of others – I am one of the many beneficiaries of his care. Alberto Jaquez and Drew Allenspach are godly brothers who also encouraged me and made each day with 9Marks a delightful one. Finally, I cannot express enough gratitude to Mark Dever. He is a great man, a great pastor and a true father in the faith.

I wrote this book as an act of love for Christ's church and with hope that it will help pastors preach Genesis 37 – 50 faithfully. I am deeply committed to the notion that biblical scholarship, in order to be truly faithful, must be done in service of the church and in submission to church authority. Much of this book was written while I was a member at Third Avenue Baptist Church. I am grateful to that congregation for watching over my soul and to the elders who served there in that time and cared for me so well: Greg Gilbert, Ben Birkholz, Bruce Kiesling, Allison Arruda, Joshua Dove, Matt Smethurst, Scott Croft and Josh. Morell.

I now serve as the senior pastor of Hunsinger Lane Baptist Church alongside three godly elders: Gary Milby, Kip Selby and Casey Groover. These men are constant sources of encouragement in my life. It is a privilege to serve the sheep at Hunsinger Lane at their side.

I would also like to thank D. A. Carson for accepting this manuscript into the NSBT series and for his feedback and guidance throughout this process. Dr Carson's books have been influencing me since high school, as has the NSBT series. It's a joy to contribute to a series with so many other volumes that have a had a profound influence on my understanding of how the Bible fits together.

Many diligent and careful editors at IVP have assisted me throughout this project. Philip Duce and Eldo Barkhuizen deserve particular mention. Their contributions to this manuscript have made it far more accurate and readable.

I'd also like to thank Brock Bittner, a faithful brother in Christ, who spent hours helping me insert edits into the manuscript, track down sources and prepare transliterated text.

God's greatest earthly gift to me has been my family. I had the unspeakable privilege of growing up in a home with parents who loved Jesus and modelled Christian maturity. My father, Saeed, is a man of great integrity, generosity and exemplary Christian character. I would be nothing without his influence. Whatever is of value in this book is a product of his faithful parenting and loving support. My mother, Theresa, is one of the most generous and faithful Christians I have ever met. Her love for the Bible is outmatched only by her willingness to serve others. I will never forget the hundreds of hours she spent working through theological issues with me in high school and college. Without my parents' financial support, I would not have been able to receive a theological education. Again, whatever is of value in this book is a credit to them.

My brothers, Matthew and Michael, also deserve special commendation. I had the privilege of going through seminary (MDiv and PhD) with Matthew. Our countless hours of discussing theology and reading Greek and Hebrew have had an impact on me that I could not begin to measure. Also, Michael has encouraged me along the way while writing this book and has lent his expertise on discourse grammar at critical moments. I am tremendously thankful for their lives, their ministries and their families.

My wife's family has also served me in significant ways in this writing project. My father-in-law and mother-in-law, Don and Mitzi James (AKA Papaw and Nami), have helped me in innumerable ways – from babysitting to fixing plumbing issues in our home. This book simply could not have been written without their loving support every step of the way. The same is true with regard to my brothers-in-law, Samuel James and Dan Maketansky, and my sisters-in-law, Emily James and Rebecca Maketansky. Their presence in my life has been a constant source of joy.

My wife, Corrie Ann, deserves more praise than these pages allow. She has been a supportive, loving wife and a true companion and friend. I cannot even begin to number the ways she has served me and spurred me on to love and good works. I cannot imagine life without her. She constantly encourages me, by both word and example, to be a more faithful follower of Jesus. She is a rare woman of great wisdom, patience and godliness. Corrie Ann, you are my greatest earthly treasure. I hope one day to love Jesus as much as you do.

Our children, Cyrus, Carson, Leighton and Lincoln, have brought much joy to my life. Kids, I could not imagine writing this book without you. I love every second we spend playing together. Every moment I spent working on this book, I would have rather spent with you. Thank you for putting up with my failures, having a forgiving spirit and bringing so much joy and laughter to our home. May God give each of you hearts that love Jesus, his church and God's glory above anything else this life has to offer.

Finally, I wish to thank the triune God who sovereignly planned, accomplished and applied his saving work to me. I do not deserve God's grace and kindness. I do not deserve his mercy. I do not deserve to read the Bible, let alone study it. I owe everything that I am to the sovereign grace of God. May this work bring glory and honour to him who delivered his Son over for my sins and raised him from the dead for my justification. My great hope is that whoever reads these pages will know and love more fully the true and better Joseph – Jesus Christ, my only hope in life and in death.

Sam Emadi

Abbreviations

1QS	*Serek Hayaÿad* or *Rule of the Community*
AB	Anchor Bible
ABD	*Anchor Bible Dictionary*, ed. D. N. Freedman, 6 vols., New Haven: Yale University Press, 1992
ABRL	Anchor Bible Reference Library
ACCS	Ancient Christian Commentary on Scripture
AnBib	Analecta biblica
ANE	ancient Near East(ern)
ANET	*Ancient Near Eastern Texts Relating to the Old Testament*, ed. J. B. Pritchard, 3rd edn with supplement, Princeton: Princeton University Press, 1969
ANTZ	Arbeiten zur neutestamentlichen Theologie und Zeitgeschichte
AOTC	Apollos Old Testament Commentary
Aram.	Aramaic
ARM	*Archives royales de Mari*
AS	*Aramaic Studies*
AUSDDS	Andrews University Seminary Doctoral Dissertation Series
AUSS	*Andrews University Seminary Studies*
BBR	*Bulletin for Biblical Research*
BECNT	Baker Exegetical Commentary on the New Testament
BETL	Bibliotheca ephemeridum theologicarum lovaniensium
BHS	*Biblia Hebraica Stuttgartensia*, ed. K. Elliger and W. Rudoph, Stuttgart: Deutsche Bibelgesellschaft, 1967–77
Bib	*Biblica*
BibInt	*Biblical Interpretation*
BSac	*Bibliotheca sacra*
BRev	*Bible Review*
BST	The Bible Speaks Today
BTB	*Biblical Theology Bulletin*

BTCB	Brazos Theological Commentary on the Bible
BTCP	Biblical Theology of Christian Proclamation
BYU	Brigham Young University
BZ	*Biblische Zeitschrift*
CBQ	*Catholic Biblical Quarterly*
CBQMS	Catholic Biblical Quarterly Monograph Series
CBR	*Currents in Biblical Research*
CC	Calvin's Commentaries
CTJ	*Calvin Theological Journal*
CTR	*Criswell Theological Review*
DOTP	*Dictionary of the Old Testament Pentateuch*, ed. T. D. Alexander and D. Baker, Leicester: Inter-Varsity Press; Downers Grove: InterVarsity Press, 2003
EDBT	*Evangelical Dictionary of Biblical Theology*, ed. W. A. Elwell, Grand Rapids: Baker, 1996
EJ	Encyclopaedia Judaica
ESEC	Emory Studies in Early Christianity
ETL	*Ephemerides theologicae lovanienses*
EvQ	*Evangelical Quarterly*
ExpTim	*Expository Times*
FAT	Forschungen zum Alten Testament
FRLANT	Forschungen zur Religion und Literatur des Alten und Neuen Testaments
HBT	*Horizons in Biblical Theology*
Hebr.	Hebrew
HDR	Harvard Dissertations in Religion
HSMM	Harvard Semitic Museum Monographs
HTKNT	Herders theologischer Kommentar zum Neuen Testament
ICC	International Critical Commentary
Int	*Interpretation*
JBL	*Journal of Biblical Literature*
JBLMS	Journal of Biblical Literature Monograph Series
JBQ	*Jewish Bible Quarterly*
JETS	*Journal of the Evangelical Theological Society*
JSNT	*Journal for the Study of the New Testament*
JSNTSup	Journal for the Study of the New Testament Supplement Series

JSOT	*Journal for the Study of the Old Testament*
JSOTSup	Journal for the Study of the Old Testament Supplement Series
JSP	*Journal for the Study of the Pseudepigrapha*
JTI	*Journal of Theological Interpretation*
JTS	*Journal of Theological Studies*
LHBOTS	Library of Hebrew Bible/Old Testament Studies
LNTS	Library of New Testament Studies
LTJ	*Lutheran Theological Journal*
LXX	Septuagint
m.	masculine
MTh	*Modern Theology*
NAC	New American Commentary
NCBC	New Cambridge Bible Commentary
NDBT	*New Dictionary of Biblical Theology*, ed. T. D. Alexander, B. Rosner, D. A. Carson and G. Goldsworthy, Leicester: Inter-Varsity Press; Downers Grove: InterVarsity Press, 2000
Neot	*Neotestamentica*
NICOT	New International Commentary on the Old Testament
NIDOTTE	*New International Dictionary of Old Testament Theology and Exegesis*, ed. W. VanGemeren, 5 vols., Grand Rapids: Zondervan, 1997
NIGTC	New International Greek Text Commentary
NovT	*Novum Testamentum*
NSBT	New Studies in Biblical Theology
OBO	Orbis biblicus et orientalis
OTE	*Old Testament Essays*
OTL	Old Testament Library
PBM	Paternoster Biblical Monographs
PCNT	Paideia Commentaries on the New Testament
PNTC	Pillar New Testament Commentary
RB	*Revue biblique*
RBJ	*Review of Rabbinic Judaism*
RBL	*Review of Biblical Literature*
ResQ	*Restoration Quarterly*
RTR	*Reformed Theological Review*
SANT	Studien zum Alten und Neuen Testament

SB	Subsidia biblica
SBJT	*Southern Baptist Journal of Theology*
SBLDS	Society of Biblical Literature Dissertation Series
SBLSCS	Society of Biblical Literature Septuagint and Cognate Studies
SBLSS	Society of Biblical Literature Semeia Studies
SBS	Stuttgarter Bibelstudien
SBT	Studies in Biblical Theology
sg.	singular
ScrTh	*Scripta theologica*
SJOT	*Scandinavian Journal of the Old Testament*
SNTSMS	Society for New Testament Studies Monograph Series
SP	Sacra pagina
STR	*Southeastern Theological Review*
TD	*Theology Digest*
Them	*Themelios*
TJ	*Trinity Journal*
TNTC	Tyndale New Testament Commentary
TOTC	Tyndale Old Testament Commentary
TynBul	*Tyndale Bulletin*
VT	*Vetus Testamentum*
VTSup	Vetus Testamentum Supplements
WBC	Word Biblical Commentary
WMANT	Wissenschaftliche Monographien zum Alten und Neuen Testament
WTJ	*Westminster Theological Journal*
WUNT	Wissenschaftliche Untersuchungen zum Neuen Testament
ZAH	*Zeitschrift für Althebräistik*
ZAW	*Zeitschrift für die alttestamentliche Wissenschaft*
ZECNT	Zondervan Exegetical Commentary on the New Testament

1

Introduction

Moses affords Joseph more time in the foreground of the Genesis narrative than any other character in the book – a striking fact given the significance of Genesis' other main characters: Adam, Noah and the patriarchs Abraham, Isaac and Jacob. This prominence is even more striking considering the apparent insignificance of Joseph in the rest of the Old Testament.[1] The Old Testament refers to the Joseph story only seven times outside Genesis: once in a summary of Israel's story (Ps. 105:17), twice in the chronicler's introductory genealogy (1 Chr. 2:2; 5:1), three times in the transition narrative between Genesis and Exodus (Exod. 1:5, 6, 8), and twice with reference to his bones' removal from Egypt (Exod. 13:19) and into Canaan (Josh. 24:32). Joseph fares no better in the New Testament, either; he is meaningfully mentioned only twice – both times in a summary of Israel's story (Acts 7:9–14; Heb. 11:21–22).

The prominence of the Joseph story in Genesis and the paucity of references to him thereafter pose a particular challenge to the biblical theologian whose aim is to read any portion of Scripture in the context of the entire Christian canon.[2] How should interpreters read the Joseph narrative in the context of the entire Genesis narrative and ultimately in canonical context?[3] This book seeks to answer that question.

---

[1] See e.g. Kugel's remarks (with which I disagree): 'Save for a passing reference to Joseph being sold into slavery in Psalm 105 and a somewhat more obscure reference to Joseph in Egypt in Psalm 81, there is scarcely the slightest allusion to the events of Joseph's life recounted in Genesis anywhere else in the Hebrew Bible' (Kugel 1994: 14).

[2] My use of the phrase 'Joseph narrative' or 'Joseph story' refers to the entirety of Gen. 37 – 50. This goes against the grain of some Joseph scholarship, which reserves those phrases only for the reconstructed source text of the Joseph story usually identified as Gen. 37 and 39 – 47 (though with some variations from scholar to scholar). See discussions in Coats 1976 and Longacre 1989. I am not concerned with the conjectural reconstructions but with the text as finally delivered in canonical form.

[3] Brevard Childs posed the same question nearly forty years ago. See Childs 1979: 156.

The question of Joseph's place in the canon is intimately associated with another, narrower biblical-theological question: is Joseph a type of the Messiah? This question, of course, is not the only one related to a canonical reading of the Joseph narrative. Yet when the church and biblical scholarship have addressed the question of Joseph's role in the canon, the conversation invariably turns towards typology.

Patristic commentators asserted that the typological relationship between the patriarch and Jesus were certain.[4] Obvious similarities between the two figures has spawned an interpretive tradition within Christianity that sees righteous Joseph, on his path to glory through suffering, as foreshadowing the life of Jesus of Nazareth. Modern scholars, however, have been less persuaded.[5]

Their hesitation arises from a number of factors. Historical-critical presuppositions, which have dominated academic treatments of the Joseph narrative for the last 200 years are inherently hostile to typological readings of Scripture.[6] Those sympathetic to typological hermeneutics have also been hesitant to affirm Joseph as a type of the Messiah given the apparent lack of textual warrant. Ultimately, the longstanding tradition

---

[4] The earliest modern summary of the interpretation of the Joseph narrative in the early church is in Argyle 1956: 199–201. Argyle notes that the Fathers employed the Joseph narrative '(1) as prefiguring the Incarnation, Passion, and Exaltation of our Lord; (2) as providing a pattern for Christian character and conduct'. For a thorough analysis of early church interpretation of Joseph, primarily in the Eastern Church up to the fourth century AD, see Fortner 2004. Fortner likewise concludes that the two primary uses of the Joseph narrative were typological (messianic) and hortatory.

[5] A good deal of modern literature on Genesis rarely even discusses the issue. Mathews' commentary is typical in that he mentions the matter only in his history of interpretation but never revisits the issue or evaluates its validity (K. Mathews 2005: 670). Victor Hamilton's analysis of the 'New Testament Appropriation' of the Joseph story does mention the potential typological relationship between Joseph and Jesus. Interestingly, Hamilton does see a sort of typological correspondence between Joseph and Stephen in Acts 7: 'Joseph is the forerunner of Stephen – God is with both, and upon both, and upon both shines the glory of God.' Furthermore, Hamilton affirms the validity of seeing Matt. 21:38 and Luke 20:14 as alluding to Gen. 37:20 but does not mention the potential Christological significance of this point (V. Hamilton 1995: 714). Marshall states regarding Acts 7, 'Whether this is a typological allusion to the way in which God delivered Jesus from his afflictions . . . is not clear' (Marshall 1983: 137). Westermann strongly opposes the typological interpretation (Westermann 1982). Likewise, Van Seters argues that the 'Joseph-Christ typology' is utterly foreign to the NT and is instead a creation of the early church (Van Seters 1965: 283–284).

[6] Lampe notes that in historical critical circles, typology was a 'historical curiosity, of very little importance or significance for the modern reader. The new emphasis upon the diversity of Scripture and the original independence of its several parts tended to overthrow the foundations upon which that method rested. This was the most important . . . effect of "higher criticism"' (Lampe 1957: 16).

that Joseph typifies Christ has not produced the exegetical argumentation needed to convince modern scholars.

This scepticism is, at least in part, warranted. Messianic interpretations of the Joseph narrative have often lacked methodological rigour or have simply failed to make a convincing case. Typically, these arguments present a 'two-dimensional' portrait of the typological relationship – one that focuses on the thematic and, potentially, linguistic correspondences between the Joseph and Jesus narratives, but without considering the Joseph narrative's function in the context of Genesis, its redemptive-historical significance, or its appropriation by later biblical authors. Defenders of the messianic reading of Joseph often draw a large arc between the Joseph narrative and the Jesus narrative without showing any of the smaller arcs that link the Joseph story to the rest of the canon.

The similarities between the lives of Jesus and Joseph are indeed striking, but does a typological reading of Joseph hold up under the scrutiny of the kinds of constraints scholars have traditionally proposed should control typological readings? Is there evidence from the original context that the story is messianic? Is there a clear connection to the covenant structure of Scripture? Is there intra-canonical development? And is there explicit New Testament textual warrant? While I do not believe each of these questions must be answered affirmatively in order to assert the presence of an Old Testament type, I have come to the conclusion that, even according to the strictest hermeneutical controls, Joseph passes the typological test.

The aim of this project is to present a more comprehensive canonical treatment of the Joseph narrative – one deserving of its theological depth and literary artfulness. As Levenson has noted, the Joseph story 'is arguably the most sophisticated narrative in the Jewish or the Christian Bibles'.[7] Similarly, Alter echoes these sentiments in the conclusion to his analysis of the Joseph story, saying that it is 'one of the best stories, as many readers have attested, that has ever been told'.[8]

---

[7] Levenson 1993: 143. Westermann designates it a 'work of art of the highest order' (Westermann 1982: 26). In Albright's estimation, 'nothing in the Ancient Near East can equal the dramatic portrayal of Joseph's career' (Albright 2006: 23). Even Speiser, whose commentary is largely committed to carving up each narrative along the lines of the documentary hypothesis, admits '[The Joseph story] is at once the most intricately constructed and the best integrated of all the patriarchal histories . . . The remarkable thing is that the whole still appears to be deceptively smooth, after so much legitimate scrutiny by modern critics' (Speiser 1964: 292–294).

[8] Alter 2011: 219.

I hope to avoid the 'two-dimensional' messianic readings of the Joseph narrative that merely focus on large-scale similarities between the lives of Joseph and Jesus. Instead, I hope to paint a three-dimensional portrait of Joseph by considering (1) Genesis 37 – 50 in its own literary and theological context, (2) intra-canonical development of the Joseph story via inner-biblical allusion and (3) references and allusions to the Joseph story in the New Testament.

Thesis

This book is not a commentary on Genesis 37 – 50. My interests are much narrower. This book will defend the notion that the Joseph story, understood according to its biblical-theological context, functions as the resolution to the plot of Genesis and that this story typologically influences how later biblical authors narrate redemptive history culminating in the New Testament's portrayal of Jesus as an antitypical Joseph. My aim is to unfold a biblical-theological account of the Joseph narrative by exploring his redemptive-historical contribution to Genesis and by examining how later biblical authors develop the story of Joseph across the Old Testament. I am particularly interested in two questions. First, what is the literary and biblical-theological significance of the Joseph narrative as the conclusion to Genesis? Second, how do later biblical authors interpret and reuse the Joseph narrative?

With regard to Joseph's biblical-theological function in Genesis, I will argue that Joseph provides the literary and biblical-theological resolution to the story of Genesis. Joseph is intimately linked to the Abrahamic covenant, functioning as the first major instantiation of the fulfilment of the Abrahamic promises. Joseph also provides resolution to (or sometimes more appropriately reversal of) the fractious, curse-ridden storylines developed in Genesis, such as fraternal conflict, famine and family deception. Furthermore, I will also demonstrate that Moses links the story of Joseph to the eschatological expectations established in Genesis (such as royal seed) and specifically to the hope for an eschatological king.

With regard to later biblical authors' appropriation of the Joseph story, I will argue that Joseph is a model-character for faithfulness in exile, a harbinger of God's exodus salvation, and an exhibition of the hope of glory through suffering. Later biblical authors saw the life of Joseph as the type of life that characterized how God worked among his people, particularly in fulfilling his promises. Some authors, such as Daniel, even modelled their autobiographies in part on the life of Joseph.

This biblical-theological treatment of the Joseph narrative lends credibility to the notion that Joseph prefigures the Messiah. Moses includes evidence within Genesis itself that Joseph foreshadows God's future work in fulfilling his promises and undoing the curses established in Genesis 3. Later biblical authors, such as the author of Psalm 105, confirm this interpretation. Other authors reuse and incorporate material from the Joseph story into their own writings in order to present themselves or others as 'new Josephs'. These 'new Josephs' develop the Joseph narrative across the pages of the Old Testament and thus provide the proper foundation for a truly canonical reading of Genesis 37 – 50. Finally, I will argue that this intra-canonical development of the story of Joseph culminates in the New Testament. The New Testament authors employ the Joseph narrative in the service of their Christological claims about Jesus of Nazareth, the one who recapitulates the life of Israel and the lives of Israel's prominent Old Testament figures in a way that brings fulfilment to the story of the Old Testament. Consequently, the New Testament itself presents Jesus as the new and final Joseph.

Joseph in canonical context in pre-modern Christian literature

Early Christian interpreters primarily read the Joseph narrative as either foreshadowing the life of Jesus the Messiah or as modelling Christian virtue.[9] Each of these interpretations shows a distinct desire to relate the story of Joseph to the larger story of redemption. Essentially, Christological reading of the Joseph narrative, universally accepted by pre-critical Christian interpreters, was assumed, largely due to the interpretive posture of early Christians as they sought to demonstrate that Jesus of Nazareth was the resolution to the story of the Old Testament.[10]

---

[9] The Joseph narrative has enjoyed a rich interpretive life in Judaism, Christianity and Islam – a point to which scholars have given quite a bit of attention. See the most recent survey of the rather significant amount of literature on this topic in Niehoff 1992: 1–14. See also the bibliography provided by Westermann on Joseph 'In Later Literature' in Westermann 1982: 17–18.

[10] Westermann identifies the 'traditional ecclesiastical view', which affirms the historicity of Gen. 37 – 50 and its typological significance as the first of three major stages in the history of interpretation of the Joseph story (Westermann 1982: 18). On the interpretive commitments and presuppositions of the early church, see Young 1997 and O'Keefe and Reno 2005.

Argyle's survey of the patristic use of the Joseph story shows that the early church at least as far back as Justin Martyr understood Joseph as a Christological type. Irenaeus, Origen, Cyprian, Jerome, Chrysostom, Ambrose, Augustine, Cyril of Alexandria and a host of other interpreters of the early church affirmed a typological reading of the Joseph narrative.[11]

The notion that Joseph foreshadowed the Messiah remained largely unchallenged throughout the early and medieval church,[12] the Reformation,[13] and among the Puritan tradition[14] and its theological heirs.[15] Some interpreters are more guarded and critical in their conclusions than others.[16] Yet examples of pre-modern Christian interpretation of the Joseph narrative that do not affirm or largely expound on the Christological character of Joseph are hard to find. A messianic reading of the Joseph narrative cemented itself early in the interpretive tradition.

Yet, while the Christological interpretation of Joseph enjoys a rich and well-attested theological heritage, the actual outworking of this notion beyond the mere notation of similarities between the lives of Joseph and Jesus is rare. Given the hermeneutical assumptions of pre-critical authors (and their theological heirs), the typological correspondence between Joseph and Jesus was largely assumed – never garnering sustained reflection or defence.

---

[11] Argyle 1956.

[12] Ibid. 200.

[13] Calvin 1996: 261, 266.

[14] Owen 1965: 203; Goodwin 1996: 161.

[15] Fuller 1988: 3.146; Edwards 2005: 2.651–653. See also the comments throughout Matthew Henry's commentary on Gen. 37 – 50 (Henry 1935) as well as Winslow 1863 on the Joseph story.

[16] Fuller e.g. cautiously observes, 'I am far from thinking that every point of analogy which may be traced by a lively imagination was designed as such by the Holy Spirit; yet neither do I think that we are warranted in rejecting the idea.' Fuller proceeds to tie his discussion to his larger examination of the nature of typology and hermeneutics. See Fuller 1988: 3.146. Spurgeon's typological interpretation is significantly less restrained: 'I need not say to you, beloved, who are conversant with Scripture, that there is scarcely any personal type in the Old Testament which is more clearly and fully a portrait of our Lord Jesus Christ than is the type of Joseph. You may run the parallel between Joseph and Jesus in very many directions, yet you need never strain the narrative so even much as once . . . in making himself known to his brethren, he was a type of our Lord revealing himself to us . . . I. Notice, first, that the Lord Jesus Christ, like Joseph, reveals himself in private for the most part . . . II. The second remark I have to make is this – when the Lord Jesus Christ reveals Himself to any man for the first time, it is usually in the midst of terror, and that first revelation often creates much sadness . . . III. Now, thirdly, though the first appearance of Jesus, like that of Joseph, may cause sadness, the further revelation of the Lord Jesus Christ to his brethren, brings them the greatest possible joy' (Spurgeon 1899: 93–97). The worst offender, in terms of typological over-reading, is Arthur W. Pink. In *Gleanings in Genesis*, Pink identifies 101 ways Joseph is a type of Christ (Pink 1922: 340–408).

Modern scholarship on Joseph's significance in Genesis

Since this book will examine the topics of (1) Joseph's literary and biblical-theological function in the book of Genesis, (2) later biblical authors' use of the Joseph narrative, and (3) ultimately the notion that Joseph is a type of Christ, I will consider modern research on each of these questions in turn.

With the publication of Jean Astruc's *Conjectures sur les mémoires originaux dont il paroît que Moyse s'est servi pour composer le livre de la Genèse* (1753), literary, canonical and typological readings of the Joseph narrative largely gave way to historical-critical approaches to the story. When scholars did examine the literary features of the Joseph story, they typically did so along source-critical lines.[17] In short, these critical treatments of the Joseph story, essentially concentrating on the source divisions (and thus internal incoherence) of the story, disengaged Genesis 37 – 50 from its place in the story of Genesis in particular and from the Old Testament in general.[18] Even as scholars challenged source-critical approaches and reasserted the narrative's synthetic unity by virtue of a thoughtful redactor(s),[19] the Joseph story was still seen as an isolated literary composition without any significant literary, theological or biblical-theological connection to the rest of Genesis. Donald Redford for example argues:

---

[17] For an overview of the development of the historical-critical treatment of the Joseph story, see Paap 1995 and de Hoop 1998: 366–450. Even source-critical approaches were driven by deeply historical interests. In other words, the goal of these source-critical efforts is not to uncover the literary features and/or interpretive rules for the Joseph saga, but to reconstruct the history behind the Joseph story – thereby situating it in the right historical context. For an example, see William F. Albright who posited that the story is a 'syncresis of two separate mythic cycles' – a fertility myth from the cult at Shechem and an Egyptian tale (Albright 1918: 114). Cf. Redford 1970: 88–98.

[18] The previous century's scholarly obsession over the genre of Gen. 37 – 50 has only further driven a wedge between the story of Joseph and the rest of the Genesis narrative. Gunkel, credited for being one of the first scholars to return scholarship to a more literary interest in the Joseph story, argues that the story's length, 'epic discursiveness', and interest in 'soul life' indicates that it ought to be read as 'romance' in contrast to the rest of Genesis, which he characterized as 'legend'. See Gunkel 1901: 80–86. Similarly, von Rad's well-received proposal that the Joseph story grew out of the wisdom tradition and is a 'didactic tale' highlights its distinctiveness in the light of the rest of Genesis given its characterization of Joseph and infrequent direct speech from God (von Rad 1966: 294–295).

[19] As Smith notes, 'It was in the study of this segment of Genesis during the 1960s and 70s that the scholarly consensus concerning the Documentary Hypothesis began to break apart' (B. Smith 2002: 3). For broader treatments on the death of the documentary hypothesis and source-critical approaches to the Pentateuch, see Wenham 1999: 116–144; Garrett 2001: 28–41.

The theological outlook of the writer of Gen. 37–50 is different from that of the Patriarchal narrator. He does not mention the Covenant or the Promise, ubiquitous in the earlier chapters of Genesis. He is not interested in supplying the reader with comment on matters theological, as the Patriarchal author was.[20]

Gerhard von Rad likewise asserted that 'the Joseph story is in every respect distinct from the patriarchal narratives which it follows'.[21] He later asserts that the Joseph story 'is ... devoid of any specifically theological interest in redemptive history'.[22] These sentiments are repeated with some force by Arnold:

> A final question about the Joseph narrative is its function in Genesis and the Pentateuch as a whole. The covenant and the ancestral promises of land and seed – so central throughout Gen. 12–36 – are absent entirely, nor do we encounter any further revelatory theophanies. This theological uniqueness combines with the literary distinctiveness we have discussed to illustrate the role of the Joseph narrative in the Bible.[23]

Given the resistance to the notion that the Joseph story bore any meaningful connection to the rest of Genesis, locating the Joseph story in canonical context was long an abandoned enterprise among scholars.[24] As Brevard Childs noted, amidst the raging debates of historical-critical

---

[20] Redford 1970: 247. Redford's criticism of previous scholarship's source-critical approach to Joseph is tapered by the fact that he himself still engages in the enterprise – positing different sources behind the story than those traditionally proposed.

[21] Von Rad 1966: 292.

[22] Ibid. 299.

[23] Arnold 2009: 316. See also the comments by Brueggemann 'The Joseph narrative offers a kind of literature which is distinctive in Genesis. It is distinguished in every way from the narratives dealing with Abraham and Jacob. The intellectual world of this narrative has much more in common with the David story of II Sam. 9–20 than it does with the ancestral tales. While we cannot be sure, a plausible locus for the narrative is the royal, urban ethos of Solomon which imitated international ways and which sharply critiqued the claims of the old tribal traditions. Its presuppositions suggest a cool detachment from things religious that is contrasted with the much more direct religious affirmation of the Abraham and Jacob stories. This narrative appears to belong to a generation of believers in a cultural climate where old modes of faith were embarrassing ... The narrative should be understood as a sophisticated literary response to a cultural, theological crisis. How does one speak about faith in a context where the older ways are found wanting? That is the issue in the Joseph narrative' (Brueggemann 1982: 288).

[24] Alexander 2007: 198.

concerns such as Gunkel's designation of the Joseph story as a novella or von Rad's argument that the wisdom tradition gave birth to the story of Joseph:

> there was little or no attention given to the canonical questions. What is the shape of the final chapters and what is their function within the book as a whole? ... If Joseph is not the bearer of the promise in the same way as his forefathers, what then is his role in Genesis?[25]

More recently, scholars have revisited the question of the relationship of the Joseph story to the rest of Genesis. Some treatments are fairly trivial, noting, for example, nothing more than the fact that Genesis 37 – 50 'deals with the same persons' as the Jacob narrative or reflects a similar economic and community structure as previous narratives.[26]

Other scholars, similiarly, have voiced minimalist accounts of the relationship of Joseph to the rest of Genesis. Coats posited the largely well-received proposal that Joseph's role in Genesis is purely etiological, providing the rationale for why the Israelites, promised the land of Canaan, found themselves in Egypt in the first place.[27] In other words,

---

[25] Childs 1979: 156.

[26] Westermann 1982: 27. Westermann expresses some dissatisfaction that 'not enough attention has been paid' to the commonalities shared between the Joseph story and the rest of Genesis. However, his own proposals on points of contact are so trivial they are hardly worth mentioning. '1. All people mentioned in chs. 37–45 (except chs. 39–41) have been the subject of narratives in the patriarchal story . . . 2. Consequently, what is narrated about the lives of these people in chs. 37–45 (except chs. 39–41) agrees with what we know from chs. 12–36 . . . 3. Conflicts, as in the patriarchal stories, are between members of the family, especially between brothers . . . 4. The Joseph story, however, differs in one very striking way from the patriarchal story – women scarcely appear in it.' In this list, the first two points are trivial and the last highlights what Joseph does not have in common with preceding narratives. Only the third point merits any significant reflection since it highlights a major literary theme woven throughout Genesis.

[27] Coats 1976. Coats has been followed by other commentators such as Brueggemann, who offers the following helpful summary of Coats's proposal: 'George Coats has shown that the Joseph narrative is a literary device to link ancestral promises to the Exodus narrative of oppression and liberation. Before this narrative, there were older traditions about the promise to the forebearers [sic] and about the deliverance from Egypt. But no way was found to link the two memories, one of which is based in Canaan and the other in Egypt. To overcome that problem, Coats suggests, this narrative was constructed. The Joseph account, then, has no independent life or function. It never existed on its own but was formed after the other materials were fixed to make a narrative linkage. It serves to carry this family from Canaan to Egypt and oppression' (Brueggemann 1982: 291). Arnold comments, 'Thus the Joseph Novel has been incorporated into the Joseph narrative as the conclusion of Genesis in order to serve as a bridge, theologically and structurally, between the ancestors and the exodus' (Arnold 2009: 317).

Joseph is purely a 'bridge' character – a man whose biography, while theologically instructive in its own way, does little more than geographically transition readers from Israel to Egypt. Joseph may change the setting of the story of Israel, but he plays virtually no role in advancing the plot of that same story. Joseph bears no relationship to the patriarchal covenants, the messianic hope initiated in Genesis 3:15 or the major redemptive-historical themes developed in primeval and patriarchal histories.

More recently, however, several scholars have dissented from these conclusions – arguing for significant literary and biblical-theological unity between Joseph and the rest of Genesis. Bruce Dahlberg's 'On Recognizing the Unity of Genesis', though only seven pages long, is the seminal work dissenting from the majority position.[28] Dahlberg argues that Genesis 1 – 11 and the Joseph story share so many common thematic and linguistic features that readers should see them as forming an inclusio around the entire Genesis narrative. Ultimately, Dahlberg argues that the two parts of the inclusio function as a call and response. Genesis 1 – 11 sets up problems that are ultimately resolved in the story of Joseph. Thus, 'Joseph appears to have been drawn intentionally as an "antitype" to Adam and, for that matter, to other main representatives of humanity who figure in chapters 1 through 11.'[29]

Other scholars, often building on the work of Dahlberg, argue that the Joseph narrative has striking connections to previous material in Genesis. Lindsay Wilson has explored the relationship of the Joseph story to the Abrahamic covenant and the intersection between the prominent wisdom theme in the Joseph story and the centrality of the covenant in Genesis.[30] T. D. Alexander has posited that the Joseph story is a 'natural continuation of the theme of royalty found in the patriarchal narratives of Gen. 12–36'[31] and 'is more than simply a bridge between Canaan and Egypt'.[32] Timothy J. Stone, building on the work of Dahlberg, has argued that the Joseph story is the culmination and conclusion of Genesis and explores that

---

[28] Dahlberg 1977: 360–367. Dahlberg published a similar work five years later, 1982: 2.126–133.

[29] Dahlberg 1982: 2.129. Similarly, Dahlberg concludes that the Joseph story 'functions as a completion and consummation to everything in the book of Genesis preceding it' (Dahlberg 1977: 363).

[30] Wilson 2004: 215–236.

[31] Alexander 2007: 202.

[32] Ibid. 212.

notion by considering how the 'story of the fall' replays several times in the lives of different figures in Genesis before 'taking a surprising turn in Joseph's story'.[33]

Finally, Brian Sigmon's dissertation 'Between Eden and Egypt', which also builds on Dahlberg's work, explores the literary relationship between the Joseph story and Genesis 2 – 4 in great detail. For Sigmon, the Joseph story represents the literary 'reversal' of the curse-induced themes of Genesis. Sigmon argues that the fraternal conflict first appearing in the lives of Cain and Abel parallels the conflict between Joseph and his brothers. Yet, whereas the first conflict results in fratricide, the latter resolves with forgiveness. Further, Sigmon argues that Joseph is portrayed as a new Adam, succeeding in his own temptation narrative (Gen. 39) and unravelling the effects of the curse by exercising knowledge of good and evil appropriate for human creatures.[34]

Overall, most scholars advocating for the 'unity with Genesis' view see Joseph as bringing happy resolution to the minor chords playing throughout earlier portions of Genesis. Joseph is a 'reversal' character. He counteracts the plot lines of fratricidal conflict, famine, infertility and a host of other problems escalating throughout the narrative since Genesis 3. Behind Joseph's part in this story – as the one who brings the hope of redemption to the frustrations and grief of the Abrahamic family – is the God who keeps his covenant and ensures the fulfilment of his promises to Abraham (Gen. 45:5–8; 50:20).[35]

The use of the Joseph narrative in later Scripture

Westermann represents the minimalist interpretive position of the role of Joseph in later biblical writings. In his estimation, 'The Joseph narrative has found a remarkable faint echo in the writings of the OT and the NT . . . He received no promise from God and so has no direct significance

---

[33] Stone 2012: 62–73.

[34] Sigmon 2013. Other works, focused more broadly on the theology of the Pentateuch or on the entire OT have also contributed to the notion that the story of Joseph authentically integrates with the rest of Genesis. Two premier examples of these types of works are Sailhamer 1992 and Dempster 2003: 88–92.

[35] The same point is also made by T. Patterson 2003, who examines the role of 'plot' in the interpretation of Genesis.

for the later history.'[36] Westermann identifies only Psalm 105, Acts 7 and Hebrews 11 as containing any significant mention of Joseph, though he notes that each passage is merely a 'historical survey'.[37]

Not all scholars, however, share Westermann's scepticism. Some have explored how later biblical authors reappropriated the story of Joseph. Arthur Van Seters attempts a comprehensive treatment of the subject in his 1965 dissertation 'The Use of the Story of Joseph in Scripture'. Van Seters examined what he considered every quotation of or allusion to the Joseph narrative in the Old and New Testaments and helpfully identified some of the most important biblical references to Joseph in later biblical literature.

My own conclusions regarding the canonical function of the Joseph narrative differ markedly from Van Seters', particularly on whether Joseph functions as a type of the Messiah. He writes, 'As for the New Testament, one cannot prove that its authors had a developed Joseph–Christ typology or viewed Christ's life as patterned to any significant degree on this particular patriarch.'[38]

Other scholars posit that the story of Joseph has influenced the rest of the Old Testament. In the law, Danny Matthews has argued that elements of the story of Moses may be modelled on the story of Joseph.[39] In the prophets, Robert Alter, Peter Leithart and James Hamilton have all noted linguistic and thematic correspondences between the stories of David and Joseph.[40] Jan Granowski, John Harvey and others have suggested that the fate of Jehoiachin in the royal court of Babylon may draw from the imagery and themes of the Joseph story.[41] Likewise, Mark Roncace has argued that the account of Jeremiah's imprisonment in 'a pit without water' echoes the story of Joseph and that the prophet shows other evidences of literary dependence on the Joseph story.[42]

More than in any other section of the canon, the writings have been identified by scholars as having the most prominent allusions to the story of Joseph – particularly in the stories of Esther and Daniel. In the modern

---

[36] Westermann 1982: 252. In this same discussion, Westermann states that Joseph is mentioned only once in the rest of the OT, in Ps. 105. A strange claim given 1 Chr. 5:1–2.

[37] Ibid. Ruppert, like Westermann, considers only the above-mentioned texts in his consideration of 'Das Nachwirken der Josephserzählung in der Bibel'. See Ruppert 1965: 239–260.

[38] Van Seters 1965: 283–284.

[39] D. Mathews 2012: 45–54.

[40] Alter 1990: 119–121; 1999; Leithart 2003; J. M. Hamilton 2008: 52–77.

[41] Granowski 1992: 173–188; Römer 1997: 10–11; Schmid 1999: 142–143; Harvey 2010: 54–55; Chan 2013: 566–577; Patton 2014: 63–64, 302–304.

[42] Roncace 2005: 81–84.

period, the recognition of a literary relationship between these three stories goes back at least as far as Ludwig Rosenthal's 1895 article 'Die Josephgeschichte, mit den Büchern Ester und Daniel Verglichen'. Rosenthal posited that the Joseph story directly influenced the literary features of Daniel and Esther. More recently, scholars have continued to affirm Rosenthal's observations but have argued for a less direct literary relationship. Instead, the similarities are largely due to a shared *ur*-genre, a literary convention controlling the author's presentation of the story.[43] This relationship has regularly been revisited by numerous scholars from various theological and hermeneutical perspectives.[44]

Joseph as a type of Christ in modern scholarship

Negative assessments

Since many scholars abandoned the notions of the unity of Scripture and the prophetic character of the Old Testament after the rise of higher criticism, the possibility that Joseph served as a type of the Messiah was largely taken off the table. Most modern scholars do not even address the question – clearly implying a 'no'.

Some scholars – prompted by their interaction with pre-critical Christian literature on the Joseph story – have criticized the typological reading of the Joseph story on two counts. First, Westermann judges pre-critical typological readings of the Joseph story as merely 'time-conditioned adaptations' of the text. This 'ecclesiastical' interpretation observes 'nothing of what happened between father, brothers, and brother, between

---

[43] Talmon, for instance, argues that 'Esther consciously borrowed from the writer of the Joseph-story.' Yet 'what is more important, they can be shown to belong basically to one literary type . . . Their similarities therefore are to be accounted for not only by their probable interdependence but also by their dependence upon one common literary tradition' (Talmon 1963: 454–455). Talmon, relying on the work of von Rad, refers to this genre type as a 'historicized wisdom-tale' (455). Morris also argues that the stories of Joseph, Daniel and Esther 'begin with the same generic convention' – what Morris calls a 'Hebrew Courtier Tale' (Morris 1994: 75).

[44] Rosenthal 1895: 278–284; Gan 1961: 144–149; J. J. Collins 1975: 218–234; Meinhold 1975: 306–324; P. R. Davies 1976: 392–401; Meinhold 1976: 72–93; Berg 1979: 123–165; Frieden 1990: 193–203; Gnuse 1990: 29–53; Labonté 1993: 271–284; Levenson 1997; Wahl 1999: 21–47; Wesselius 1999: 24–77; Wahl 2000: 59–74; Bezalel 2002: 10–16; Nel 2002: 780–798; Wesselius 2005: 241–283; Segal 2009: 123–149; Shepherd 2009; Rindge 2010: 85–104; Olojede 2012: 351–368; Milán 2013: 335–362; J. M. Hamilton 2014b: 221–235; Widder 2014: 1112–1128.

family and state, and between all these and God'. Ultimately, in Westermann's estimation, 'the Joseph narrative itself did not live on' in typological readings of the figure of Joseph.[45] In other words, Westermann sees the typological reading of Joseph as the very death of the real significance of the Joseph narrative.

Second, Van Seters and Westermann posit that such a reading is foreign to the authors of the New Testament. The identification of Joseph with Jesus does not emerge from Scripture, but is an imposition promulgated by the early church.[46]

Positive assessments

Gary Anderson's essay 'Joseph and the Passion of Our Lord' integrates the life of Joseph with the themes of election and the trials of the 'beloved' son in Genesis.[47] While Anderson has a number of suggestive comments on the Joseph narrative, he largely assumes rather than defends a typological reading of Joseph. In some senses, his work is largely a homiletical reproduction of Levenson's *Death and Resurrection of the Beloved Son* (1993).

James Hamilton's article 'Was Joseph a Type of the Messiah?' is the most robustly textual defence of the messianic character of the Joseph narrative and the only one that attempts to show canonical development of the Joseph narrative in the Old Testament itself. Hamilton argues that 'the story of Joseph in Genesis 37 – 50 was a formative influence on the account of David produced by the author(s) of Samuel'.[48] If this is the case, it shows that biblical authors considered the story of Joseph as establishing a pattern that later biblical authors employed to describe other major figures in the life of Israel. As Hamilton argues, once this pattern is established 'it is plausible that expectations for more of the same would be generated'.[49] Further, Hamilton considers New Testament evidence for Joseph as a type of Christ, principally the testimony of Stephen in Acts 7 and possible allusions to the Joseph story in the Gospels that identify Jesus with Joseph.[50]

---

[45] Westermann 1982: 253.

[46] Van Seters 1965: 283–284; Westermann 1982: 252–253.

[47] Anderson 2003: 198–215.

[48] J. M. Hamilton 2008: 52.

[49] Ibid.

[50] Schrock who mainly commends Hamilton's treatment criticizes him on the grounds that Hamilton does not tie his view of typology (specifically, the typological reading of the Joseph

Nicholas Lunn's 'Allusions to the Joseph Narrative in the Synoptic Gospels and Acts' examines whether the New Testament warrants a typological reading of Joseph. As Lunn explains:

> Joseph is not expressly termed a type or a prefigurement by any New Testament writer, nor is any part of the text of Genesis concerning Joseph expounded in a typological fashion in the New Testament, evidence can nonetheless be adduced which points to the fact that both Jesus and certain of the New Testament authors viewed the Joseph story typologically.[51]

Lunn sees allusions in Luke-Acts – particularly the parable of the tenants and the parable of the prodigal son – as portraying Jesus in Josephite imagery.

Finally, Timothy Stone argues that Joseph reverses the curse as it is played out through the story of Genesis, arising as a new and successful Adam.[52] In this role, Joseph foreshadows Christ, the consummate curse-reverser. While Stone's article is brimming with interesting connections between Joseph and early narratives in Genesis, he does not attempt to show any connections between Joseph and the Gospels. Instead, Stone argues that since Christ fulfils all of Scripture (Luke 24) and since Adam is a type of Christ, then Joseph, a new Adam, must likewise foreshadow the Messiah.

Other scholars have also made minor contributions to the discussion and have voiced their approval of a messianic reading of the Joseph story. Greidanus's commentary on Genesis has been the most forward, effectively summarizing the exegetical evidence both from within Genesis and from the New Testament.[53] Others have followed pre-critical exegetes, noting 'obvious similarities' between Joseph and Jesus without reference

---

narrative) to the covenantal structure of Scripture. 'It is significant that Hamilton grounds his redemptive historical points in the larger story of salvation outlined in the Old Testament. For instance, he traces the covenantal promises of God when he recounts the Patriarchal history leading up to Joseph, yet he does not make explicit mention of the biblical covenants. Hamilton convincingly proves the relationship between Joseph, David, and Jesus. Yet, greater support for Joseph's status as a type of Christ can be found by relating Joseph and David to the covenantal structures of the Old Testament. Both figures, in different ways and at different times, carried on the Abrahamic promises of land, people, and blessing' (Schrock 2014: 10).

[51] Lunn 2012: 30.

[52] Stone 2012.

[53] Greidanus 2007: 335–473.

to methodological constraints, intra-canonical development or exegetical evidence. Gerard Van Groningen,[54] R. R. Reno[55] and others[56] are representative of this position. Still other scholars approve the messianic reading in passing without further commentary or defence.[57]

Preview of the argument

Chapter 1 has explained the rationale for this project and introduced readers to the canonical 'problem' of the Joseph narrative – namely, his prominence in Genesis and apparent absence elsewhere. This chapter also surveyed the history of the interpretation of the Joseph narrative, discussing why pre-modern interpreters used Joseph *primarily* as a typological character while historical-critical scholars largely rejected those conclusions. Further, this chapter explored recent scholarship on Joseph's role in Genesis and the Joseph story's influence on later Scripture.

Chapter 2 discusses the methodology of this project, particularly in relation to the study of biblical theology, typology and inner-biblical allusion/intertextuality. This chapter establishes my interpretive commitments and also makes a case for typological reading, as regulated by the interpretive practices of the New Testament authors, as a legitimate hermeneutical enterprise. I also articulate the hermeneutical controls of the project, particularly for discerning the presence of inner-biblical allusion. Furthermore, I synthesize this typological approach with recent discussions on the literary phenomenon of inner-biblical allusion/intertextuality and the role of the canon in biblical-theological exegesis.

Chapters 3–6 focus on the Joseph narrative in the context of Genesis. I establish the literary structure of Genesis and examine Joseph's place in it. By demonstrating Joseph's literary relationship to the rest of Genesis and the intratextual connections between the Joseph story and previous

---

[54] Van Groningen 1990: 150–153, 166–167. Alexander also seems to register his agreement with the messianic reading of the Joseph narrative in citing Van Groningen approvingly (Alexander 1995: 36).

[55] Reno 2010: 258–265.

[56] Keil and Delitzsch 1989: 329–334; Patterson 2007: 164. Wenham hints along these lines in his commentary though without calling Joseph a 'type'. Wenham writes, 'This principle of salvation being brought to all through the suffering of the one finds its clearest expression in the NT in the life, death, and exaltation of our Lord (cf. Mark 10:45)' (Wenham 1994a: 493).

[57] Kidner 1967: 191; Wenham 1994a: 360; Waltke 2001: 523.

episodes in the lives of Adam, Cain and Abel, Abraham and others, my analysis shows that Joseph is indeed tied to the larger story of Genesis found in both primeval and patriarchal narratives. The majority of these chapters examine how Joseph develops and relates to the Abrahamic promises of kingship, seed, land and blessing. Furthermore, an analysis of this evidence demonstrates that, even within the context of Genesis itself, Joseph is a typological figure – a messianic character.

Chapter 7 examines the mentions of Joseph in the Old Testament in order to discern how later biblical authors interpreted the Joseph story. This chapter also examines allusions to the Joseph narrative in the account of Daniel and how Joseph contributes to the canonical pattern of the exiled Jew in a foreign court. Finally, I explore how these allusions and patterns contribute to a canonical understanding of the Joseph story.

Chapter 8 examines two references to Joseph in the New Testament: Acts 7 and Hebrews 11. This chapter proposes that there is explicit New Testament warrant for the assertion that Joseph is a type of the Messiah. Furthermore, this chapter examines a possible allusion to Joseph in the parable of the tenants – an allusion that ties the story of Joseph to the larger typological structures of the Old Testament. Finally, Chapter 9 offers a summary of my proposal and of the biblical-theological implications of my argument.

2

Biblical theology and typology

Defining biblical theology

This book is an exercise in biblical theology – a discipline I understand as 'faith seeking understanding of the redemptive-historical and literary unity of the Bible in its own terms, concepts, and contexts'.[1] According to this definition, biblical theology is more than simply tracing themes through Scripture. Doing biblical theology means attempting to understand the logic of Scripture's unfolding drama and make sense of how each part fits into the whole.

Therefore, integral to biblical theology is understanding how later biblical authors interpret earlier ones, particularly how New Testament authors interpret the Old Testament in the light of Christ. Indeed, understanding the exegetical logic of biblical authors is of such importance, Hamilton posits that biblical theology is nothing less than understanding and embracing 'the interpretive perspective of the biblical authors'.[2] By 'interpretive perspective' Hamilton means 'the framework of assumptions and presuppositions, associations and identifications, truths and symbols that are taken for granted as an author or speaker describes the world and the events that take place in it'.[3]

This focus on the interpretive perspective of the biblical authors means that biblical theology essentially emerges from exegesis. Again, as

---

[1] Treat 2014: 35. Rosner provides another helpful definition of biblical theology: '[Biblical theology is] theological interpretation of Scripture in and for the church. It proceeds with historical and literary sensitivity and seeks to analyze and synthesize the Bible's teaching about God and his relations to the world on its own terms, maintaining sight of the Bible's overarching narrative and Christocentric focus' (Rosner 2000: 10). Some of this chapter originally appeared in my dissertation and was later adapted in my contribution to an article on typology in Sequeira and Emadi 2017 (11–34).

[2] J. M. Hamilton 2014a: 15.

[3] Ibid.

Hamilton notes, 'the only access we have to the *interpretative perspective of the biblical authors* is what they wrote. Rather than try to go behind the text to get at what really happened, as though the text is mere propaganda, we are trying to understand what the biblical authors have written.'[4] Thus, biblical theology considers not only a text's immediate context, but the context of the entire canon – the ultimate boundary for a text's meaning. Only in the light of later revelation and through the interpretive perspective of Christ and the apostles is the redemptive-historical significance of an Old Testament text fully revealed. Thus, whereas much previous work on the Joseph story regards it as an insulated composition, this book aims to read the Joseph narrative on its own terms by allowing the *literary* and *canonical* contexts of the Joseph story to have their voice in the interpretation of Joseph's theological significance.

Defining typology

More narrowly, this project is an exercise in typological exegesis.[5] Regrettably, as Moo notes, 'typology is much easier to talk about than to describe',[6] and even among evangelicals, competing definitions of typology are legion. These matters are further complicated by related (and equally polarizing) issues such as the nature of biblical theology, the New Testament's use of the Old Testament, the structure of the canon, authorial intent, the relationship of the divine and human authors of Scripture, and other knotty theological and hermeneutical issues. Given the debate surrounding typology, even in evangelical circles, this section discusses competing definitions of typology, my proposal for the essential features of a biblical type, and the criteria necessary for discerning types in Scripture.

---

[4] Ibid. 21.

[5] Moo argues that the phrase 'typological exegesis' may be unhelpful since 'typology is not an exegetical technique, nor even a hermeneutical axiom, but a broad theological construct with hermeneutical implications' (Moo 2007: 82). I believe, however, the phrase can be appropriate in a project like this that seeks to uncover how later biblical authors understand Joseph in the light of (1) continuing revelation and (2) the revelation afforded by the coming of Christ and the inauguration of the new covenant. Beale notes that typology 'can be called contextual exegesis within the framework of the canon since it primarily involves the interpretation and elucidation of the meaning of earlier parts of Scripture by later parts' (Beale 2012: 25).

[6] Moo 2007: 81.

Competing definitions of typology

The nature of typology is one of the most fundamental hermeneutical questions in biblical theology.[7] Since the publication of Goppelt's seminal work *Typos: Die typologische Deutung des Alten Testaments im Neuen* (1939),[8] scholars have published an enormous amount of literature explaining typology as either a New Testament phenomenon or a hermeneutical method. The number of qualifications and distinctions between scholars on this issue can be truly dizzying. Nevertheless, most approaches can be broadly categorized into one of two major schools of thought: (1) traditional/evangelical typology or (2) post-critical neo-typology.[9]

Traditional approaches to typology (often rooted in the work of Patrick Fairbairn[10] and Leonhard Goppelt) ground typology textually, according to Scripture's character as progressive revelation of God's saving acts. On this foundation, proponents of traditional typology assert that a type must be characterized by (1) historical correspondence, (2) escalation, and (3) Christological fulfilment. Thus, traditionalists are concerned to distinguish typology from allegory, understanding the latter as essentially unconcerned with textual warrant or with the historicity of Old Testament persons, events and institutions.

In contrast, post-critical neo-typology eschews the methodological and textual restrictions of traditional typology. Some advocates of this position often describe their approach as 'figural reading',[11] which, in recent years, has been championed by the diverse and multifaceted Theological Interpretation of Scripture (TIS) movement.[12] Proponents of TIS and figural reading posit that typology employs readers in creating typological (or 'figural') associations. As a result, the New Testament's use of the Old Testament is perceived as an imaginative, Christological reappropriation of Israel's Scriptures. In the language of Hays, the New Testament authors

---

[7] The following presentation of typology is heavily influenced by Parker 2011; 2017: 20–68; Schrock 2014: 3–26.

[8] Goppelt 1939. Goppelt's work was later published in English as Goppelt 1982.

[9] Davidson was the first to employ this terminology to describe those who wanted to recover a typological reading of Scripture within the framework of historical-critical commitments (Davidson 1981: 111).

[10] Fairbairn 1900.

[11] Frei, for instance, conflates 'typology' and 'figural reading' in Frei 1974: 1–7.

[12] For a description and balanced criticism of the modern TIS movement(s), see Carson 2011: 187–207. See also Treier 2008; Vanhoozer 2005.

engage in a 'retrospective hermeneutical transformation of Israel's sacred texts'.[13] In this view, New Testament authors (and by implication modern interpreters) are not uncovering Old Testament types intended as prospective historical events, persons or institutions that culminate in Christ. Instead, they are creating correspondences between the Old Testament and Christ through sanctified interpretive imagination. The Old Testament is 'Christianly contextualized'[14] by reading Christological correspondences *into* it – correspondences unintended by the human author. As a result, proponents of figural reading also support allegory as a legitimate hermeneutical enterprise. They posit that many instances of what scholars have typically designated 'typology' in the New Testament are better understood as allegory.[15]

As will become more evident below, neo-typology fails to do justice to the nature of Scripture, as progressive revelation is incompatible with the hermeneutical assumptions of New Testament authors evinced in their use of the Old Testament, discounts divine inspiration and lacks any real methodological constraints. Figural reading suffers from the same problems inherent in all postmodern interpretive agendas: it muffles the voice of the author and discounts a text's character, making the task of interpretation a subjective enterprise. Reader-activated correspondences between Old Testament and New Testament reveal nothing about Scripture's own redemptive-historical claims. As a result, figural readings of Scripture often reveal little more than an interpreter's imaginative prowess. The true message of Scripture as developed through the promise–fulfilment structure of the covenants is bartered away for a two-dimensional interpretive freedom that licenses interpretive communities to shape and reshape Scripture as they see fit. The result is 'Theological Interpretation' that eschews the Bible's own approach to both theology and interpretation.

In contrast, this project attempts to understand Scripture on its own terms and according to its nature as a text of both human and divine production. My aim is to account for Genesis 37 – 50 by engaging in author-oriented exegesis that simultaneously recognizes the ultimate context of a text's meaning is the entire canon of Scripture. My

---

[13] Hays 2014: xv. See also Hays's comments on interpretive imagination in *Conversion of the Imagination* (2005).

[14] R. W. L. Moberly 2007: 100.

[15] Gignilliat 2008: 140. See also Wilken 1998: 197–212.

understanding of typology, then, is very much 'traditional' – particularly as that method has been developed within the evangelical and Reformed traditions.

Essential features of a type

In their recent work on the covenants, Gentry and Wellum represent this traditional approach to typology within the Reformed tradition. They define typology as 'the study of the Old Testament salvation-historical realities or "types" (persons, events, institutions) which prefigure their intensified antitypical fulfillment aspects (inaugurated and consummated) in New Testament salvation history'.[16] This definition usefully highlights the essential features of a biblical type. First, types are historical ('salvation-historical realities'). Second, types are prospective ('prefigure'). Third, types exhibit escalation in moving from type to antitype ('intensified antitypical fulfillment'). Fourth, types are textual ('Old Testament' and 'New Testament salvation history'). Finally, as Wellum and Gentry imply throughout the book, types are unfolded through the covenants. They are shaped and interpreted by the covenantal structure of Scripture. In the remainder of this section, I will discuss the significance of each of these features as part of the New Testament's conception of typology.

Historicity. The New Testament evidence indicates that types are actual historical events, persons and institutions. This historical dimension to typology is critical for New Testament theology given how many apostolic claims concerning the person and work of Christ are rooted in his fulfilling the patterns of Israel's history.

In this respect, types are not mere products of literary art.[17] If the apostles' typological claims about Christ are purely allegorical, Christ is not necessarily the actual solution to any historical plight. He does not remedy our exile from the garden or meet Israel's need of a Davidic king. Instead, he is merely a figure to whom the apostles, via their own literary artfulness, assigned allegorical or kerygmatic significance. Put simply, if types are not historical, then Christ is not the culmination of a providentially ordained history or the fulfilment of any actual, historical promise.

---

16 Gentry and Wellum 2012: 103.
17 Contrast Sparks who posits that a 'theological reading of the Bible [may be performed] even when Scripture's ostensible historical content turns out to be either wrong or fictional in some way' (Sparks 2008: 178).

The New Testament attests to this fact repeatedly where the significance of an Old Testament type depends upon its historicity. The Adam–Christ typology in Romans 5, for instance, hangs on the notion that Adam is a figure of historical consequence – the federal head of the human race. Paul's typological argument is stripped of any real significance if Adam is merely metaphorical or mythological. Similarly, when New Testament authors mention other typological events (see 1 Cor. 10 and 1 Peter 3), their arguments hang on the historicity of the Old Testament person, event or institution discussed. Wherever New Testament authors employ typological exegesis they do so in a way that highlights the historicity of the Old Testament. Their aim is not merely to describe Christ by using theological or kerygmatic categories but also to demonstrate that he is the *telos* of history, the one who fulfils Israel's expectations and resolves humanity's plight.

Prospective/author-intended. The biblical data also indicate that Old Testament types are prospective in nature, which is to say that they were intended by the author. This means that types are 'indirect prophecy';[18] they are designed and described by God to forecast something about his redemptive work in Christ. This claim contrasts with the post-critical view of typology, which asserts that types are formed by New Testament authors retrospectively, who posit correspondences between Christ and patterns in Israel's history. In this 'retrospective' view, types have no prophetic, predictive or promissory function. Instead, they are theological constructs rooted in post-resurrection rereadings of the Old Testament.[19]

The prospective nature of types is borne out by the way both Old Testament and New Testament authors speak about them. Throughout the Pentateuch Moses portrays persons, events and institutions in the mould of God's prototypical design for creation in Genesis 1 – 2, evidencing that both prototype and the types patterned after them anticipate some eschatological resolution. In fact, the Pentateuch ends with typological expectations of a new Moses (Deut. 18:15–18; 34:10–12) and a new exodus (Deut. 30:1–10). Moses understands his own life and experiences in the exodus as prospectively foreshadowing something to come.

Similar evidence for the prospective nature of types is found in the New Testament. In Romans 5:14, Paul refers to Adam as a 'type of the one who

---

18 Beale 2012: 17–18.
19 France 1998: 39–40.

was to come'. As Schreiner notes, 'the reference to "the coming one" (*tou mellontos*) should be understood from the perspective of Adam. In other words, from Adam's standpoint in history Jesus Christ was the one to come.'[20]

Similarly, in 1 Corinthians 15:1–3 Paul understands the life, death and third-day resurrection of the Messiah to be events fully attested to by the Old Testament Scriptures. Clearly, Paul does not have any specific predictive prophecy in view. In fact, one would be hard pressed to find any prophecy that speaks to Jesus' rising on the third day.[21] Instead, Paul is appealing to the prospective patterns of Old Testament redemptive history that Jesus fulfils.[22] According to Paul, Jesus' death is not retroactively made to fit with Israel's Scriptures. Rather, his death and resurrection are carried out 'in accordance with' their prophetic expectations.

Jesus and the New Testament authors also attest to the prospective nature of Old Testament types by the way they expect others to interpret Scripture. Jesus, for example, rebukes the Jews for not believing what Moses wrote of him (John 5:46–47). Paul uses 'the law of Moses and the Prophets' to convince an audience of Jesus' work as Messiah (Acts 28:23). Apollos, too, 'refuted the Jews in public, showing by the [Old Testament] Scriptures that the Christ was Jesus' (Acts 18:28; cf. 9:22). These instances, which could easily be multiplied, demonstrate that the promise–fulfilment character of the Old and New Testaments is not something imposed by later Christian readers. Instead, it is essential to progressive revelation. Jesus' words in John 5 and Apollos's defence of Jesus' messiahship in Acts 18 are only intelligible if the typological structures of the Old Testament genuinely anticipate their new-covenant fulfilments.

The fact that Old Testament types anticipate new-covenant realities does not negate that Christ often fulfilled the Old Testament in surprising, unexpected ways. Additionally, affirming the prospective nature of Old Testament types does not mean that interpreters prior to Pentecost could

---

[20] Schreiner 1998: 280. I am grateful to Brent Parker, who first brought Schreiner's comments on this text to my attention.

[21] Dempster 2014 considers the OT typological roots of Paul's 'third day' statement in 1 Cor. 15.

[22] In the same vein, Treat comments on Luke 24, saying, 'When Jesus said, "thus it is written, that the Christ [Messiah] should suffer" (Luke 24:46), he was not merely proof-texting Isa. 52:13–53:12 or some other elusive individual prophecy of a suffering Messiah. He was interpreting his life, death, and resurrection as the fulfillment of a pattern in the story of Israel, a pattern characterized by humiliation and exaltation, shame and glory, suffering and victory' (Treat 2014: 54).

have discerned all that the Old Testament typologically anticipated. As Paul states, even though the law and the prophets bore witness to Christ (Rom. 1:2; 3:21; 15:8; Gal. 3:8), the gospel was a 'mystery that was kept secret for long ages' (Rom. 16:25–27). Thus, Christian interpreters after the resurrection have a privileged interpretive location in redemptive history. Christ's death, resurrection and ascension, coupled with his apostles' ministry and the work of illumination by the Spirit, shed light on the typological structures of the Old Testament. Certain Old Testament types are only discernible retrospectively. This retrospection, however, does not 'create' the type. The association is not reader-imposed.[23] Instead, this retrospection is a recognition that some Old Testament types were 'hidden in plain sight' – only intelligible by the light of later revelation.

Escalation. Given the progressive nature of special revelation, types also undergo escalation from Old Testament anticipation to New Testament fulfilment. In other words, the pattern of God's acts in the Old Testament bears witness to a final act that will not just reflect his previous dealings with his people but also consummate his work with them. Since biblical history develops towards an eschatological goal, antitypes are not merely analogous with earlier episodes in biblical history. New-covenant antitypes are the *telos* of biblical history. The new covenant fulfils Old Testament expectations within the framework of inaugurated eschatology. Thus, the New Testament indicates that Jesus (and by implication the church) fulfil all Old Testament expectations, leaving no further room for redemptive-historical development aside from the consummation of the kingdom.[24]

Textual. As Berkhof notes, 'Accidental similarity between an Old and New Testament person or event does not constitute the one a type of the other. There must be some Scripture evidence that it was so designed by God.'[25] This means that types are rooted in the *text* of the Old and New Testaments and are exegetically discerned. Any posited correspondence between persons, events or institutions that is not rooted in Scripture imposes an extratextual grid over Scripture's message and thus silences Scripture's own self-interpretation.

---

[23] See also Beale 2012: 13–25 for helpful comments on retrospection.
[24] Lints 1993: 305.
[25] Berkhof 1952: 145.

Schrock explains that the *textual* dimension of typology recognizes that types 'must arise from the language, sequence, and storyline of the Bible itself. [They] cannot be imported from an "extratextual hermeneutical grid," but must be verified by the Bible's own language or imagery.'[26] This means that typology must be 'tethered' to the text of Scripture.[27] Correspondences between events that contravene or go beyond scriptural testimony cannot be considered types since these correspondences emerge from readers' imaginations and not from the exegetical data. Again, as Schrock explains, 'true typology' is built on the foundation of 'the intratextual relationship between one historical figure in one biblical epoch and another later, (usually) greater historical figure'.[28]

Reading Scripture typologically is not an 'imaginative' task but an exegetical one. This proposal takes seriously Scripture's claims concerning itself and its nature as 'word–act' revelation. God designs persons, events and institutions to foreshadow the culmination of redemptive history in Christ (act) and then attests to these through his own commentary on those persons, events and institutions in Scripture (word). Types, then, can be uncovered only through grammatical-historical and canonical exegesis, which reveals the divine author's intention for a text. As Beale explains:

If typology is classified as partially prophetic even from the OT human author's viewpoint, then it can be viewed as an exegetical method. This is true because such an anticipatory aspect of an OT passage can be discerned by a historical-grammatical approach . . . And . . . if we assume the legitimacy of an inspired canon, then we should seek to interpret any part of that canon within its overall canonical context (given that one divine mind stands behind it all and expresses its thoughts in logical fashion) . . . In this regard, typology can be called contextual exegesis within the framework of the canon since it primarily involves the interpretation and elucidation of the meaning of earlier parts of Scripture by later parts.[29]

---

[26] Schrock 2014: 5.
[27] Ibid. 6.
[28] Ibid. 6–7.
[29] Beale 2012: 24–25.

Typology, therefore, is rooted in a *canonical* understanding of redemptive history. Scripture bears witness to types, and readers uncover those types through the discipline of exegesis. This exegesis focuses on the intent of both the human author (revealed via the grammatical-historical method) and the intent of the divine author (revealed via exegesis that takes into account earlier *as well as* later revelation; i.e. canonical context). Further, the intents of the human and divine authors never contradict each other. The divine intent, discovered through canonical context, always grows out of and is consistent with the human author's intent. Thus, types are textual because they are not products of 'imaginative' rereadings of Scripture but exegetical facts, rooted in Scripture by divine intent.

Covenantal. Finally, types are covenantal. As many scholars have posited throughout the history of interpretation, covenants shape the biblical storyline and provide the essential building blocks for biblical theology. With each new covenant, God unfolds his eternal plan, filling out the details and developing earlier promises while bringing Israel's eschatological hopes into sharper focus. As a result, 'the Bible's typological and covenantal structures are interdependent'.[30] Types (i.e. the law, the temple, the land, etc.) are part and parcel of God's covenants, and covenants provide the interpretive context necessary to understand a type's significance in redemptive history.[31]

Interpreting types according to their covenantal context is particularly important when examining Old Testament historical narrative, since, typically, it lacks explicit theological commentary.[32] Readers often understand the full significance of characters' actions only in the light of covenant stipulations and promises laid out elsewhere in the Old Testament. Covenants, thus, provide the inner-biblical interpretive and theological grid needed to evaluate historical narratives. Reading Old Testament history according to covenantal unfolding and context reveals the deeper, theological significance that often goes unstated in narrative. For example, Chapter 3, below, notes that Genesis 39:4–5 indicates that Joseph is a 'blessing' to Potiphar the Egyptian. This detail takes on much richer theological significance when read in the light of the covenant promise that Abraham's children would be a 'blessing to the nations' (Gen. 12:2–3).

---

[30] Schrock 2014: 6.
[31] For a full development of this point, see Gentry 2016: 9–33.
[32] This is particularly true of the Joseph story.

Criteria for discerning types

Equally important in this discussion is how types are discerned in the Old Testament. Or, more pointedly, what criteria must be used to establish Old Testament types? This question is paramount in a project such as this, where strict methodological controls are needed in order to avoid 'domesticating the evidence'[33] and becoming a 'hyper-typer'.[34]

The primary task for establishing the existence of a type is showing how it accords with the nature of a type as outlined above. Scripture must attest that a proposed type, rightly understood in covenantal context, is a historical person, event or institution anticipating an escalated reality. If these features can be established from the original context or from later biblical reflection, then a type is present. My purpose in this chapter is not to rehearse the many different ways Scripture can attest to these features. Beale, Wellum and Gentry and others have already enumerated the types of exegetical and theological evidences that establish historicity, prospection, escalation and the other elements of typology.[35] My work builds on their proposals and stands on their shoulders.

In summary, I hope to show that the typological reading of the story of Joseph is textually rooted and canonically developed within Scripture itself. I will demonstrate the typological character of Joseph by considering (1) the exegetical, literary and thematic features that relate Joseph to the larger storyline of Genesis and the Abrahamic covenant, (2) linguistic and thematic points of contact between the Joseph story and earlier episodes in Genesis, (3) how later Old Testament authors appropriate the language and imagery of the Joseph story, and (4) the ways New Testament authors allude to or employ the Joseph narrative in their retelling of the Gospel accounts and their biblical-theological commentary on Joseph. With each of these points, I aim to demonstrate concrete *textual* warrant for my proposal. I also hope to reveal the biblical authors' 'interpretive perspective' on the Joseph story in the light of unfolding revelation, particularly as it climaxes in the person and work of Jesus Christ.

---

[33] Carson 2007.

[34] Currid 1994: 121.

[35] Beale 2012: 13–27; Gentry and Wellum 2012: 102–108; Naselli 2012; Schrock 2014.

3

The Joseph story in Genesis' *tôlĕdôt* structure

The primary literary structuring device in Genesis is the *tôlĕdôt* formula, the demonstrative pronoun (usually *'ēlleh*) followed by *tôlĕdôt* in a construct relationship with a noun (usually a proper name).[1] The phrase *'ēlleh tôlĕdôt* (these are the generations of) occurs ten times in Genesis (2:4; 5:1; 6:9; 10:1; 11:10, 27; 25:12, 19; 36:1, [9];[2] 37:2). Scholars who adopt a literary approach to Genesis generally agree that the *tôlĕdôt* mark new sections within the book. As some recent studies have shown, however, the *tôlĕdôt* are much more than generic chapter headings in Genesis. Instead, they provide a reading strategy for the book by signalling major plot developments while simultaneously tracing the development of the singular theme of redemption through the seed of the woman.[3]

Furthermore, as many scholars have noted, the *tôlĕdôt* formula signals not only the beginning of a new section but also its subjects – the descendants of the person named in the *tôlĕdôt* formula. As DeRouchie explains, the purpose of these 'transitional headings' is to 'progressively direct the reader's focus from progenitor to progeny and narrow the reader's focus

---

[1] The anomaly in this pattern is Gen. 5:1. Though still clearly a *tôlĕdôt* structural marker, 5:1 reads, 'This is the book of the generations of Adam.' On this anomalous *tôlĕdôt*, see the discussion in DeRouchie 2013: 242–244.

[2] While 36:9 does repeat the phrase *'ēlleh tôlĕdôt*, most scholars agree that this should not be read as an independent (or eleventh) *tôlĕdôt* structural marker but as some type of substructural unit within Gen. 36 separating the genealogy recording Esau's time in Canaan (36:1–8) from the genealogy of Esau's descendants in the 'hill country of Seir' (36:9–43). Garrett reads the repetition of 36:9 as an inclusio with 36:1 (Garrett 1991: 96, n., 97). More persuasively, as both Matthew Thomas and Jason DeRouchie have observed, a second use of *tôlĕdôt* within a section already introduced by the phrase occurs three times (Gen. 10:32; 25:13; 36:9). Notably, these genealogies share two traits: (1) each follows a segmented (as opposed to linear) genealogy, which (2) traces the descendants of the nations surrounding Israel, not the seed of promise. See Thomas 2011: 74–76; DeRouchie 2013: 219, n. 1.

[3] See Thomas 2011 and DeRouchie 2013.

from all the world to Israel, through whom all families of the earth will be blessed'.[4] Thus, excluding the segmented genealogies of the sons of Noah (10:1 – 11:9), Ishmael (25:12–18) and Esau (36:1–8; 36:9 – 37:1), the *tôlĕdôt* sections trace the story of the promise from Adam and Noah through the funnel of Abraham and Isaac into the nascent nation of Israel, represented by Jacob and his twelve sons.

But the *tôlĕdôt* formula does more than mark sections and introduce new subjects. These markers also signal, at least in part, how each section of Genesis relates to the previous ones. As DeRouchie notes, the *tôlĕdôt* 'witness a progressive narrowing that places focus on the line of promise and the centrality of Israel in God's kingdom-building program'.[5] The Genesis story moves from (1) the heavens and the earth (1:1 – 2:3) to (2) Adam (2:4 – 4:26) to (3) Noah (5:1 – 6:8) to (4) Shem (11:10–26) to (5) Terah (11:27 – 25:11) to (6) Isaac (25:19 – 35:29) and finally to (7) Jacob (37:2 – 50:26). In other words, the story moves from all creation to humanity, and then to a specific family line within humanity.[6] The seven divisions move from larger to smaller units until the readers arrive at the central vehicle through which God will accomplish redemption – the nation of Israel represented by its twelve patriarchs.[7] Thus the *tôlĕdôt* ensure that the

---

[4] DeRouchie 2013: 225. See also Hamilton, 'The *tôlĕdôt* structure . . . suggests a movement from a starting point to a finishing point, from a cause to an effect, from a progenitor to a progeny who is the key individual at that point in either implementing or perpetuating God's plan and will in his heavens and earth' (V. Hamilton 1990: 10).

[5] DeRouchie 2013: 235.

[6] Ibid.

[7] DeRouchie and Thomas argue on the basis of discourse grammar that the five asyndetic *tôlĕdôt* introduce major divisions within Genesis while waw-initial *tôlĕdôt* serve as co-ordinating subsections. In this light, the *tôlĕdôt* in Genesis do not mark ten sections of equal rank but, rather, five major sections marked by asyndeton with waw-initial subsections underneath these main headings (Gen. 2:4; 5:1; 6:9; 11:10; 37:2). Previous scholars have also argued for five major divisions on the basis of asyndeton, though not on the same text-linguistic grounds as Thomas and DeRouchie. See Cassuto 1964: 188, and Weimar 1974: 65–93.

In this scheme, the major divisions marked by the asyndetic *tôlĕdôt* appear to fall along covenantal lines. The first *tôlĕdôt* records the story of the Adamic covenant, from its initiation, through its undoing (Gen. 3:1–7), to the glimmers of hope (Gen. 3:15; 4:26) and despair (4:1–16) that follow as God responds in both salvation and judgment. The second *tôlĕdôt* does not record the beginning of a new covenant but instead seems to hold out the implications of the failed Adamic covenant (Gen. 6:1–7). This section focuses on 'stage two' of the Adamic administration, highlighting the ruin caused by Adam's failed administration. The third and fourth asyndetic *tôlĕdôt* (with their corresponding waw-initial subsections) focus on successive covenants. The third asyndetic *tôlĕdôt* highlights the Noahic covenant, whereas the fourth traces the history of the Abrahamic covenant. Like the second major *tôlĕdôt* section (Gen. 5:1 – 6:8), the Joseph story does not record the inauguration of the next covenant in redemptive history. The likely reason is because it fulfils the same function for the story of the Abrahamic covenant as 5:1 – 6:8 did for the Adamic covenant. The Joseph story is 'stage two'

narrative does not 'wander aimlessly' but focuses attention on a line of promise commissioned to carry out God's purposes in the world.[8] This structure thus emphasizes the essential unity of Genesis. Each linear *tôlĕdôt* advances the same promises and the same redemptive-historical expectations, even as those promises and expectations develop as God initiates new covenants with increasingly smaller family units (e.g. Adam, Noah, Abraham).

Function of the *tôlĕdôt* formula: tracing God's promise through each generation

As M. Johnson observed in his seminal work on genealogies in 1969, genealogies (like those represented in the *tôlĕdôt* of Genesis) develop 'a sense of movement within history toward a divine goal'.[9] The linear genealogies delineating the royal line of blessing in Genesis trace the development of God's covenantal promises through specific family lines in exclusion to all others. From a biblical-theological perspective, Moses uses the *tôlĕdôt*, with its emphasis on genealogy as part of the very meaning of the word, as a way of tracing the story of God's commitment to fulfil his eschatological goal of a world populated with image bearers (Gen. 1:28) that must now come through an act of redemption and warfare by a 'seed of the woman' (Gen. 3:15). The tenfold *tôlĕdôt* propels forward the genealogically driven storyline represented by Genesis 1:28 and 3:15, while also identifying family lines excluded from covenant participation – the nations of the world to whom Israel must carry out its missiological purpose.[10] The very use of the word *tôlĕdôt* as a structural marker indicates that Moses highlights the inseparable connection between the main characters of Genesis (the 'seeds or 'begotten ones' [*yld*]) and the redemption story. Each 'seed' in the line of promise is indelibly linked to the eschatological hope of Genesis 1:28 and 3:15 as well as to Adam, Noah, Abraham and the covenants their narratives represent.

---

of the Abrahamic covenant. Yet, unlike 5:1 – 6:8, this final *tôlĕdôt* is not meant to show the failure of the Abrahamic covenant, but its success. As we will see more fully below, the fourth major section establishes the *promises* given to Abraham, Isaac and Jacob, but the final *tôlĕdôt* (Joseph's story) highlights the partial *fulfilment* of those promises.

8 Thomas 2011: 42; see also 72–73.

9 M. Johnson 1969: 60.

10 DeRouchie 2013: 239–242.

Within Genesis, the seven *tôlĕdôt* units made up of linear genealogies and narrative work hand in hand to disclose how, through a
particular line of descent climaxing in Israel, God preserved his
blessing-commission (Gen. 1:28) and the hope for a curse-defeating,
regal offspring (Gen. 3:15). In contrast, the three segmented *tôlĕdôt*
establish Israel's 'mission field'. In other words, Moses uses narratives and linear genealogies to highlight the ancestry of Israel as the
chosen line of promise, but uses segmented genealogies to give ever-
present reminders to Israelite readers that their image-bearing
purpose is for the sake of the nations and that their longed-for
deliverer will be the agent of blessing to all the families of the earth
(12:3; 22:17b–18). The world was not created for Israel but Israel for
the world.[11]

These observations on Genesis' internal structure further advance the
proposal, already affirmed by many scholars, that the patriarchal stories
must be read with an eye towards God's larger creation purposes established in the primeval narratives and that those purposes play out along
covenantal lines.[12] The result is that the interpretive influence between the
patriarchal and primeval histories is bidirectional. Whereas the patriarchal narratives clarify and refine our knowledge of God's purpose to
create for himself a people with whom he dwells and over whom he rules,
the primeval history highlights that these are God's intentions not only
for the nation of Israel but also for all humanity. Genesis 1:1 – 11:9 establishes the universal scope of God's work in creation and redemption,
whereas the patriarchal narratives (officially beginning with the *tôlĕdôt* of
Shem in 11:10) focus on the means God will use to effect that redemption.
Thus, while the patriarchal narratives focus on Israel, they remain in
the cosmic framework of God's purposes for his creation established by the
first eleven chapters.

---

[11] Ibid. 240–241.

[12] E.g. Arnold states, 'Cosmic beginnings and Israel's national beginnings are thus tied
together theologically as one story in Genesis . . . By tying it together through the genealogies
and *tôlĕdôt*-structuring device, Abraham and the nation Israel serve as the means of salvation
for all humanity, indeed for the entire cosmos . . . The book of Genesis took a dramatic turn
with Terah's genealogy at 11:27 (that is with Terah's *tôlĕdôt*-structuring clause) . . . This
ingenious macrostructure is made possible by five occurrences in the primeval history (2:4;
5:1; 6:9; 10:1; 11:10) and five more in the ancestral narratives (11:27; 25:12; 25:19; 36:1; 37:1; plus
one extra in 36:9)' (Arnold 2009: 229).

A number of smaller literary and textual features demonstrate the interplay between creation, the Noahic and the Abrahamic covenants. As Hamilton notes, the promises of the Abrahamic covenant in Genesis 12:1–3 provide a 'direct answer' to the curses of Genesis 3:14–19.[13] Along the same lines, the fivefold repetition of 'blessing' in Genesis 12:1–3 appears to be Yahweh's response to the fivefold curse in Genesis 3 – 11 (Gen. 3:14, 17; 4:11; 5:29; 9:25).[14]

Similarly, the promise that God will bless all the 'families' (*mišpāḥôt*) of the earth hearkens back to the proliferation of 'families' in the Table of Nations (10:5, 18, 20, 31, 32). On this point Carrol R. notes, 'Continuity is thus complemented by contrast: Abram and the nation which will spring from him are not to exhibit the same sort of disobedience and prideful aspirations as were exhibited at Babel; greatness will come by divine grace, not human pretense.'[15]

Also, at the seam between the primeval and patriarchal narratives, linguistic links between the Babel story in Genesis 11 and the initial promises to Abraham (cf. Gen. 11:4 with 12:2) indicate the author's purpose that readers see each event in the light of the other. The Babelites desire to make a name for themselves and are thwarted by God, but Yahweh will make a name for Abraham.[16] The very contours of the Abrahamic promises also demonstrate the interpretive dependence between primeval and patriarchal narratives. For example, Dempster notes that Yahweh's promise to bless 'all the families of the earth' through Abraham exhibits Israel's essentially missiological (hence global) *raison d'être*.[17]

At the beginning of Israel's history, then, is the fundamental fact that it has been made for the benefit of the world. Israel's calling is fundamentally missiological; its purpose for existence is the restoration of the world to its pre-Edenic state. Genesis 12:1–3 is thus the 'aetiology of all Israelite aetiologies', showing that 'the ultimate purpose of redemption which God will bring about in Israel is that of bridging the gulf between God and the entire human race'.[18]

---

[13] J. M. Hamilton 2007: 253–273.

[14] Wolff 1974: 54–55; Dempster 2003: 77.

[15] Carroll R. 2000: 21.

[16] Arnold 2009: 132.

[17] Dempster 2003: 23.

[18] Ibid. 76–77. The final phrase of Dempster's quotation comes from von Rad 1966: 65. A host of other scholars have also posited this type of 'call–response' or 'problem–solution' relationship between the primeval and patriarchal histories. See Dumbrell 1993: 68; Arnold 2009: 229.

The *tôlĕdôt* structure and the story of Joseph

Genesis' *tôlĕdôt* structure, as well as the thematic and textual linkages between primeval and patriarchal history, attests to an essential and unbroken unity to the Genesis story. God's covenantal promises, reflecting his purpose for all of creation, are traced from generation to generation in a single family through the *tôlĕdôt*. Joseph does not discontinue Genesis' focus on creation and covenant, but advances it. If the *tôlĕdôt* formula does, in fact, 'witness a progressive narrowing . . . on the line of promise and the centrality of Israel in God's kingdom-building program' then the Joseph story is the climax of that genealogical unfolding, at least as far as Genesis is concerned.[19] Since the *tôlĕdôt* trace the development of the seed promise through the unfolding of the covenants, Joseph's story must be interpreted according to this authorially constructed framework.

Thus, as the final section in Genesis, the Joseph story exhibits both continuity and discontinuity with what precedes it. As the final *tôlĕdôt*, Joseph's story is the end point of Genesis' racing, genealogy-driven narrative. In this sense, considering Genesis as a self-contained literary unit, Genesis 37 – 50 represents the final act of the book. So far from being wholly discontinuous from the primeval and patriarchal narratives, this final *tôlĕdôt* presents Genesis 37 – 50 as the final plot piece in a story developing as early as Genesis 2:4 – cementing the Joseph story into the unfolding drama of God's covenantal promises. In other words, the structure of Genesis clearly roots the Joseph story as being in essential literary and biblical-theological continuity with all that precedes.

Joseph, however, is also discontinuous from earlier narratives. Just as previous *tôlĕdôt* marked, at least in some sense, a 'new stage' in redemptive history (especially through the inauguration of new covenants), so also Joseph's story is a new stage. As argued below, the Joseph story marks a transition from the establishment to the fulfilment of promises. Consequently, the point is not that the covenant story here ceases, but with this final *tôlĕdôt* that story turns towards new developments. The same covenantal promises are still in view, yet instead of linear developments that trace the passing of covenantal promises from a father to a single heir,

---

19 DeRouchie 2013: 235.

the covenant blessings now diffuse to all twelve sons of Jacob and hence to their eponymous tribes.[20] With previous *tôlĕdôt* sections, the line of promise narrowed. Now those covenantal promises fan out to the blossoming nation of Israel. Thus far in the story the promise has transferred from a father to his singular seed. Now those promises develop along corporate lines.[21] The time of the patriarchs has come to an end. Now the story turns to the nation of Israel.

The new direction of the story also includes other biblical-theological developments. Thomas, for instance, posits that one reason Genesis 37:2 – 50:26 is its own *tôlĕdôt* is due to the 'reconciliation of the brothers in the Joseph cycle':

> In the earlier stories of brothers in Genesis, there was always some problem: Cain killed Abel, Ishmael 'played with' Isaac, and Esau wanted to kill Jacob, for example. Here, in the story of Jacob's sons, however, after the initial problems, the brothers are able to reconcile on the basis of Joseph's forgiveness of them. This opens up a new type of relationship among different groups of people. Perhaps, this is the basis on which all 12 tribes are able to be together the focus of the narrative from here on. Perhaps, it is the next stage of covenant: people covenanting among themselves in imitation of the covenants with God.[22]

Thomas is right to look for a theological explanation as to why the story of Joseph receives its own *tôlĕdôt*. As I will show, reconciliation as a

---

[20] Joseph himself recognizes this fact when he refers to the covenant's being administered to 'Abraham, Isaac and Jacob' (Gen. 50:24), not 'Abraham, Isaac, Jacob and Joseph [or Judah]'. As Thomas notes, 'As we move into the following generation [the *tôlĕdôt* of Jacob], the process of narrowing stops with the sons of Jacob. All 12 are taken as the focus of the story from that point on, so no narrowing process is necessary ... Given that in each of the previous narrowings there is a decision made among siblings as to who will be the next focus, the focus on all 12 brothers from here on is significant. The *tôlĕdôt* section of Jacob begins with his 12 sons' (Thomas 2011: 116–117).

[21] 'That Jacob has twelve sons may have further significance. It is common for key figures in Genesis to have two or three sons ... Jacob's fathering twelve sons distinguishes him, therefore, from the other patriarchs. Yet it has been noted that one son in particular usually takes up the position of the main line and that secondary lines are presented first, whereas the main line is presented last. That Jacob has twelve sons, rather than two or three, and that there is no reversal of primogeniture in the genealogy seems to indicate that Gen. 35:22b–26 marks a new stage in the genealogical schema. The implication appears to be that all twelve sons constitute the main line' (Kaminski 2004: 112).

[22] Thomas 2011: 46.

resolution to the theme of fraternal conflict is indeed part of the answer. This theme, however, is part of a much larger picture, one of a regal seed of Israel beginning to fulfil the covenantal promises.

The patriarchal narratives and covenantal promises have set up an expectation for God to act through and for Jacob's descendants in fulfilment of those promises. Genesis 37:2 marks a turning point in the narrative and as a result new questions emerge: what new challenges are posed to the fulfilment of God's promises? What will the fulfilment of those promises look like? What will happen to the covenantal promises given the Cain-like behaviour of the covenant family and their eventual dislocation out of Canaan into Egypt?

In sum, the *tôlĕdôt* structure highlights the continuity of God's covenant purposes as they pass from Adam through Abraham to the nation of Israel. Moses' use of *tôlĕdôt* thus gives biblical-theological unity to Genesis and emphasizes the continuity between the parts. But, as demonstrated above, the final *tôlĕdôt* signals a new stage of development in the story of the Abrahamic covenant.[23]

---

[23] Similarly, Childs, reflecting on why Joseph receives his own *tôlĕdôt*, writes, 'Joseph is clearly set apart from the earlier patriarchs. He does not form part of the triad to whom the promise of land and posterity is given, rather he becomes the first (Gen. 50:24) to whom the promise to Abraham, Isaac, and Jacob is reiterated . . . Joseph became the means of preserving the family in a foreign country (50.20), but also the means by which a new threat to the promise of the land was realized. Conversely, Judah demonstrated an unfaithfulness which threatened to destroy the promise of posterity, which was only restored by the faithfulness of a Canaanite wife. In sum, the final section of the book of Genesis turns on the issue of the threat to the promise which leads inevitably to the book of Exodus' (Childs 1979: 156–157).

4

Joseph and covenant: kingship

In this chapter and the two following I unfold the biblical-theological significance of the Joseph story along several lines.[1] First, I briefly examine how Moses introduces Joseph in the Genesis story and discuss some of the hermeneutical challenges in interpreting Genesis 37 – 50. Second, I argue that kingship is an essential element of the Abrahamic covenant and that Joseph is a truly royal figure in the Abrahamic line. Third, I argue that Moses portrays Joseph as instrumental to the fulfilment of the Abrahamic seed promise. Fourth, I show how the Joseph story develops the Abrahamic land promise and how his death signals the nation's hope for the exodus and the return to the Promised Land. Fifth, I examine how Joseph fulfils covenantal expectations by mediating blessing to the nations. Sixth, I briefly examine how other, less prominent features of the Joseph story develop his role within Genesis. Finally, I synthesize all these exegetical arguments in a brief biblical-theological account, explaining the contextual and covenantal purpose of the Joseph story.

Introducing Joseph and Genesis 37 – 50

Moses' initial mentions of Joseph in Genesis 30 – 36 foreshadow Joseph's coming prominence in the rest of the book. Joseph is first mentioned in the birth narratives of the twelve sons of Israel, with his birth acting as the final event in the chiastic centre of the Jacob cycle.[2]

---

[1] Material in this chapter and the following two has been adapted from S. Emadi 2018: 1–24.
[2] Chiasm adapted from Arnold 2009: 264. For a defence of this chiastic proposal, see Fishbane 1998: 40–58; Fokkelman 1991: 86–241; Wenham 1994a: 169–170.

A   29:1–14, Jacob arrives in Paddan-aram
  B   29:15–30, Laban gains an advantage over Jacob
    C   29:31 – 30:24, birth of Jacob's children
        (Conclusion: Joseph's birth)
  B' 30:25–43, Jacob gains an advantage over Laban
A' 31:1–55, Jacob departs from Paddan-aram

Joseph's place in the chiastic structure portends his later significance in Israel's history. Other features of the Jacob narrative continue to anticipate this reality. For example, the account of Jacob's placing Joseph and Rachel in the back of the caravan to meet Esau hints at the favouritism that will later ignite the conflict between Joseph and his brothers (Gen. 33:2, 7), as does Joseph's being introduced to Esau before Rachel (Gen. 33:7).

Similarly, in the Genesis 35:22–26 genealogy,[3] Moses arranges Jacob's children by mother (Leah, Rachel, Bilhah, Zilphah) rather than birth order, thus putting Joseph in the seventh position in the genealogy. As Sasson notes, the seventh position in a genealogy regularly marks a person of great significance (cf. Gen. 5:21–24; Matt. 1:17) and may here signal Joseph's centrality in the following narrative.[4]

Joseph reappears next in his own story, Genesis 37 – 50. These chapters are notoriously difficult to interpret – most probably because they have almost no theological commentary embedded in the story itself. In this sense Joseph's story resembles Esther's. The narrator embraces a primarily 'secular' outlook in his retelling of the events by providing little explicit theological evaluation on the meaning of this small portion of Israel's history.

---

[3] Bailey argues that this text is also chiastic and that the structure emphasizes Rachel's sons (and her handmaiden Bilhah's sons), specifically Joseph and Benjamin:

A Now the sons of Jacob were twelve (v. 22b).
  B The sons of Leah: Reuben (Jacob's firstborn), Simeon, Levi, Judah, Issachar and Zebulun (v. 23).
    C The sons of Rachel: Joseph and Benjamin (v. 24)
    C' The sons of Bilhah, Rachel's maid: Dan and Naphtali (v. 25)
  B' The sons of Zilpah, Leah's maid: Gad and Asher (v. 26a).
A' These were the sons of Jacob who were born to him in Paddan-aram (v. 26b).

See Bailey 1994: 270–271. Kaminski concurs with Bailey's argument (Kaminski 2004: 114).

[4] Sasson 1978: 171–185, particularly 183. Arnold likewise agrees that 'this list may illustrate the honor accorded the seventh position in genealogies, placing Joseph there by narrating Rachel's and Bilhah's sons, before returning to Leah's sons through Zilpah' (Arnold 2009: 306).

In a few important instances the narrator does interject theological interpretation of the unfolding events. Moses mentions Yahweh's response to the wickedness of Judah and his sons in Genesis 38. He also notes Yahweh's presence with Joseph and blessing of Potiphar's house in Genesis 39.[5] These references to Yahweh are enormously important for our understanding of the story – both for their theological content and as a literary device cementing the stories of Judah and Joseph together. Strangely, however, these final 14 chapters refer to 'Yahweh' only 12 times (0.85 times per chapter), in comparison to 153 references in chapters 1 – 36 (4.25 times per chapter). 'Elohim' occurs 35 times in the Joseph story (2.5 times per chapter) but 184 times in the first 36 chapters (5.11 times per chapter).

Just as explicit divine activity decreases after Genesis 37, theophanic visions are also much less frequent in the Joseph story than in the patriarchal narratives. Even Joseph's dreams differ from his father's: they employ figurative imagery, contain no direct speech from Yahweh and are not attributed to Yahweh (initially). Yahweh resumes his more active role only after Joseph and his family are reunited, when the dramatic tension is resolved. At this point, only Jacob hears directly from Yahweh (Gen. 46:1–4) – the final theophanic vision in the book.

Further, the most salient theological interpretation of the narrative comes from the mouth of Joseph himself (Gen. 45:4–9; 50:19–21), leaving readers to discern whether the narrator shares his interpretation of the events.[6] As a result, scholars divide over both large and small interpretive matters. For example, commentators posit a number of central themes in the story: reconciliation, providence and preservation, covenantal fulfilment, sapiential embodiment or idyllic leadership, among others.[7]

---

[5] Gen. 38:7, 10; 39:2, 3(×2), 5(×2), 21, 23(×2). Jacob invokes the name of Yahweh after the blessing of Dan (Gen. 49:18).

[6] Pirson argues that the narrator's silence towards Joseph's interpretation of his own destiny (Gen. 45:5–11) makes it impossible to know whether the narrator affirms Joseph's statement as true. 'It should be noted that it is his [Joseph's] interpretation of the events; the narrator nowhere denies nor confirms it' (Pirson 2002: 138). See also Miscall 1978: 31.

[7] On reconciliation, see Fischer 2001: 242–271; B. Smith 2002; 2005: 158–174. On providence and preservation, see Kidner 1967: 179; Scullion 1992: 955; Dillard and Longman 1994: 48–56; Garrett 1996; LaSor et al. 1996: 48; Hoffmeier 1997; P. R. House 1998: 82–85; Schreiner 2013: 25–27. On covenantal fulfilment, see Wenham 1994a: 344. On sapiental embodiment or idyllic leadership, see von Rad 1953: 120–127. This article later appeared in English as 'The Joseph Narrative and Ancient Wisdom' in von Rad 1966. See also Smothers 1964; Loader 1974: 21–31; Coats 1980: 15–37; Wessels 1984: 39–60; L. Wilson 2004. By referencing these works in correspondence with a particular theme, I do not mean that these scholars posit that these themes

Scholars also divide on more specific interpretive matters. Some, for example, see Joseph in Genesis 37 as a bratty, tattling upstart who needs a lesson in humility,[8] while others advocate a more sympathetic or agnostic reading.[9] Some see the narrator's silence about Judah and Tamar as approbation,[10] while others infer an unfavourable comparison to Joseph's purity (Gen. 39).[11] Similarly, scholars variously interpret Joseph's 'testing' of his brothers (Gen. 42 – 44) as either the actions of a man prudently and patiently pursuing reconciliation with his estranged family or the torturous power play of a maniacal, self-absorbed tyrant.[12]

Similar disagreement exists over Joseph's administration in Genesis 47:13–26. According to McKenzie, this passage portrays a seed of Abraham's blessing the nations through judicious policy.[13] According to Watt, this passage shows Joseph as 'a tyrant wielding power as a corrupt form of leadership'.[14] In short, the 'interpretive space' created by the lack of explicit theological commentary from the narrator makes the meaning and function of the Joseph story more ambiguous than previous sections of Genesis.

The prominence of other characters also poses interpretive challenges. Obviously, Joseph is the main human actor in this drama, but Jacob and Judah both play prominent roles as well – so much so that, as opposed to being just the story of Joseph, some scholars argue that Genesis 37 – 50 is really the story of all three men.[15] What do we make of a story that seemingly features one character but constantly shifts attention to the

---

(note 7 *cont.*) are the only or even the primary themes of the Joseph story. Indeed, many of these scholars articulate other minor themes in addition to the major themes mentioned. Also, not every scholar fits neatly into each of their assigned categories, since each develops his proposed theme along different lines and with a number of permutations.

[8] Sternberg e.g. comments, 'God's future agent and mouthpiece in Egypt could hardly make a worse impression on his first appearance: spoiled brat . . . braggart' (Sternberg 1985: 98). See also Wenham 1994: 350; Waltke 2001: 499.

[9] Westermann 1982: 36; B. Smith 2002: 226, 229; L. Wilson 2004: 55–56; Goligher 2008: 17–18; Arnold 2009: 318; Gonzales 2009: 213–215.

[10] Brueggemann 1982: 308–309; Westermann 1982: 54.

[11] B. Smith 2002: 53.

[12] Indeed, Wildavsky, Fung and Pirson make Joseph out to be little more than a maniacal, self-absorbed, ladder-climbing tyrant with a god complex. See Wildavsky 1993; Fung 2000; Pirson 2002.

[13] McKenzie 1983: 386–399.

[14] Watt 1995: 68–69. See also Lerner 1989: 278–281. The thesis of Lerner's article is that the Torah condemns Joseph's actions. With remarkably strong language he asserts, 'Joseph is here portrayed as ruthlessly pursuing a course of coercive economic centralization . . . The Torah's account of Joseph's early life presages his moral failure as ruler of Egypt' (278–279). The Egyptians under Joseph's reign did not share such a negative assessment (Gen. 47:25).

[15] Dempster 2003: 88–92. Smith refers to Gen. 37 – 50 as the 'Joseph-Judah story' and argues that these chapters present a 'double plot'. B. Smith 2002; 2005.

'supporting roles'? Do all of these characters and storylines integrate into a single 'Joseph story'?

Perhaps the most infamous challenge along these lines is the so-called 'excursus' of Genesis 38, the account of Judah's promiscuity. Scholars have produced a mountain of literature trying to account for the rationale of this story so seemingly out of place in the context of Genesis 37 – 50.[16]

While some scholars overstate the dissimilarity between the Joseph story and the rest of Genesis, the Joseph story does bear some distinguishing marks. As noted, explicit divine activity and theological interpretation are much scarcer here than before. The shape of the narrative also distinguishes it from other patriarchal stories. These previous stories are fairly episodic,[17] whereas the Joseph story is a 'single unit that traces the development of a single conflict'.[18]

These interpretive challenges are, indeed, daunting but not insurmountable. While Moses has constructed a complex and subtle narrative, assiduous attention to the details of the text will reveal just how the Joseph story fits within the storyline of Genesis and within redemptive history.

Joseph in biblical-theological perspective

What is Joseph's contribution to redemptive history in Genesis? As chapter 1 demonstrated, much previous scholarship concedes little, if any,

---

[16] For a small sampling of this literature, see Coats 1972: 461–466; Cassuto 1973: 29–40; Goldin 1977: 27–44; Emerton 1975: 338–361; 1979: 403–415; G. R. H. Wright 1982: 523–529; Mathewson 1986; 1989: 373–392; Curtis 1991: 247–257; Lockwood 1992: 35–43; Fokkelman 1996: 152–187; Lambe 1998: 102–120; B. Smith 2002; 2005. The traditional historical-critical response to this problem is simply to assert that Gen. 38 has been shoehorned into its current location by a sloppy redactor. E.g. von Rad argues, 'every attentive reader can see that the story of Judah and Tamar has no connection at all with the strictly organized Joseph story at whose beginning it is now inserted' (von Rad 1972: 351). See also Brueggeman's comments 'This peculiar chapter stands alone, without connection to its context. It is isolated in every way and is most enigmatic. It does not seem to belong with any of the identified sources of ancestral tradition. It is not evident that it provides any significant theological resource. It is difficult to know in what context it might be of value for theological exposition' (Brueggemann 1982: 307–308). Additionally, as one might expect, Gen. 38 has quite a sordid history of interpretation – with some even refusing to render commentary on the chapter. This tradition goes back as far as Josephus, who passed over the episode entirely in his *Antiquities*, likely in order to portray Israel favourably to a Gentile audience. This tradition of excising Gen. 38 from the Joseph story continues even in the modern period. The 1948 Eerdmans edition of Calvin's commentary, for instance, omits Calvin's comments on Gen. 38:9–10.

[17] Wilson notes, 'The earlier patriarchal accounts are composed of smaller stories, generally no longer than 20 or 30 verses. The Joseph story arguably contains 392 verses' (Wilson 2004: 45).

[18] B. Smith 2005: 158. See also Sarna 1966: 211; Humphreys 1988: 8; Kugel 1994: 13.

real theological correspondence between the Joseph story and preceding narratives. Redford's comments are worth repeating on this point:

> The theological outlook of the writer of Gen. 37 – 50 is different from that of the Patriarchal narrator. He does not mention the Covenant or the Promise, ubiquitous in the earlier chapters of Genesis. He is not interested in supplying the reader with comment on matters theological, as the Patriarchal author was.[19]

As noted in chapter 1, Brevard Childs states the dilemma more pointedly when he asks, 'What is the shape of the final chapters and what is their function within the book as a whole? . . . If Joseph is not the bearer of the promise in the same way as his forefathers, what then is his role in Genesis?'[20]

This chapter and the two that follow are primarily a response to that question. Joseph's story is an anticipatory fulfilment of the Abrahamic covenant. By 'anticipatory fulfilment' I mean that while God indeed uses Joseph to fulfil his promises to Abraham, this fulfilment is only partial and incomplete, thus 'anticipating' a greater fulfilment to come. Joseph shows the type of work God will do in the future, pointing forwards to a more complete fulfilment of the patriarchal hopes. In this way, Joseph's story also provides literary and redemptive-historical resolution to the Genesis narrative.

By examining the Joseph story in the biblical-theological framework of Genesis, I also hope to answer another question pertinent to the entire project of reading Joseph in canonical context: Does the Joseph narrative itself indicate that Joseph's life ought to be read as a pattern of God's future saving activity? Or, to put it another way, does Moses understand Joseph to be a type of the serpent-crushing, royal seed promised in Genesis 3?

Royal seed: primeval types and promises

T. D. Alexander argues that 'the entire book of Genesis is especially interested in highlighting the existence of a unique line of male descendants

---

[19] Redford 1970: 247.
[20] Childs 1979: 156.

which will eventually give rise to a royal dynasty'.[21] This interest in kings and their kingdoms begins as early as the creation narrative (Gen. 1 – 2) and continues throughout the primeval history (3 – 11). The Abrahamic covenant heightens this interest, enshrining the hope for godly human dominion in the covenantal promises given to Abraham and his seed.

Genesis 1 establishes God's royal prerogatives over his creation. In contrast to other ANE creation accounts, which focus on cosmic struggle, Genesis highlights God's unchallenged authority simply to speak the world into existence. As other scholars have demonstrated at length, Yahweh commissions Adam to share in the royal task, and Moses depicts Adam in Genesis 1 – 2 as a priest-king.[22] Yahweh invests in Adam a right to rule that, if rightly administered, reflects God's own kingly glory as creation's life-giving sovereign and continues his creative and animating rule described in Genesis 1.[23] The end result is that 'God not only reigns over people, he also reigns through them.'[24]

Several features of the creation narrative point to Adam's royal position.[25] Moses' identification of Adam as God's 'image' (ṣelem) carried royal overtones in the ANE. Furthermore, 'image' (ṣelem) coupled with 'likeness' (dĕmût) indicate that Adam as king bore a covenantal as well as a filial relationship with the Creator (cf. Gen. 5:1–3).[26] As a result of his image-bearing identity, Yahweh commissions Adam with the regal duties of 'subduing' and 'ruling' creation (Gen. 1:26–28). In other words, Adam bears God's image *so that* he might rule.[27] Later biblical reflection on the creation account, such as Psalm 8, also affirms the notion that Adam is king among God's creatures and mediator of God's rule. Dempster summarizes the evidence: 'the rest of the canon assumes the royal overtones of Genesis 1, indicating the unique authority assigned to the primal couple, and thus to all humanity'.[28] All in all, Adam's identity is

---

[21] Alexander 1997: 366.

[22] Dumbrell 1994: 25; Beale 2004: 81.

[23] 'Adam and Eve's rule was not … to be an abusive, life-stealing rule. God did not commission them to inaugurate all great acts of colonialism, imperialism, or authoritarianism that would follow. Just the opposite. Adam and Eve's rule was to be a fruit-bearing, cultivating, empowering, equipping, authoring-life-in-others rule' (Leeman 2010: 143).

[24] Treat 2014: 55.

[25] For fuller discussions of these arguments, see Wenham 1994b: 399–404; Dempster 2003: 55–75; Walton 2003; Beale 2004: 29–121; Payne 2008; Beckerleg 2009; Gentry and Wellum 2012: 177–221; Beetham 2013: 237–240.

[26] Kline 2000: 45–46.

[27] For a defence of the resultative translation of wĕyirdû, see Gentry and Wellum 2012: 187–189.

[28] Dempster 2003: 60.

defined by his place in God's covenantal dealings. Adam is a beloved son and servant king.[29]

Further development of Adam's royal commission in Genesis 2 closely ties his regal work to the duties of a priest. Yahweh places Adam in a garden-temple where Adam must 'serve' (*'ābad*) and 'guard' (*šāmar*). These two words, in combination, only refer to the work of priests elsewhere in the Old Testament (Gen. 2:15; cf. Num. 3:7–8; 8:26; 18:5–6).[30] Summarily Adam is a priest-king. 'He is to rule (Gen. 1:26–28) by serving in the Edenic temple and guarding it from intruders (Gen. 2:15).'[31]

Significantly, the creation account, as well as later biblical texts' reflection on Genesis 1 – 2, indicate that Adam's royal office was eschatological. Notably, Adam's reign was not a static enterprise – the maintenance of a status quo. It came with an inherent *telos*. Adam only rightly administered his rule as he expanded the borders of Eden and, with Eve, populated that acquired territory with other image bearers. Adam's royal labours worked towards joining the Creator in eternal Sabbath rest – the endgame of creation. The reigning was for the resting.

This eschatological character of Adam's royal duties not only explains God's purposes in the 'creation project' (as Alexander calls it)[32] but also God's purposes in the work of redemption. As God acts to reclaim humanity and restore his kingdom in a post-Genesis 3 world, the restoration of human vicegerency is vital to that end. As demonstrated below, a post-Genesis 3 hope for royal seed expressed prophetically in passages such as Genesis 3:15, typologically in characters such as Noah or Melchizedek, or covenantally in the promises to Abraham, Isaac and Jacob does not merely point to the promise of earthly power for the nation of Israel but also indicates God's commitment to reinstate his rule over creation – and to do so through a new human mediator. God will resurrect the hope of Sabbath rest by restoring the throne of Adam.

This hope for royal restoration begins as early as the curse itself. Yahweh prophesies that a child will crush the head of the serpent, undoing the serpent's damage and restoring creation's Edenic character

---

[29] Gentry sums up his examination of *ṣelem* in the ANE stating, 'the term "the image of god" in the culture and language of the ancient Near East in the fifteenth century B.C. would have communicated two main ideas: (1) rulership and (2) sonship' (Gentry and Wellum 2012: 192). See also Alexander 2008: 77.

[30] Dempster 2007: 135.

[31] Treat 2014: 55. See also Dempster 2007: 136; Beale 2011: 32.

[32] Alexander 2008: 22, 37, 72.

(Gen. 3:15).[33] While the royal character of the seed is not immediately apparent, his ability to accomplish what royal Adam failed to achieve (making him a new Adam) and his ability to wage war against 'the serpent'[34] at least hint at his royal character. The development of the seed theme in Genesis confirms this conclusion. Relying on the work of Alexander, Treat shows that the promised victory of the seed over the serpent is a '*royal* victory' because this promise is 'progressively revealed in a lineage of kings'.[35] More specifically, Moses and other biblical authors tie Genesis 3:15 to royal imagery, particularly in Numbers 24 and the Psalms (i.e. Pss 72, 89), which also confirms a royal reading of the text.[36]

More forcefully, Genesis develops the royal-seed promise typologically through characters who emerge as 'new Adams'. These figures advance God's work of restoration and foreshadow the ultimate royal seed both through their successes and failures. As Beale notes, 'After Adam's failure to fulfil God's mandate, God raises up other Adam-like figures to whom his commission is passed on.'[37]

The first recipient of that royal commission is Noah, whom Moses pictures as a new Adam, with kingly responsibilities over creation.[38] The very name 'Noah' derives from the intersection of the two eschatological hopes of (1) 'rest' in the land (2) through the mediation of a seed (Gen. 5:29). Adam's royal commission to be fruitful and multiply passes to Noah (Gen. 9:1, 7; cf. 1:28). Additionally, as Hahn observes, the Noahic covenant gives Noah 'a dynastic authority over "all flesh" (9:16, 17)'.[39]

Royal seed: Abrahamic types and promises

Just as Noah was the tenth generation from Adam, Abram enters the narrative as the tenth generation from Noah – the new heir in God's lineage of royal covenant mediators. God's promises in Genesis 12:1–3 clearly

---

[33] Dempster 2003: 68–69.

[34] Robert Gonzales's rather thorough treatment of the identity of the serpent shows that the serpent of Genesis (*hanāḥāš*) may not simply be a regular snake possessed and animated by Satan, but Satan himself in Seraph form – a dragon-like, supernatual angelic entity. See Gonzales 2009: 21–28. See also Ronning 1997: 126–142.

[35] Treat 2014: 58; emphasis original.

[36] Wifall 1974: 361–365; Alexander 1998a: 204–205; J. M. Hamilton 2006b: 30–54.

[37] Beale 2004: 93.

[38] G. Smith 1977: 307–319; Gentry and Wellum 2012: 161–165.

[39] Hahn 2009: 97.

point to the kingly destiny of Abram and his seed. In Genesis 12:2–3, Yahweh promises Abram that he will make him a great nation (*gôy*) and will bless the 'families' (*mišpāḥâ*) of the earth. As Gentry explains, the word *gôy*, particularly in contrast with *mišpāḥâ*, connotes royalty:

> The basic meaning of *gôy* is an *organised* community of people having *governmental, political,* and *social structure.* This contrasts with the fact that the other nations are derogatorily termed *mišpāḥâ* in Genesis 12. This word refers to an amorphous kin group larger than an extended family and smaller than a tribe ... This shows that the author has a real purpose in Genesis 12:3 in using the term *mišpāḥôt* [for the nations]: he wants to indicate that the kingdoms of this world will never amount to anything; only the kingdom of God will last forever. The author's choice of terms emphasises that the family of Abram is a real kingdom with eternal power and significance while the so-called kingdoms of this world are of no lasting power or significance.[40]

God's promise to make Abram's name great (Gen. 12:2) also portends royal status – 'to have a great name given to one by God is to be viewed as a royal figure (2 Samuel 7:9)'.[41] In short, in Genesis 12:1–3, 'Abram was promised ... the hope of many an oriental monarch.'[42] In biblical-theological terms, 'the promises to Abraham renew the vision for humanity set out in Gen. 1–2. He, like Noah before him, is a second Adam figure.'[43]

Later developments of the covenant blessings also focus on the royal features of Abraham's identity. Yahweh promises Abraham that he will sire a line of kings (Gen. 17:6). Abraham's inherited royal Adamic identity will transfer to a line of sons. Similarly, Abraham's wife bears a regal name. Both Sarai and Sarah mean 'princess', a name Yahweh highlights when he promises to make her the matriarch of a royal line (Gen. 17:16).

Moses continues to *show*, not so much *tell*, Abraham's royal identity in subsequent narratives. In Genesis 14 Abraham marshals a military

---

[40] Gentry and Wellum 2012: 243–244; emphases original.
[41] Arnold 2009: 132.
[42] Wenham 1987: 275. See also Ruprecht 1979: 444–464; V. Hamilton 1990: 372–373; Gentry and Wellum 2012: 224.
[43] Wenham 2000: 37.

conquest against other ANE kings. As Wenham writes, 'In these scenes Abram is portrayed not merely as the archetypal Israelite who has faith in God, but as a conquering king who has been promised victory over his foes and a great territory.'[44]

Further, in this episode the enigmatic Melchizedek appears as a priest-king after the order of Adam and Noah. The close associations between Melchizedek and Abraham hint at the royal-priestly identity Abraham shares with this king of righteousness in proto-Jerusalem.[45]

Later the Hittites identify Abraham as 'a prince of God' (Gen. 23:6). Abraham treats kings as an equal (Gen. 20; 21:22–34). Similar features are found in the Isaac and Jacob stories, though less prominently (cf. Gen. 26:26–31). Most importantly, in all these activities Abraham bears Adam's royal commission to be fruitful and multiply, though now mediated to him in the form of covenantal promises (Gen. 12:2; 17:2, 6, 8; 22:17).

Yet in Abraham's life, the theme of a royal seed is strongest in the covenantal promises. In fact, the promise of royal seed is 'a central feature to the patriarchal promises'.[46] Through Abraham, God promises not only to restore the land, fruitfulness and blessing of Eden but also to restore human vicegerency.[47] Thus God repeatedly promises future royalty when he reiterates the covenant to Isaac and Jacob (Gen. 17:6; cf. 17:16; 22:17b–18; 35:11).

Scholars generally organize the Abrahamic covenantal promises according to the categories of land, seed and blessing. While these themes are primary, the theme of a royal seed also clearly emerges in the covenant ceremonies of Genesis 15 and 17 (and in reaffirmations to Isaac and Jacob). The promise of royal offspring is so thoroughly folded into the Abrahamic expectation that it becomes part of the very fabric of the covenant. Abraham's covenantal promises included land, seed, blessing and kingship – these four notions are intimately and inseparably linked.[48]

Three passages in Genesis (17:6; 17:16; 35:11) demonstrate this connection by mentioning all four promises together. Diffey rightly notes that:

---

44 Wenham 1987: 335.

45 Hahn 2009: 130–134; M. H. Emadi 2016.

46 Diffey 2011: 316.

47 With regard to God's restoring land, fruitfulness and blessing through the Abrahamic covenant, see J. M. Hamilton 2007: 253–273.

48 See Diffey 2011: 313–316. I arrived at these conclusions independent of Diffey. I was pleased to find his stimulating article on this subject as further confirmation that the promise of kingship in the Abrahamic covenant deserves more attention.

these three 'royal promise' narratives share common features: 1) each of these promises occurs within the context of a narrative in which the character is given a new name; 2) within each of these narratives the promise of kings is intertwined with the themes of fruitfulness, seed and land.[49]

Additionally, (3) each promise of future royalty is tied to a specific recipient: Isaac (not Ishmael) in Genesis 17 and Jacob (not Esau) in Genesis 35.[50]

In Genesis 17 'God Almighty' appears to Abram and recommits himself to the three promises established in Genesis 12 and 15: seed, blessing and land.[51] Yahweh promises to make Abraham the 'father of a multitude of nations' (17:5) and 'exceedingly fruitful' (17:6). He assures Abraham that by establishing an everlasting covenant he will 'be God to you and to your offspring after you' (17:7). Finally, Yahweh promises to give Abraham and his offspring 'the land of your sojournings, all the land of Canaan, for an everlasting possession' (17:8).

Two features stand out in this reaffirmation of the covenant. First, Yahweh changes Abram's name to Abraham, signifying his role as a father of nations. Second, Yahweh promises that 'kings shall come from you' (17:6) – a hope inseparable from the already established triad of covenantal promises.

The same pattern appears just a few verses later as God reconfirms his commitment to give barren Sarai a son (17:16) and to make her progeny into 'nations' (17:16). Again, amidst this reaffirmation of the covenant, two important features emerge. God gives Sarai the name Sarah and promises that 'kings of people shall come from her' (17:16). Furthermore, Yahweh explains that while Ishmael will also give birth to royalty (by fathering 'twelve princes', 17:20), this is *not* the fulfilment of God's royal-seed promise to Abraham and Sarah. Instead, Yahweh will fulfil that promise through Isaac (17:19, 21). This explicit rejection of Ishmael and election of

---

[49] Ibid. 314.

[50] Ibid.

[51] Diffey notes, 'This title [God Almighty] is used of God only five times in the book of Genesis, two of which occur in the passages at hand. Each of these occurrences are [*sic*] found in direct speech. In Genesis 17:1 and 35:11 the name is proclaimed by God himself. These are the only two times in Genesis that God refers to himself as God Almighty. Furthermore, four of the five times this name is used it is in the direct context of fruitfulness (Gen. 17:1; 28:3; 35:11 and 48:3). There is one instance in Genesis where the title Almighty is used (Gen. 49:25), this too is in the context of procreative activity and blessing' (ibid. 314–315).

Isaac has biblical-theological significance. Yahweh will not fulfil his royal seed promise to Abraham and Sarah generically, as if any kings among Abraham's progeny will do. A specific royal house is in view – one that participates in God's redemptive work in restoring creation by reclaiming a people that enjoy God's blessing in the Promised Land. Only the royal seed through Isaac share in that redemptive agenda.

These same elements emerge in Genesis 35. God appears to Jacob and reaffirms the covenantal promises to Abraham – promises that recapitulate God's original purposes for humanity. God commands Jacob to 'be fruitful and multiply' (*pĕrēh ûrĕbēh*) – a repetition of the original mandate to Adam and Eve (Gen. 1:28; cf. 9:1, 7). Along with the command comes a promise that Yahweh will grant what he commands: 'A nation and a company of nations shall come from you, and kings shall come from your own body. The land that I gave to Abraham and Isaac I will give to you, and I will give the land to your offspring after you' (Gen. 35:11–12). Again the promises of kingship, seed and land are explicit.

As in Genesis 17, this reaffirmation of the covenant includes a name change (Jacob to Israel, 35:10) and the promise that 'kings shall come from your own body', nestled between the promises of seed and land. Diffey rightly summarizes the evidence as follows:

> The intertwining and repetition of these themes in parallel narratives reveals that every aspect of the promise is an integral part of the whole. The promise of kings is no less important than fruitfulness or land in these passages. All three coalesce into one and the same promise that is given to each of the characters at his or her renaming. These promises of fruitfulness, kingdom and land are not intended for just any offspring though. The context of each of the narratives reveals that the promise of kingship was intended for a specific child's lineage. The context also reveals that there were offspring that were rejected or excluded from this promise.[52]

Joseph: Abraham's royal seed

With these observations, we are now in a place to explore how the Joseph story picks up the theme of kingship in Genesis and the Abrahamic

---

[52] Ibid. 315.

covenant. Strikingly, Joseph's introduction in Genesis 37 bears a number of royal features. His special treatment by his father and his 'bad report' (Gen. 37:2) about his brothers plant seeds of animosity in the family, but, ultimately, what incites his brothers to action are Joseph's dreams of royal destiny. These dreams become Joseph's defining characteristic in the eyes of his brothers, who ridicule him as 'this lord of the dreams' (37:19). Genesis 37:20 also demonstrates the centrality of the dreams to the conflict in Genesis 37 and to Joseph's identity among his brothers, 'Come now, let us kill him and throw him into one of the pits. Then we will say that a fierce animal has devoured him, and we will see what will become of his dreams.'

In the first dream, Joseph's sheaf is exalted above those of his brothers and even receives obeisance from them. Such bowing (*ḥāwâ*) suggests an action done for a royal figure, which is exactly how the brothers interpret the dream. Their incredulous response makes this explicit: 'Are you indeed to reign over us [*hămālōk timlōk 'ālênû*] or are you indeed to rule over us (*māšôl timšōl bānû* [37:8])'? In the context of the Joseph story, both *mālak* and *māšal* carry explicit connotations of royalty. Further, *mālak* and *māšal* occur in the same context only three other times in the Old Testament, each instance clearly denoting royalty (Judg. 9:2, 6, 8; Jer. 33:21, 26; 2 Chr. 9:26, 9:30).[53]

Joseph's second dream continues in the same vein. In this instance the sun, moon and eleven stars bow down before Joseph. While these celestial bodies represent Joseph's family, the imagery itself is suggestive. Only the king of creation would have the obeisance of the cosmos. Joseph again uses the word *ḥāwâ* (Gen. 37:9), as does Jacob when he rebukes Joseph for his dreams (*lĕhištaḥăwōt lĕkā 'ārĕṣāh* [Gen. 37:10]).

While the dream sequences contain the most explicit royal imagery, other features of chapter 37 also foreshadow Joseph's future royal status. Joseph is a leader among his brothers. Though he is eleventh in birth order, Jacob looks to him for the supervision and administration of his other children (Gen. 37:2, 12–14).

Joseph's famous 'coat of many colours' (*kĕtōnet passîm* [37:3]) may signify some sort of royal garb.[54] The translation of *kĕtōnet passîm* is

---

[53] On the brothers' response to Joseph's dream, Westermann comments, 'The question of kingship is only hinted at, but it runs through the narrative' (Westermann 1982: 38).

[54] Brueggemann 1982: 300; Waltke 2007: 500. Wilder shows that clothing in the ANE is often closely associated with ruling and kingship. See Wilder 2006: 51–69.

notoriously difficult.[55] Regardless, as others have noted, the Old Testament mentions this type of clothing elsewhere only once: when describing the 'long dress with sleeves' worn by one of David's daughters – the typical garb of the virgin daughters of the royal family (2 Sam. 13:18).[56] Further, as Wilson notes, the dream and the robes represent the same reality of Joseph's future royal pre-eminence: 'As far as the brothers are concerned, the robe and the dream are one, for their reaction to *both* is the hatred of Joseph. The robe will carry the meaning of, and will symbolize the dreams for the rest of the chapter.'[57]

Genesis 37:3 may reveal even more about Joseph's leadership in the family. Jacob loves Joseph more than his other sons because Joseph is a 'son of old age to him' (*ben zĕqunîm lô*). Many commentators understand this to mean that Joseph was beloved because he was born late in Jacob's life.[58] This explanation of the phrase 'son of old age', however, is inadequate. If this were the case, shouldn't Jacob's favouritism extend to Joseph's *younger* brother Benjamin, who was also a son of the favoured wife, Rachel, and later identified as *yeled zĕqunîm*, the 'child of [Jacob's] old age' (Gen. 44:20)?

Lowenthal posits that in this instance *ben* connotes a 'word of quality' or expresses a 'characteristic' rather than genealogy.[59] If that is the case, then *ben zĕqunîm* refers to someone who bears the characteristics of a sage or an elder, or is, as Lowenthal suggests, 'a born leader'.[60] Lowenthal's solution, however, is problematic. The phrase *ben* + plural *zāqēn* occurs in only two other places in the Old Testament, both in reference to Isaac (Genesis 21:2, 7, both *ben lizqunāyw*). Lowenthal's notion that this phrase represents a wise son or 'a born leader' works for seventeen-year-old Joseph, but could not be applied to Isaac, who is only a few days old in Genesis 21. A more likely interpretation is that *ben zĕqunîm* typecasts

---

[55] *Kĕtōnet passîm* is one of the most notorious *crux interpretums* in the OT. The 'coat of many colours' tradition comes from the LXX's *chitōna poikilōn* and the Vulgate's *tunicam polymitam*. For a full discussion of the translational problems and history, see V. Hamilton 1995: 407–409; Pirson 2002: 33–35; Gonzales 2009: 215.

[56] Mathews notes, 'The giving of a garment is a well-known theme in cultural studies and a standard item in royal correspondence from Mari' (V. Mathews 1995: 30). Mathews cites *ARM* 1.8.31; 10.17; 29.10; 46.15.

[57] Wilson 2004: 67, 69–70; emphasis original. See also V. Mathews 1995: 30; Green 1996: 51.

[58] Westermann 1982: 37; D. Baker 2014: 14.

[59] Lowenthal 1973: 167.

[60] Ibid. 168.

Joseph with an Isaac-like identity.[61] Joseph appears on the scene much like the first son of promise, and, as such, the covenantal and dynastic expectations for Isaac (and Jacob) are now linked to him.[62]

If these introductory comments do describe Joseph with royal imagery, or at least foreshadow his future royal position, then his brothers' animosity is always linked to his position of leadership. This leadership (which enables him to give a 'bad report' about his brothers to Jacob), along with his position as Jacob's favourite (signified by the *kĕtōnet passîm*), incites the animus of the eleven. Later, the brothers 'hated [Joseph] even more' (Gen. 37:8) because his dreams signified regal destiny.

Whether all or just some of these features associate Joseph with royalty, the dream sequences rather unambiguously portray him as the potential first royal seed of Abraham.[63] As Alexander notes, 'kingship is

---

[61] I am indebted to Aubrey Sequeira for this insight. This conforms with Fretheim's observation on Jacob's favouritism: 'Joseph evidently now has a relationship with his father that the others do not have. It suggests that Joseph becomes the chosen son of the promise; the eleven are "Esau"' (Fretheim 1994: 598).

[62] Alexander notes that another possible evidence of Joseph's royal stature is the description of Joseph as *rō'eh 'et 'eḥāyw baṣṣō'n* in Gen. 37:2 (Alexander 2007: 202). While most translations render this phrase, 'He was shepherding the flock with his brothers', some commentators posit that *'et* may function as the direct object marker, changing the phrase to read, 'He was shepherding his brothers who were with the flock' (Lowenthal 1973: 15; Christensen 1983: 261–263). Hamilton, for instance, indicates that this may be 'anticipatory paronomasia' and that the sense of *rō'eh 'et* is 'to rule over', as in 2 Sam. 5:2; 7:7 (V. Hamilton 1995: 406). The primary evidence for this interpretation is Gen. 37:12, the only other instance where *rō'eh* is followed by both *bêt* and *'et*. In that passage *'et* very clearly functions as the direct object marker and the *bêt* denotes location.

As a result, Pirson argues, 'It is not unlikely that v. 2 on first reading reads, "he was shepherding the flock with his brothers," whereas on second (or further) reading – when readers know about Joseph's food policy and the salvation of his relatives – the feasibility of reading "he was shepherding his brothers with the flock" urges itself upon those readers' (Pirson 2002: 30).

The evidence, however, points away from this proposal, which Pirson himself admits is only on the 'margins of possibility' (29). The verb *hāyah* + the qal m. sg. participle *rō'eh* is a periphrastic construction. If the *'et* is marking the direct object, then the *bêt* prefix on 'flock' must denote 'with' or 'near' – both of which are rarely in the semantic domain of the *bêt*-preposition. 1 Sam. 16:11 is another example of the qal m. sg. participle *rō'eh* taking a transitive *bêt* – interestingly, with the same word, 'flock' (*ṣō'n*). See also 1 Sam. 17:34, where the same construction, qal m. sg. participle *rō'eh* + *bêt* with 'flock', occurs. Given the use of the same periphrastic construction, these 1 Samuel passages are much closer structurally to Gen. 37:2 than 37:12, which employs the infinitive construct form of *rō'eh* . Finally, the LXX, Vulgate, Peshitta, Targum Onkelos and Targum Neofiti are also uniform in supporting the reading 'Joseph was shepherding the flock with his brothers.'

[63] Alexander rightly notes that while these features of Joseph's introduction in Gen. 37:2–4 do not 'establish Joseph's royal credentials' with the same sort of certainty as do the dreams, 'due consideration should be given to them in the light of the acknowledged artistry of the Joseph Story' (Alexander 2007: 202).

the "dominant motif"' of the dreams.[64] This characterization is surely suggestive.

In light of the royal expectations found prior to Gen. 37, it is hardly a coincidence that the plot of the Joseph story should rely so heavily on the theme of royalty for its development. Since the narratives in Gen. 12–36 associate kingship with the patriarchs and their descendants, the manner of Joseph's introduction in Gen. 37 is significant.[65]

Readers of Genesis have awaited – prophetically, typologically and by covenant promise – the arrival of a royal seed through the line of Abraham. Now, in the opening verses of the final *tôlĕdôt* section, the introduction of Joseph heightens that anticipation. Readers in touch with the royal theme cannot help but question, 'Are you the one who is to come or should we expect another?'

The following narrative continues to hint, and then finally affirm, Joseph's regal destiny. Joseph becomes a slave to Potiphar, 'an officer of Pharaoh' (Gen. 39:1) but eventually rises to the rank of chief-of-staff in Potiphar's house. Even as Joseph sinks deeper into suffering and humiliation through incarceration, the narrator never allows the audience to disassociate Joseph from the royal imagery that marked his introduction, reminding them that Joseph's prison is 'the place where the king's prisoners were confined' (Gen. 39:20). In hindsight, readers can see that, in God's providence, the further Joseph descends in social rank, the closer he moves to the royal court. Though in prison, he moves one step closer to the palace, as Potiphar appoints him custodian of the chief cupbearer and baker of the 'king of Egypt' (40:1, 4).

Finally, Pharaoh exalts Joseph to his right hand, including him in the royal court. Joseph may not be king, but Moses describes him with royal attributes. Joseph's dreams come to fruition when his brothers 'bow down' (*ḥāwâ*) before him three times (42:4; 43:26, 28), matching the three uses of *ḥāwâ* in the dream sequence in Genesis 37:7, 9–10.[66]

---

[64] Alexander 1998a: 206.

[65] Alexander 2007: 201.

[66] This type of number matching is characteristic of Moses' writing in Genesis. See e.g. the fivefold use of 'blessing' in Gen. 12:1–3 (*bārak*), which seems to be a response to the fivefold use of 'curse' (*'ārar*) in Gen. 3 – 11. Number matching also fits with the overall

The brothers who once scoffed at the notion that Joseph would 'rule' (*māšal*) over them (Gen. 37:8) report to their father that Joseph is alive and 'ruling' (*māšal*) over Egypt (Gen. 45:26). Joseph even describes himself as a 'father to Pharaoh, lord [*'ādôn*] of all his house, and ruler [*mōšēl*] over all the land of Egypt' (Gen. 45:8; cf. 45:9, 26) – a description that 'appears to be overly stated', perhaps in order to cast Joseph as a regal figure.[67]

Joseph's royal status is the first hope for resolution to an eschatological expectation burgeoning since Genesis 1 and now mediated through the promises of the Abrahamic covenant (Gen. 17:6; cf. 17:16). Alexander correctly notes:

> When viewed as part of the book of Genesis as a whole, Joseph's regal connections take on a deeper significance. His dreams and their fulfilment come in the context of a family tradition that has royal expectations embedded within it.[68]

Joseph's rise to royalty, therefore, is not merely evidence of God's vindication or approbation of his faithfulness. It is the first tangible evidence of God's unswerving commitment to restore human vicegerency through a son of Abraham. God promised Abraham a dynasty, a royal seed. Joseph is the first of that seed, a new Adam mediating God's blessings to the nations – a beloved son and servant king.

(note 66 *cont.*) literary character of the Joseph story, which regularly uses numbers as a literary device. Though I disagree with a number of his conclusions, see Pirson's comments on the significance of numbers in the dreams in Pirson 2001: 561–568.

The number three also seems to be a significant literary device throughout the Joseph story. For instance, Moses records three incidents involving robes with Joseph (Jacob, Potiphar's wife, Pharaoh), three blessings from Jacob (Pharaoh, Ephraim/Manasseh, the twelve tribes), three pairs of dreams (Joseph, baker-cupbearer, Pharaoh), and three trips of the brothers to Egypt. Furthermore, the ages of the patriarchs also seem to follow a rather complex pattern built on the product of decreasing odd numbers with increasing squares: Abraham dies at 175 (7×5^2), Isaac at 180 (5×6^2) and Jacob at 147 (3×7^2). Joseph both continues and alters the pattern by continuing the decrease in odd numbers but by being the sum of the squares. Joseph dies at 110 ($1 \times [5^2 + 6^2 + 7^2]$). As Labuschagne notes, 'Joseph is the *successor* of the pattern (7, 5, 3, 1) and the *sum* of the predecessors ($5^2 + 6^2 + 7^2$)' (Labuschagne 1989: 126; emphases added). See also Wenham 1994a: 491; V. Hamilton 1995: 709–710.

67 Alexander 1998a: 206.
68 Alexander 2007: 200.

Joseph and Judah: present and future royal seed

Given the contours of Genesis thus far, readers might expect that the identity of the royal line is now clear: Joseph and his progeny. Yet a final plot twist shatters those expectations. At the end of his life, Jacob blesses his children by prophesying concerning the 'last days' (Gen. 49:1) and identifies *Judah* as the father of the royal line: 'The sceptre shall not depart from Judah, nor the ruler's staff from between his feet, until tribute comes to him; and to him shall be the obedience of the peoples' (Gen. 49:10).

Joseph and Judah in Genesis 37 – 50

While readers might assume Joseph will be the father of Abraham's royal line, the revelation that Judah is the line of Israel's royal seed is not entirely unexpected. Judah is more than a supporting actor in the Joseph story. Literary interplay between Judah and Joseph emerges as early as Genesis 37 and the subsequent juxtaposition of their stories in Genesis 38 (Judah's story) and Genesis 39 – 41 (Joseph's story).[69]

Both sons are prominent characters in Genesis 37. At first Moses foregrounds Joseph, the favourite, as Jacob's most significant child. Joseph's dream reports dominate the content of verses 1–17. After verse 18, however, Joseph recedes into the background. He no longer contributes any dialogue to the story and is largely an object acted upon rather than a subject performing actions. In fact, only later, in Genesis 42:21, do we learn that Joseph pleaded for his life while his brothers dined. In the latter half of the chapter, Moses foregrounds two other characters: Reuben (Gen. 37:21–22, 29–31) and Judah (Gen. 37:26–27), presenting Judah as the more prominent and influential of the two.

Genesis 37 thus highlights the four main characters of Genesis 37 – 50 (Jacob, Joseph, Judah and Reuben) as well as the fraternal conflict that

---

[69] Alter's work seems to have renewed contemporary scholarly interest on this point (Alter 2011). Yet, as Alter points out, his observations are as ancient as *Bereshit Rabba*. Modern commentators also noted the literary interplay between the Joseph and Judah stories in the initial chapters of the Jacob *tôlĕdôt* prior to Alter's work. In an article that originally appeared in 1929 in Hebrew, Cassuto also noted these same parallels in the narratives (Cassuto 1973: 29–40). Redford noted these same parallels in 1970, though he determined they were not intentional and were therefore irrelevant (Redford 1970: 17). Smith's explanation of the history of interpretation on this point is worth noting: 'It seems that much of the success of Alter's article should be attributed to the fact that scholarship was ready for his perspective by the mid-1970s, whereas in 1929 it was not' (B. Smith 2002: 40–41).

characterizes their story. After chapter 37, the two primary characters, Judah and Joseph, each have their own individual but parallel narratives. While a number of scholars have seen Genesis 38 as only an excursus (or worse, the product of a sloppy redactor), its linguistic and thematic features link it to Joseph's story in both 37 and 39. For example, in 37:31 the brothers deceive Jacob with a 'goat of the flock' (*śĕʿîr ʿizzîm*), whereas in 38:17 Tamar's deception of Judah involves Judah's pledge of a 'goat of the flock' (*gĕdî ʿizzîm*) in exchange for sex. Even more forcefully, the phrase 'reckon please . . . And he reckoned' occurs in both accounts. In Genesis 37:32–33, the brothers ask Jacob to identify the blood-soaked garment of the supposedly dead Joseph (*hakkēr nāʾ . . . wayyakîrāh*), while in Genesis 38:25–26 Tamar makes Judah identify his signet cord and staff (*hakkēr nāʾ . . . wayyakēr*). Additionally, in Genesis 37 Jacob mourns over the supposed loss of a son, while Judah loses two sons in Genesis 38, seemingly without a hint of mourning.

Yet, even more forcefully, Moses links the story of Judah's fall in Genesis 38 to the story of Joseph's rise to power in Genesis 39 – 41. Both stories begin with each brother 'going down' from the land of promise – Judah of his own accord (*wayyēred* [Gen. 38:1]) and Joseph against his will (*hûrad* [Gen. 39:1]). A number of scholars have noted the theme of illicit sex shared between these chapters.[70] Joseph's purity is the foil to Judah's promiscuity. 'Whereas Joseph refuses temptation that accosts him "day after day" (Gen. 39:10), Judah is tempted because his temptress knows that he is the kind of man to pursue immorality repeatedly.'[71]

The parallels continue to the end of each narrative. Both Genesis 38 and 39 – 41 culminate in the birth of two sons (Gen. 38:27–30; 41:50–52) – the naming of which portends hope for both characters. Perez and Zerah mark a significant moment of change for Judah on account of his repentance, while Ephraim and Manasseh signify Joseph's rescue out of both the pit and the prison. Also, as is customary in Genesis, both sets of brothers will experience a reversal of the primogeniture.

Moses ensures that readers will see these narratives as mutually interpretive by repeating the name Yahweh. Of the twelve occurrences of Yahweh in Genesis 37 – 50, all but one occur in Genesis 38 – 39. The last occurrence of the divine name (Gen. 49:18) comes on the lips of Jacob.

---

[70] See discussion in B. Smith 2002: 102–105.
[71] Ibid. 104.

Thus, these eleven occurrences constitute the only times in the entire Joseph story where the narrator references Yahweh.

This rare instance of theological interpretation from the narrator highlights the antithesis between Joseph and Judah. In Genesis 38, 'each of the three occurrences of the divine name in Genesis 38 presents God as Judah's antagonist'.[72] 'But Er, Judah's firstborn, was wicked in the sight of the LORD, and the LORD put him to death . . . And what [Onan] did was wicked in the sight of the LORD, and he put him to death also' (Gen. 38:7, 10). In Genesis 39, however, Yahweh is an agent of blessing. He twice causes Joseph to prosper (Gen. 39:3, 23), blesses Potiphar on account of Joseph (Gen. 39:5) and Moses indicates four times that he was 'with Joseph' (Gen. 39:2, 3, 21, 23). The juxtaposition is clear: Yahweh blesses the one and opposes the other. Joseph is the foil to Judah.[73]

The subsequent chapters continue to focus on both Joseph and Judah, and in the remaining chapters their paths will intersect again. Judah (a changed man after the events of ch. 38) continues to play a prominent role in the remaining chapters.[74] Judah convinces Jacob to allow Benjamin to return with the brothers to Egypt (Gen. 43:8–10). Judah's speech (the third longest in Genesis) and sacrificial offer to save his brother ultimately

---

[72] Ibid. 112.

[73] Other narrative contrasts abound: 'Finally, . . . whereas Joseph suffers for a sin he did not commit, Judah refuses to take responsibility for a sin he did commit . . . When, however, it comes time for Judah to pay for his immoral deed, he does not search out the prostitute himself. He sends his friend Hirah the Adullamite. Joseph is therefore presented as a martyr who would rather suffer for an immoral act he never committed than to live prosperously with a guilty conscience. Judah, on the other hand, is presented as a coward who embraces immorality while shunning its shame . . . Judah's remarkable failures become even more profound as one looks at the life of Joseph. Joseph lacks the advantages that Judah enjoys. Unlike Judah, Joseph is not streetwise. He tends to assume the best of people, even when he has reason to assume the worst. He zealously and ingenuously agitates his brothers' hatred of him by sharing with them his dreams of supremacy and dominion. Freedom is another advantage that Judah enjoys over Joseph. The end of Gen. 37 and the beginning of 39 tell the reader that, like Judah, Joseph leaves his family for another land, but unlike Judah he goes there as a slave – a victim of Judah's shrewd scheming. Like Judah, Joseph in his chapter encounters opposition, but unlike Judah, who is opposed only by his inferiors (Onan in v. 9 and Tamar in vv. 12–25), Joseph is opposed by Potiphar's wife and Potiphar, his superiors. And whereas Judah comes to his moment of crisis with a crowd of friends supporting him, Joseph comes to his crisis friendless. He begins chapter 39 as a slave in a rich man's house. He ends the chapter as a slave in prison. Amazingly, however, Joseph is the one who succeeds. While Judah's world is getting turned upside down, Joseph is prospering. Three times the text uses the מַצְלִיחַ to refer to Joseph' (B. Smith 2002: 104–111).

[74] For a thorough defence of the notion that Gen. 38:26 represents Judah's repentance, and that the names of Perez and Zerah represent a hopeful, spiritually brighter future for Judah, see ibid., esp. 99–108.

convinces Joseph of the possibility of reconciliation with his brothers (Gen. 44:18–34). Further, Smith has argued on a number of fronts that Judah takes Joseph's place of favour in the family. For example, Smith notes that 'Genesis 37:4, 14 presented Joseph as Jacob's favored information-gatherer. In 46:28, however, Jacob sent Judah to gather information for him regarding the family's settlement in Goshen.'[75] He concludes:

> In this plot analysis, the presence of Judah throughout the narra-
> tive is taken as a proof of unity and not of fracture because Judah,
> together with Joseph, played a central role in the unifying plot
> action of reconciliation. He and Joseph together dominate the nar-
> rative at its three most crucial points. First, they appear together at
> the story's beginning, creating the exciting force and thus giving the
> plot the direction and shape that the rest of the narrative develops.
> Second, they appear together at the story's crisis moment, the narra-
> tive's most decisive turning point, where Judah pleaded for Benjamin,
> and Joseph responded by assuring the brothers of his forgiveness.
> And third, they appear together in the most important scene of the
> story's resolution, Genesis 49. Here they dominate Jacob's prophecies
> concerning the twelve tribes of Israel, the prophecies into which all
> of Genesis flows and from which all subsequent biblical history
> issues.[76]

Judah and Joseph in Genesis 49:8

Significantly, this Joseph–Judah association climaxes in Genesis 49:8: 'Judah, your brothers shall praise you; your hand shall be on the neck of your enemies; your father's sons shall bow down before you.' Jacob depicts the coming Judahite with imagery that closely resembles the life of Joseph. Judah's brothers will praise him and even 'bow down' (ḥāwâ) before him – the same word used three times of the brothers' obeisance to Joseph in the dreams (Gen. 37:7, 9, 10) and another three times when they actually bow before him (Gen. 42:4; 43:26, 28).[77] Indeed, the image of eleven

---

[75] B. Smith 2005: 167.
[76] Ibid. 169–170.
[77] I came to this conclusion independent of Smith's excellent work on the Joseph story. Smith, however, also argues that Gen. 49:8 is part of the literary interplay between Joseph and Judah. Further, Smith sees this as part of the 'transformation' of favouritism from Joseph at the beginning of the story to Judah at the end (B. Smith 2002: 169–170).

brothers 'bowing' to their royal sibling in Genesis 49:8 reads like a summary of the preceding Joseph story. This similarity is deliberate. Joseph is a 'narrative prefiguration' of Judah's seed.[78] In other words, the first frame of reference the original audience would use to interpret the phrase would be the story of Joseph. Should those readers ask what the coming Judahite will look like, they have an answer provided in Genesis 49:8 – he will look like Joseph.[79]

While this Josephite imagery in the blessing on Judah can seem unexpected initially, after review, Genesis 49:8 clearly is the climax of the Joseph–Judah juxtaposition that begins as early as chapter 37. Sailhamer, one of the few scholars to comment on the connection between this prophecy and the preceding narrative, summarizes it well:

> It is difficult not to see in this statement an intentional allusion to the dream of Joseph (37:10) in which his father's sons would come to

---

[78] I have adopted the language of 'narrative prefiguration' from Shepherd 2009: 13. Shepherd's summation of the Joseph story and its relationship to Gen. 49:8 is insightful and worth reproducing: 'Throughout the narrative, Joseph stands as the Spirit-filled source of life for all the land (Gen. 41:38–57). His dream in which his brothers bow to him (Gen. 37:7–8) finds fulfillment in Egypt (Gen. 42:6, 9; 43:26) and connects him to what was said to Jacob in Gen. 27:29: "be a lord to your brothers, that the sons of your mother may bow down to you." By means of this the author sets forth a pre-figuration of the future messianic kingdom from Judah to whom the brothers will bow (Gen. 49:8). The poem in Genesis 49 highlights Judah (Gen. 49:8–12) and Joseph (Gen. 49:22–26) by the amount of text devoted to them in contrast to the other brothers. It is no surprise that Joseph – the main character of the preceding narratives – figures so prominently in this poem. As for Judah, he appears as the main character in the Judah and Tamar narrative of Genesis 38, inserted so curiously between the otherwise continuous narratives of Genesis 37 and 39. Judah also steps into the place of the firstborn, Reuben, in the course of the Joseph narratives (Gen. 37:21–22, 26–27, 29–30; 42:37; 43:3–4, 8–10), and his offering of himself as a substitute for Benjamin leads to the climax of the first half of the story (Gen. 44:16–34). Thus, Judah appears in Genesis 49 as the one from whom the messianic king will come, and Joseph stands as a pre-figuration of this individual through whom the blessing will be restored.'

[79] Pirson notes other verbal similarities: 'There is a strange phenomenon to be seen in Jacob's prediction about Judah. In his words to Judah, he uses the verbs חוה ("bow down", v. 8), טרף ("tear", v. 9), אסר ("bind", v. 11) as well as the noun גפן ("vine", v. 11). These words are encountered elsewhere, but in all of these instances they were used in connection with Joseph.' Pirson then notes, 'הוה in 37:7, 9, 12 (cf. when the brothers come to see Joseph in Egypt and bow down before him); טרף in 37:33; 44:28; אסר (qal) in 39:20; 40:3, 5; 42:24; 46:29; גפן in 40:9, 10' (Pirson 2002: 128). These linguistic points of contact are indeed suggestive, given the literary relationship between Joseph and Judah throughout the story and the strong connection between Gen. 49:8 and Gen. 37, 42–45. Further, many of these words appear in only these instances in Genesis. Perhaps these linguistic points of contact further colour the Judahite blessing with Joseph imagery. I am sceptical, however, as to how strong these linguistic connections are. E.g. ṭārap is also used in the blessing of Benjamin (49:27). Further, the binding of the Judahite's foal to the vine (49:11) seems to bear little meaningful connection to the binding of Joseph in prison (40:3) or Joseph's binding of Simeon (42:24).

bow down before him. In other words, that which was to happen to Joseph, and did happen in the course of the narrative (e.g., 42:6), has been picked up by way of this image and transferred to the future of the house of Judah. That which happened to Joseph is portrayed as a picture of that which would happen to Judah 'in the last days' (49:1).[80]

Moses' association of Joseph and Judah is particularly fecund for a biblical theology of the Joseph narrative. Even if, as some scholars claim, Genesis 49:8–12 is not messianic, the point remains the same.[81] Moses patterns the life of the future royal seed of Israel on the life of Joseph. Joseph is the *type* of king Israel will see again. As Alexander notes:

> The existence of close parallels between Joseph and the future king anticipated by the writer of Genesis is a natural consequence of their both belonging to the same 'seed'. As we have noted above, there is running through Genesis the idea that progeny will resemble its progenitor. If a future king is to arise from the main line of 'seed' in Genesis, then it is to be expected that he will resemble his predecessors. However, it is apparent that for the writer of Genesis the achievements of this future king will far surpass those of his ancestors.[82]

By drawing a typological line from Joseph to the future king from Judah, Moses folds the Joseph narrative into Israel's larger story, which will

---

[80] Sailhamer 1992: 235. Other scholars have noted the relationship but do so in passing or with limited biblical-theological reflection. In fact, these words from Sailhamer are the sum total of his commentary on the relationship between Joseph and the messianic Judahite. Shepherd's observations have been noted above. Stone argues along the same lines in a footnote. He writes, 'Joseph is a type of the ruler to come from the line of Judah . . . The image invoked by Joseph's dreams sets the stage for Joseph's rule, playing a central role in its culmination. Transferring this image to Judah's blessing may suggest that in the latter days a ruler will arise from Judah who will look like Joseph' (Stone 2012: 69). Hamilton also notices the relationship only in passing: 'Genesis closes with promises of a king from the line of Judah, in the splendor of Joseph reigning over Egypt, a pattern of the coming seed of the woman, seed of Abraham, in whom all the nations of the earth have been blessed' (J. M. Hamilton 2010: 89). See also short references to this association in Alexander 1995: 36–37. Wenham notes, '"Your father's sons will bow down to you," just as earlier they had bowed down to Joseph (cf. 37:7, 9; 42:6; 43:26; 43:28)' but does not provide any further commentary or mention the significance of this observation (Wenham 1994a: 476). Also Dempster 2003: 91.

[81] Westermann 1982: 232. See Alexander's analysis and response to Westermann in Alexander 1995: 34–36.

[82] Alexander 1995: 37.

culminate with the Messiah. This association retrospectively informs our reading of the story. To ensure that his readers see Joseph as a royal figure with eschatological significance, Moses now makes that point plainly. The account of Joseph is not an end in itself. It is a pattern for God's work in the future.

In short, Jacob's prophecy is the most explicit evidence from Genesis that Joseph should be read typologically – his life is a pattern of things to come. Genesis 49:8 crystallizes his biblical-theological significance. This text effectively 'eschatologizes' the preceding Joseph narrative. The king from the line of Judah will be *Joseph redivivus* – the Joseph of 'the last days'.

Genesis 49:8 may also allude to another royal figure in Genesis. Whereas the first and third lines of Genesis 49:8 employ imagery from the Joseph story to describe the coming king, the second line may also faintly echo Genesis 3:15 with the words 'your hand shall be on the neck of your enemies'. No verbal parallels exist between this text and the *proto-evangelium*, but the image of a king who overcomes his enemy through violent, personal conflict (hand on the neck) parallels the warfare described in Genesis 3:15 (heel crushing the head). This association would certainly not be unexpected. Throughout Genesis, Moses has traced the lineage of the royal seed of Genesis 3:15 meticulously through Seth, Noah, Abraham, Isaac and Jacob, culminating in Genesis 49:8–12. As a result, while Genesis 49:8 may further develop earlier 'seed' promises in Genesis, the promised Judahite seed is still the same hoped-for conqueror mentioned as far back as Genesis 3:15. Further, as Alexander notes in tracing the promise of a royal seed through Genesis, 'the members of the family line often resemble each other'.[83] Readers should thus expect similarities between the seed of the woman, Seth, Noah, Abraham, Isaac, Jacob, Joseph and the coming Judahite.

Inner-biblical exegesis of Genesis 49:8–12 in Numbers 24 (which contains the very next instance of Moses' use of 'the last days' [Num. 24:14]) appears to confirm this conclusion. In Numbers 24, Moses records that Balaam identifies the king of Genesis 49:8–12 (cf. Num. 24:9) with the enigmatic serpent-crushing seed of Genesis 3:15 (Num. 24:17). This figure, who embodies the promises of the Abrahamic covenant (Num. 24:9) will conquer Israel's enemies, making the people of God an Edenic

---

[83] Ibid. 24.

paradise (Num. 24:5–9).[84] If it is the case that Genesis 49:8 contains allusions both to Genesis 3:15 and the figure of Joseph, Jacob depicts the
coming Judahite with imagery from the first and last kingly figures of
Genesis, perhaps indicating that this new king will be the summation of
the royal hope that runs throughout Genesis.

---

[84] Dempster 2003: 113–117; Beale 2011: 92–102.

5

Joseph and covenant: seed

The 'seed' theme in Genesis

As already noted in my discussion of the *tôlĕdôt* formula, family lines are enormously important in Genesis. In fact, the word *zeraʿ* is a *Leitwort* in Genesis, appearing 59 times despite only appearing 171 times in the rest of the Old Testament (including the Aramaic equivalent in Dan. 2:43).

Like the theme of kingship, the theme of 'seed' (i.e. numerous offspring) extends as far back as the creation account. Adam's royal and priestly duties included populating the earth with image bearers (Gen. 1:28). By having children, Adam would extend God's reign and visible glory to the far reaches of the earth. By becoming one flesh, Adam and Eve engage in an eschatological pursuit – the creation of a people who reflect the image and glory of the Creator.

In fact, the climactic 'blessing-commission' of Genesis 1:28 is paradigmatic for understanding all of Genesis. God's intention for humanity is the global proliferation of image bearers.[1] Thus Genesis 1:28 functions as the Bible's first 'Great Commission'.[2] In the Edenic state, reproduction was the central component needed for fulfilling God's eschatological programme. After the fall, however, the proliferation of 'kingdom' seed can only come through the redeemed line of promise and, even then, only through great difficulty. In a Genesis 3 world, obstacles litter the path of

---

[1] I have adopted the language of 'blessing commission' from DeRouchie (2013: 226). Depending on the work of Cynthia Miller, DeRouchie notes that the command is framed as a blessing since 'introductory speech frames will often include an additional finite verb before the primary verb of saying in order to characterize the type of speech that is made. Here the commission to fill and oversee the earth is framed as a divine blessing, which throughout Scripture is always dependent on God to fulfil' (DeRouchie 2013: 227; cf. Miller 1996: 51–52, 186, 192–194; 1995: 155–182). For more on the notion that Gen. 1:26–28 is the climax of Gen. 1:1 – 2:3, see Dempster 2003: 56–58 and DeRouchie 2013: 226.

[2] Beale 2011: 57.

seed-bearing. Even more, as Genesis 3:15 intimates, serpentine assaults will imperil the seed's survival. For God to fulfil his promises, the covenant seed must not only prosper but also be preserved through many dangers.

Adam's failure in his confrontation with the serpent not only corrupts the quality of the image but also makes reproduction difficult. The hope for numerous offspring is curtailed by Yahweh's words of judgment against the woman, 'I will surely multiply your pain in childbearing; in pain you shall bring forth children' (Gen. 3:16). As Turner observes, 'In [Gen.] 1:28, humans had been commanded to "multiply" . . . in 3:16 what actually multiplies . . . is "your pain in childbirth."'[3] This minor chord reverberates throughout Genesis as barrenness plagues the women of the covenant (Gen. 16:2; 25:21; 29:31).[4]

Yet in spite of, and even through, these barren wombs, the eschatological hope of creation lives on both in the commands and corresponding promises of Yahweh. Adam's commission to 'be fruitful and multiply' (*pĕrēh ûrĕbēh*) passes through Noah (Gen. 9:1, 7) to the patriarchs Abraham (Gen. 12:2; 17:2, 6, 8, 16; 22:18), Isaac (Gen. 26:3–4, 24) and Jacob (28:3–4, 14; 35:11–12). As we might expect, the command to produce numerous offspring is transposed into a promise of the Abrahamic Covenant (Gen. 12:2; 17:6; etc.).[5] Whereas Yahweh once said, 'be fruitful and multiply', in the Abrahamic covenant he says, 'I will multiply you exceedingly . . . I will make you exceedingly fruitful' (Gen. 17:2, 6).

This promise develops slowly through the first three quarters of Genesis. God promises in Genesis 12 that Abraham will sire a great nation. Yet by the time of his death Abraham has only one son in the covenant line. Isaac and Jacob, therefore, function as down payments on the promise, giving hope for future fulfilment. But even as Jacob bears twelve sons (29:31 – 30:24), the question remains as to how his fledgling family will flourish into a nation in the light of the constant threats that imperil their proliferation, both external (famine) and internal (family conflict).

---

[3] Turner 1990: 23–24. The connection between 1:28 and 3:16 may exceed mere thematic correspondence. Kim argues that 'the use of הרבה ארבה ("I will surely multiply") in Gen. 3:16 suggests an allusion to the *rābâ* ("multiply") in Gen. 1:28', particularly given how the hiphil form of the word is used throughout Genesis (M. M. Kim 2010: 42).

[4] M. M. Kim 2010: 63–65; J. M. Hamilton 2012a: 6–13.

[5] For a full discussion, see Beale 2011: 46–58.

Preservation and proliferation

Once again the story of Joseph changes the melody of Genesis from the music of promise to that of fulfilment. Through the ministry of Joseph, the Abrahamic hope of nationhood is first realized. In this sense, Joseph catalyses God's creation of new humanity.

The theme of preservation of the seed marks Joseph's ministry to his family and characterizes Joseph's own self-understanding. In Genesis 45:5–8, a rare moment of theological interpretation from within the story, Joseph informs his brothers (and readers) of the redemptive-historical significance of the events of his life:[6]

> And now do not be distressed or angry with yourselves because you sold me here, for God sent me before you to preserve life. For the famine has been in the land these two years, and there are yet five years in which there will be neither ploughing nor harvest. And God sent me before you to preserve for you a remnant on earth, and to keep alive for you many survivors. So it was not you who sent me here, but God. He has made me a father to Pharaoh, and lord of all his house and ruler over all the land of Egypt.
> (Gen. 45:5–8)

The primary theme of Joseph's statement is God's superintending providence over all human affairs, a theme that will reappear more concisely in Genesis 50:20: 'What you meant for evil, God meant for good.'[7] Joseph emphasizes divine providence three times in his speech in Genesis 45, each time with increasing intensity and theological specificity.

The third time, Joseph not only affirms that God sent him to Egypt but also even downplays his brothers' role. He is eager to highlight God's sovereign providence. Climactically, in Genesis 45:8b, Joseph explains

---

[6] Some scholars question whether Joseph's interpretation of his destiny is shared by Moses or God himself. Miscall 1978: 31; Clines 1995: 195; Pirson 2002: 138. Also see throughout Fung 2000. The problem with this position is that it fails to reckon with later biblical affirmation of Joseph's words (cf. Ps. 105:17–24).

[7] This point is even further highlighted by comparing Pharaoh's words in Gen. 41:41 ('I have set you over all the land of Egypt') with Joseph's in Gen. 45:8 ('God . . . made me . . . ruler over all the land of Egypt'). For this insight I am indebted to my former pastor, Greg Gilbert.

that God not only 'sent' him but also even 'established' (*śîm*) him in his positions of power.[8]

Joseph also escalates the reason God sent him to Egypt. First, he says God sent him merely to preserve life (Gen. 45:5). Then he adds that God sent him, more specifically, to preserve a 'remnant' (Gen. 45:7). Finally, he explains that God sent him in order to establish him in his position of power over Egypt.[9]

Joseph's affirmation in verse 7 that God sent him to 'preserve a remnant [*šě'ērît*]'[10] and to 'keep alive . . . survivors [*pělêṭāh*]' is particularly interesting given how these words are 'freighted with theological significance'[11] in the Prophets, particularly when used in tandem (2 Kgs 19:31; Isa. 10:20;

---

[8] Joseph's statement that God made him a 'Father to Pharaoh' (45:8) may also hearken back to the promise to Abraham that he would be the 'father of many nations' (Gen. 17:4). While many scholars take the plural 'nations' in Gen. 17:4 to refer to the progeny Abraham fathered through Hagar and Keturah, others reject this notion since the same promise is repeated to Sarah in Gen. 17:16 (cf. Dumbrell 1993: 73; Alexander 1994: 17–18; Lee 2009: 473–474).

Alexander, for instance, notes that the fatherhood of Abraham does not merely refer to 'natural descendants' but to any for whom Abraham is a 'channel of divine blessing' – even indicating that this explains the 'unusual comment that Joseph "was a father to Pharaoh"' (Alexander 1994: 17). This interpretation is certainly possible, particularly given that such a non-biological nuance of the Hebrew term *'āb* is also reflected elsewhere in the OT (see Williamson 2000a: 158, see the whole discussion from 157 to 160; cf. N. T. Wright 1997: 219–223).

[9] The literary features of Joseph's speech suggest a sophisticated three-part structure. Vv. 3–4 are bookended with the phrase 'I am Joseph' (*'ănî yôsēp*). Vv. 5–8 each begin with the exclamation 'now' (*'attāh*), which, in conjunction with the shared language of vv. 5–8, unites these verses as their own section and may suggest a chiasm. The fact that a waw + finite verb mainline narrative marker occurs only in v. 7 (*wayyišlāḥēnî*) may suggest v. 7 as its own line within a chiasm. Finally, vv. 9–13 are bookended by the imperatives 'hurry and go up' (*mahărû wa'ălû*) and 'hurry and bring down' (*ûmihartem wěhôradtem*). Many of these literary features have already been noted by K. Mathews (2005: 809–810). Visually the structure looks as follows:

Section 1
V. 3a: 'I am Joseph'
Vv. 3b–4a
V. 4b: 'I am Joseph'
Section 2
Vv. 5–6: 'Now [*wě'attāh*] . . . God sent me . . . to preserve life'
V. 7: 'God sent me [*wayyišlāḥēnî*] . . . to preserve . . . a remnant'
V. 8: 'Now [*wě'attāh*], not you who sent me . . . but God [sent me]'
Section 3
V. 9: 'Hurry and go up'
Vv. 10–13a
V. 13b: 'Hurry and bring down'

If the chiasm in section 2 is indeed valid then the centrality of v. 7 in the chiasm may suggest the importance of the statement that God sent Joseph in order to preserve a 'remnant'.

[10] This is the only instance of *šě'ērît* in the Pentateuch.

[11] V. Hamilton 1995: 576.

Table 1 Theological interpretation in Genesis 45:5–8

Verse 5	God sent me . . . to preserve life	*lĕmiḥyāh šĕlāḥanî 'ĕlōs*
Verse 7	God sent me . . . to preserve a remnant	*wayyišlāḥēnî 'ĕlōhîm . . . lāśûm . . . šĕ'ērît*
Verse 8	It was not you who sent me here, but God [sent me] and placed me [followed by three things]	*lō' 'attem šĕlaḥtem 'ōtî hēnnāh kî hā'ĕlōhîm [šĕlāḥēnî] wayśîmēnî . . .*

37:32; cf. Joel 2:32). Additionally, 'remnant' and 'survivor' in Genesis 45:7 signify that God saves the covenant community from destruction as a sign of future hope for the nation – essentially the same idea found in the Prophets. In both the exilic era and in Genesis, Yahweh preserves a 'remnant of Israel and . . . survivors of the house of Jacob' (Isa. 10:20). The apparent connection to the prophetic corpus is so arresting that critical scholars view it as evidence of post-exilic theology's influence on the Joseph story.[12]

Of course, the evidence is insufficient to posit that prophetic-remnant theology emerged wholly out of Genesis 45:7 or that Isaiah intends an allusion to this passage in Isaiah 10:20 or 37:32.[13] But given the verbal and conceptual similarities, it is not out of the question that Genesis 45 could easily have influenced prophetic writing about God's preserving a remnant – even muscling its vocabulary into the prophetic writings from time to time.

As Currid notes, God's intention to preserve a remnant or seed 'has been the primary purpose of the book of Genesis'.[14] God has preserved the seed through child-bearing in the face of violence (Gen. 4:1–26), through an ark in the face of judgment (Gen. 6:9 – 9:29), through divine intervention in the face of foreign corruption (Gen. 12:10–20) and even through sacrifice in the face of certain death (Gen. 22:1–19). Now, through Joseph, God protects the covenant line in the face of famine, a perennial enemy endangering the covenant line throughout Genesis (Gen. 3:17–19;

---

12 Heaton 1947: 134–136; Westermann 1982: 145.

13 The bare presence of *šĕ'ērît* and *pĕlēṭāh* is insufficient to establish the presence of an allusion, particularly given that the verb *śārāh* occurs with *pĕlēṭāh* together in contexts clearly not related to the OT's remnant theology (Gen. 32:9). This is one reason Wenham prefers not to see any biblical-theological significance to these words, preferring the translation 'surviving descendant' (Wenham 1994a: 428).

14 Currid 2003: 2.324.

12:10; 26:1; 42:1–2). Thus, Joseph's use of 'remnant' and 'survivor' in Genesis 45:7 is, in part, an embryonic manifestation of the Old Testament's remnant theology – a subtle foreshadowing of a theme more prominently developed in later revelation.[15] Further, God's purpose 'to preserve life' (v. 5 [lĕmiḥyāh]) and to 'keep alive' (v. 7 [ûlĕhaḥăyôt]) may correlate Joseph to Noah, the archetypal seed-preserver in Genesis. As Wenham notes, '"to preserve" (life) is a key phrase in the flood story (6:19–20; cf. 7:3; 50:20), implying that Joseph is like Noah, an agent in the divine saving plan'.[16]

Even aside from these biblical-theological considerations, the most basic meaning of the passage is that God preserved humanity, particularly the covenant line, through Joseph. Joseph then instructs his brothers to bring their father and his entire family to Egypt (Gen. 45:9–10) and makes provision for the journey (Gen. 45:21). Further, Joseph ensures they will flourish in Egypt: 'I will provide for you, for there are yet five years of famine to come, so that you and your household, and all that you have, do not come to poverty' (Gen. 45:11).[17]

Genesis 46 – 47 focuses on the covenantal promises, particularly seed and blessing. These chapters are rich with covenantal language and imagery from the patriarchal narratives, particularly the introductory verses of Genesis 46. Jacob's dream in verse 1 reintroduces theophanic communication from Yahweh, a characteristic of the patriarchal narratives, notably absent in the Joseph story thus far.[18] This is God's third (and final) appearance to Jacob in a dream and notably each dream highlights the Abrahamic seed promise. As Smith explains:

---

[15] Hamilton notes, 'It may well be that in the deliverance of his brothers and his father Joseph perceives that far more is at stake than the mere physical survival of twelve human beings. What really survives is the plan of redemption announced first to his great grandfather. At least the reader is cognizant of that fact' (V. Hamilton 1995: 576). Hasel also comments, 'If the essential kernel of the prophetic remnant motif is given when the election of Israel is referred to, then we have here already an inkling of the remnant motif of the eighth century prophets' (Hasel 1972: 159; see entire discussion, 154–159).

[16] Wenham 1994a: 428; also K. Mathews 2005: 813. See also Hasel's analysis linking the Noah story to the remnant motif in Hasel 1972: 135–147.

[17] These words show that Joseph preserves the line and fulfils the seed promise. As Wilson points out, God's seed promise demands not only the multiplication of Abraham's progeny but, even more fundamentally, its 'survival . . . despite dangers and threats' (Wilson 2004: 227).

[18] 'This vision occurs not simply at a turning point in Jacob's life; it is also the last time God is recorded as speaking to the patriarchs. The next recorded revelation takes place in the time of Moses. This, then, is the culmination of all the promises made to the patriarchs, and it picks up motifs from other great moments of revelation (e.g., 15:1–21; 17:1–21; 22:1–18). God, as it were, reminds Jacob of all the promises made to him in his own lifetime and to his forefathers Abraham and Isaac before him' (Wenham 1994a: 440).

When God first spoke to Jacob, he was alone, *en route* to Padan Aram to escape the wrath of Esau. In the dream that He gave Jacob, He promised that his seed would be 'as the dust of the earth' (Gen. 28:14). The next time Yahweh appears to Jacob, the patriarch is again in Bethel, this time *en route* to his father's home in Hebron. Similarly God tells him that 'a nation and a company of nations' would come from his offspring (Gen. 35:11). Unlike Genesis 28, however, which presents Jacob alone, Genesis 35 concludes with a list of Jacob's descendants, the twelve sons of Israel (vv. 22b–26). The next time God appears is Genesis 46:2–4, when Jacob is in Beersheba, *en route* to Egypt to escape the famine in Canaan. Again Yahweh reiterates the promise that Jacob would become a 'great nation,' but this time the dream is followed by twenty verses listing not twelve but *seventy descendants*. As Jacob journeys into Egypt, he is not yet the great nation that Yahweh has promised he will one day be. But the growth of his seed in Genesis from zero, to twelve, to seventy, provides a compelling argument for trusting that what remains unfulfilled in the Abrahamic covenant will most certainly come to pass in every detail.[19]

Beersheba, the location of the vision, is also profoundly important in the patriarchal narratives. Abraham resided in Beersheba when God told him to sacrifice Isaac and also returned to live there at the conclusion of that ordeal (Gen. 22:19). Both Abraham and Isaac were at Beersheba when they built altars and 'called on the name of the Lord' (Gen. 21:32–33; 26:23–25, 32–33).[20] Jacob follows suit, offering sacrifices at Beersheba, the text notes, 'to the God of his father Isaac' (Gen. 46:1) – another suggestive annotation drawing attention to the patriarchs. Also in Genesis 46:2 is a double call ('Jacob, Jacob') from Yahweh followed by *hinnēnî*, which echoes the double call of Abraham in Genesis 22:11 – the only other name repetition in Genesis.[21]

In Jacob's dream, God recommits himself to his covenantal seed promise. He assures Jacob about the decision to go into Egypt (Gen. 46:3)[22] and indicates that 'there' – in Egypt(!) – God will begin to fulfil his promise to

---

[19] B. Smith 2002: 283–284.
[20] See discussion in Beale 2004: 96–103.
[21] Wenham 1994a: 441; Alter 1996: 273; Wilson 2004: 184–185.
[22] A needed assurance, perhaps, given Yahweh's strict commands to Isaac in Gen. 26:1–5 against travelling to Egypt.

make Jacob's line 'into a great nation' (*gōy gādôl*). This phrasing recalls the promise God made when he first spoke to Abraham in Genesis 12:2.[23] Alter's conclusion is right: 'both the language and the action of this whole scene are framed as an emphatic recapitulation of the earlier Patriarchal tales'.[24] Further, in verse 4 God promises his presence with the patriarch ('I myself will go down with you to Egypt') and to bring him up again to Canaan. Thus, the three-step drum beat of land, seed and blessing continues. Here, however, Yahweh reveals that the multiplication of Israel's progeny will begin *outside* Canaan.[25]

Yahweh's rationale for sending Israel to Egypt in order to multiply may be alluded to later in the Joseph story. Genesis 46:33–34 indicates that the Egyptians considered the Israelites an abomination because they were shepherds. Thus, unlike the Canaanites, the Egyptians would not likely seek out Israelite sons and daughters for marriage, nor would the Israelites be able to turn to the Egyptians for spouses. Safeguarded by the prejudices of the Egyptians, Israel would develop as a nation without the dangers posed by intermarriage with foreign peoples. Yahweh thus sent Israel into the 'womb of Egypt' where they could safely develop away from foreign cultural influences.[26]

The rest of Genesis 46 is an outworking of God's promise to make Jacob a 'great nation'. Verses 5–7 establish this point generally, while verses 8–27 accomplish the same task in greater detail. Almost each line in the chapter makes some reference to the seed's preservation and proliferation.

In verse 5, for example, Jacob is carried in Pharaoh's wagons not only by the 'sons of Israel' but by 'their little ones [*ṭappām*] and their wives'. The reference to 'little ones' (*ṭap*) is particularly interesting given its previous usage. In Genesis 43, after Reuben's failed attempts to persuade his father, Judah pleads with Jacob for permission to return to Egypt, 'that we may live and not die, both we and you and also our little ones [*ṭappēnû*]' (v. 8). Later, after the brothers reconcile, Pharaoh unwittingly honours Judah's concern for the covenant line by providing wagons to bring the

---

[23] Brueggemann 1982: 353; Westermann 1982: 156; Wilson 2004: 185.

[24] Alter 1996: 273. Later Alter notes again, 'The language of the dream-vision strongly echoes the language of the covenantal promises to Jacob's father and grandfather' (ibid). Similarly, White, '[Gen. 46:1–4] stitches the Joseph narrative to the previous unifying theme of the history of the promise' (White 1991: 237.

[25] See also Dempster's comments 'The aged patriarch is promised that in exile the family will mushroom from the size of a small family into a huge nation. God will then bring the nation back and re-establish it in the land of promise' (Dempster 2003: 89).

[26] For this insight and phraseology I am indebted to Peter Gentry.

'little ones' (*lĕtappĕkem*) safely to Egypt. Moses then records the transport of 'the little ones' (Gen. 46:5 [*tappām*]) and Joseph's provision for them in Egypt (Gen. 47:12 [*haṭap*]). Finally, when Jacob dies and his sons worry about Joseph's intentions for the family, Joseph again pledges to provide for 'the little ones' of the family (Gen. 50:21 [*tappĕkem*]).[27]

Verses 6–7 also highlight the seed theme, indicating that those who travelled to Egypt were 'Jacob, and all his offspring with him, his sons, and his sons' sons with him, his daughters, and his sons' daughters. All his offspring he brought with him into Egypt.' Moses here uses *zeraʿ* as the bookends around a chiastic construction. The *waw*-initial [*Wayyābōʾû*] in verse 6b continues the mainline narrative, indicating that Jacob went to Egypt with his 'seed', whereas the asyndetic verse 7 provides subordinate (offline) information further describing the *zeraʿ*. The resulting chiasm highlights that Jacob's sons and daughters who come to Egypt are part of the seed promise, the nascent 'great nation' God promised in verse 3.[28]

After verse 7, the text names all the descendants who journeyed with Jacob to Egypt (Gen. 46:8–27). This section begins yet another dual mention of offspring: 'These are the names of the descendants of Israel [*bĕnê yiśrāʾēl*; cf. v. 5],[29] who came into Egypt, Jacob and his sons [*ûbānāyw*]' (46:8).[30] As Smith notes, 'In Genesis 46:3, God promised to make Jacob a "great nation." In the list of Genesis 46:8–27, Moses demonstrates that before Jacob even reached Egypt, the fulfilment of that promise was already well under way.'[31]

	A	Jacob and all his seed came with him to Egypt	*wayyābōʾû miṣrāyĕmāh yaʿăqōb wĕkol zarʿô ʾittô*	A
	B	His sons and his sons' sons	*bānāyw ûbĕnê bānāyw*	B
	B'	His daughters and his sons' daughters	*bĕnōtāyw ûbĕnôt bānāyw*	B'
	A'	[Jacob] brought all his seed with him to Egypt	*wĕkol zarʿô hēbîʾ ʾittô miṣrāyĕmāh*	A'

---

[27] *Ṭap* is used only three other times in Genesis (34:29; 47:24; 50:8).

[28] 'The double mention of *zeraʿ*, "his descendants" (vv. 6–7), a word used elsewhere in the patriarchal narratives of the promised offspring, underlines God's fidelity to his covenant' (Wenham 1994a: 442).

[29] Both vv. 5 and 8, which introduce respective sections of ch. 46, begin with the phrase *bĕnê yiśrāʾēl*, marking the primary interest of the chapter.

[30] Gen. 46:8 is recapitulated in Exod. 1:1.

[31] B. Smith 2002: 283.

The colophon at the end of the genealogy totals Jacob's descendants at 'seventy' (Gen. 46:27) – a highly suggestive annotation. Dempster notes:

> remarkably, this list includes seventy members, the same number as the nations enumerated in the Table of Nations (Gen. 10), which were eventually dispersed across the earth. Here is Abraham's new humanity, a new 'Table of Nations', called into being to restore the nations to the fulfillment of the divine purpose.[32]

Yahweh is both preserving (Gen. 45:5–8) and multiplying Israel. Jacob's descendants are emerging as a nation. Under Joseph, the promise of offspring begins to be fulfilled.

Genesis 46 slows down the pace of the story significantly at just the moment we might expect it to race to its emotional resolution: the reunion of Joseph and Jacob. Verses 5–7 record in some detail the journey of Jacob and his family to Egypt while Verses 8–27 'amplify the general information given in verses 6–7, and thus do not serve to advance the storyline at all'.[33] The genealogy does highlight the seed, but what purpose does it play in the larger Joseph story? Wilson rightly explains:

> The fact that [the genealogy] immediately follows verses 1–7, which were bursting with echoes of the patriarchal promises, suggests that this element in the narrative is being reinforced. The implied reader has been immersed in Joseph's rise to power, and wise use of it, coupled with his scheme to achieve reconciliation with his brothers. Now the editor is drawing back from this specific focus in order to show the larger picture of God's purposes for the world through his covenant people.[34]

---

[32] Dempster 2003: 89. See also Sailhamer, 'The list of names in these verses appears to have been selected to total "seventy" (47:27). It can hardly go without notice that the number of nations in Genesis 10 is also "seventy". Just as the "seventy nations" represent all the descendants of Adam, so now the "seventy sons" represent all the descendants of Abraham, Isaac, and Jacob – the children of Israel . . . Thus the writer has gone to great lengths to portray the new nation of Israel as a new humanity and Abraham as a second Adam. The blessing that is to come through Abraham and his seed is a restoration of the original blessing of Adam, a blessing which was lost in the fall' (Sailhamer 1992: 225). See also Thomas 2011: 109.

[33] Wilson 2004: 186.

[34] Ibid.

Genesis 46 – 50 shows how Joseph relates to Genesis' larger story of creation and covenant. Covenantal and patriarchal themes emerge quite prominently in Joseph's story, but only *after* the reconciliation between Joseph and his brothers. This order is significant. Fraternal conflict has plagued the covenant family and endangered the seed promise as far back as Cain and Abel. Joseph's reconciliation with his brothers, however, triggers an advance in covenant history. God, by his gracious providence, undoes the fraternal hostility impeding the success of his promises. As a result, God begins to fulfil his promises and the covenant seed flourishes. This narrative progression 'makes it clear that more is at stake than simply the fate of a wandering family'.[35] In Joseph God reverses the status quo of violence against the covenant line. The reconciliation of the family is a demonstration that God is reversing the curse, turning evil in on itself, and advancing his cause in the world – as a result the covenant seed blossoms.[36]

The focus on covenant fulfilment in Genesis 46 – 50 may also reveal why Moses adopts a largely secular perspective in Genesis 37 – 45. The absence of Yahweh's name and lack of theological interpretation heighten the sense of drama as readers wonder whether the covenant line will be able to recover from what is perhaps the greatest set of challenges it has faced thus far: family violence, separation, famine and exile. Joseph's provision, forgiving spirit and reconciliation with his brothers in Genesis 45 resolve all these problems, undoing the tensions of the previous eight chapters. This resolution, in turn, triggers a return to a pattern of narration more consistent with earlier sections in Genesis, including mentions of the Abrahamic covenant, patriarchal blessings, more frequent use of covenant terminology and theophanies.

This focus on the seed promise intensifies in Genesis 47:27. The preceding narrative records the devastation of the famine. As Genesis 47:13 indicates, 'There was no food in all the land, for the famine was very

---

[35] Ibid. 187.

[36] Also Wilson: 'The literary effect of including this and the following section is very revealing. While the implied reader would expect Joseph and Jacob to be reunited quickly after 45:28, the journey (and the travelers) are described in great detail. This inevitably alerts the reader to the twin function of Jacob's descent to Egypt. On a family plane, it enables the reuniting of a fractured family. However, the detail and patriarchal overtones of 46:1–27 also serve to recall the broader context of the Abrahamic promises before Joseph meets Jacob. As the story comes to a conclusion, both the resolution of the family conflict and the partial fulfilment of the broader promises are coming to a climax' (Wilson 2004: 185).

severe, so that the land of Egypt and the land of Canaan languished by reason of the famine.' Through his careful planning, Joseph not only saves Egypt and Canaan, but also acquires more territory for Pharaoh (47:13–26; esp. 47:25).[37] Even in the midst of famine, God brings life and prosperity to Israel. Counter-intuitively, the Israelites increase even as the curses of Genesis 3 press against them in full force. Joseph's planning and God's blessing cause Israel to prosper.

Significantly, Moses describes the state of the Israelites in Goshen with words reminiscent of the Garden of Eden: 'thus Israel settled in the land of Egypt, in the land of Goshen. And they gained possessions in it, and were fruitful and multiplied greatly [*wayyiprû wayyirbû mĕʾōd*]' (Gen. 47:27). Up to this point, the word pair 'fruitful and multiply' (*pĕrû ûrĕbû*) has either been imperative or promissory (see Table 2 below).[38] In other words, God has either commanded people to be fruitful and multiply (Gen. 1:28; 9:1, 7; 35:11) or promised that they will do so (16:10; 17:2, 6; 22:17; 26:4, 24). But now, for the first time, fruitfulness and multiplication are a reality. Furthermore, under Joseph's reign Abraham's seed not only flourishes but does so exceedingly (*mĕʾōd*).

What began as a command to Adam transformed into a promise to Abraham and has now become a reality under Joseph. In Genesis 47:27, the Israelites participate in the long-awaited fulfilment of the commission originally given to Adam in Genesis 1:28 and in the promises restated to Abraham. Through the mediation and leadership of Joseph – the royal seed – the people of God flourish into a new humanity. The Adamic commission to multiply image bearers begins, not in the garden, but in exile – and this because of the reign and provision of the rejected, royal son.[39]

At the same time, other narrative features show that Genesis 1:28 is only partially fulfilled – it is an anticipatory fulfilment. God restates his seed promise to Jacob at Luz (Gen. 48:4), revealing that something more is still expected. Additionally, as Kaminski notes, 'nowhere is it stated in Genesis that they have "*filled* the *land*" (cf. Gen. 1:28; 9:1)'[40] – a narrative development that does in fact occur in Exodus 1:7.

---

[37] See Brian Sigmon's argument that Gen. 47:13–26 is a 'slideshow', a picture of what might have happened to Jacob and his family were it not for Joseph's intervention (Sigmon 2011: 454–470).

[38] This table excludes irrelevant references to *pārâ* and *rābâ*, such as when God commands animals to multiply (Gen. 1:22; 8:17) or promises fruitfulness to the line of Ishmael (Gen. 17:20).

[39] See similar observations by Stone 2012: 70.

[40] Kaminski 2004: 123.

Table 2 *Pārâ* and *rābâ* in Genesis

1:28	Imperative
9:1	Imperative
9:7	Imperative
16:10 (*rābâ* only)	Promise
17:2, 6	Promise
22:17 (*rābâ* only)	Promise
26:4 (*rābâ* only)	Promise
26:24 (*rābâ* only)	Promise
28:3	Benediction
35:11	Imperative
48:4	Promise
47:27	Indicative

Nevertheless, the language of the 'be fruitful and multiply' blessing-commission bookends Genesis. In Genesis 1:28 we see the initial command, and in Genesis 47:27 we find its fulfilment, though presented such that readers expect more to come. Kaminski, who traces the development of Genesis 1:28 throughout Genesis, summarizes the evidence well: 'Genesis 47:27 may be seen, therefore, as the first explicit statement that the primaeval commands to "be fruitful and multiply" (Gen. 1:28; 9:1; cf. Gen. 35:11) have been executed. Thus we may conclude that Gen. 47:27 marks the initial fulfilment of the promise of increase and of the primaeval commands.'[41]

Joseph's crucial role in fulfilling the seed promise is confirmed by later biblical authors. Psalm 105, depending on Joseph's interpretation of his own story in Genesis 45:4–8, records that Yahweh 'sent' Joseph ahead of the Israelites (Ps. 105:17), presumably to preserve them through the famine (Ps. 105:16, 20–22). As a result, 'Israel came to Egypt . . . and the LORD made his people very fruitful [*Wayyeper*] and made them stronger than their foes' (Ps. 105:23–24). The psalmist thus identifies Joseph as Yahweh's agent, preserving and prospering the seed of Jacob in the midst of famine. Joseph's preserving influence on Israel is also highlighted in Exodus 1:8, when a new Pharaoh oppresses Israel because he 'did not know Joseph'. Even the memory of Joseph in the court of Egypt prospered Israel. Once that memory faded, the blessing and prosperity Joseph mediated to his family vanished.

---

[41] Ibid.

Seed conflict and sibling rivalry

Another major feature of the Genesis narrative as it pertains to the preservation and proliferation of the seed is the motif of conflict between seeds. The earliest expression of this 'seed conflict' occurs in Genesis 3:15, where God indicates that a seed of the woman and a seed of the serpent will be at odds to the point of violence. As already discussed, while this passage ultimately points to a singular seed of the woman who will undo the serpent's work, 'within the overall context of Genesis the "seed of the woman" refers to those who are righteous, whereas the "seed of the serpent" denotes those who are wicked'.[42]

The conflict between the two seeds develops between brothers in the very next chapter. Cain, the seed of the serpent, kills Abel, the seed of the woman.[43] Given the close linguistic parallels between Genesis 3 and 4,[44] and the fact that the next *tôlĕdôt* section does not begin until after Genesis 4, the Cain and Abel story is paradigmatic for Genesis' portrayal of the effects of the fall. Many of Genesis' major motifs originate in this episode – particularly sibling rivalry, jealousy and the favouring of the younger son.

This sibling conflict is recapitulated numerous times in Genesis.[45] Ishmael mocks the younger and favoured son Isaac, leading to an estrangement between the two. Jacob and Esau fight even while in the womb (Gen. 25:21–23). Jacob deceives Esau, who in turn plots his brother's murder. Even when Jacob returns to Canaan and is greeted happily by Esau, the two are far from reconciled. Jacob lives in Canaan while Esau turns to the land of Seir. As Mathews notes, 'Although no conflict occurred in patriarchal times, the attention in Genesis to Esau's future generation, the Edomites and their rulers (chap 36), reflect the trouble Israel experienced in their wilderness passage (Num. 20:14–21; cp. Num. 24:18; Deut. 23:7).'[46] Moreover, even Leah and Rachel share a rivalry that incorporates the themes

---

[42] Alexander 1998b: 18.

[43] For a defence of the notion that Cain and Abel are representative of the two seeds described in Gen. 3:15, and for a general survey of the seed conflict traced out in Genesis, see Hamilton 2010: 80–86. For a survey of modern literature on sibling conflict in Genesis, see Sigmon 2013: 18–35.

[44] See e.g. the analysis in Sigmon 2013: 120–126.

[45] Genesis also witnesses to other, more indirect, forms of sibling conflict. For instance, Shem and Japheth are set at odds with Ham. Abraham quarrels with Lot, the son of his brother Haran. Likewise, Jacob (the representative of Abraham) quarrels with Abraham's other brother Nahor (K. Mathews 2005: 75).

[46] Ibid. 76.

of favouritism for the younger and jealousy (cf. Gen. 30:1). Each of these sibling rivalries or 'seed conflicts' develops the paradigmatic conflict first announced in Genesis 3:15 and then portrayed in Cain's murder of Abel. While only the Genesis 4 conflict ends in murder, the threat of fratricide against the covenant seeds looms throughout each of these conflicts.

The seed conflict between Joseph and his brothers is thus climactic in Genesis. As a number of commentators note, the brothers' intense animosity for Joseph evokes the first fratricidal conflict in Genesis 4.[47] Gonzales goes so far as to label Genesis 37 'Cain *Redivivus*'.[48] He summarizes the evidence:

> In both cases, the unrighteous despised the righteous because God favors the latter (4:4–5; 37:4, 5, 8, 11). As Cain's anger and hatred intensify to the point of plotting murder (4:7), so the hatred of Joseph's brothers mounts (37:4, 5, 8, 11) until it results in an assassination conspiracy (37:18–20). Cain actually murders Abel (4:8); Joseph's brothers stop short of murder and sell him into slavery (37:21–28). Yet their deed amounts to a virtual murder.[49]

Other aspects of the conflict also parallel Cain and Abel.[50] The word brother (*'āḥ*) is prominent in both narratives, occurring eight times in the Cain and Abel story and twenty-one times in Genesis 37. Likewise 'blood'

---

[47] Dahlberg 1982: 131; Ronning 1997: 206; Brodie 2001: 358; Wilson 2004: 222; Stone 2012: 67–68; Mathews 1996; Sigmon 2013.

[48] Gonzales 2009: 213.

[49] Ibid. 219. On the notion of 'virtual murder', Gonzales notes, 'First, the unwarranted theft of a man's freedom and consignment of his life to slavery is treated with the same gravity in the ancient Near East as the unwarranted theft of a man's life – as a capital offense punishable by death (Exod. 21:16; Deut. 24:7). Compare also stipulation no. 14 in "The Code of Hammurabi", which reads, "If a seignior has stolen the young son of a(nother) seignior, he shall be put to death." *ANET*, 166. Second, one of the most painful elements of death is the prospect of being separated from those whom the person loves, especially family (Gen. 21:16; 23:2; 50:1; 2 Sam. 12:16–18, 22; Isa. 38:11, 17–19). Joseph had to suffer this pain (41:51–52), as did his father (37:34–35; 42:36, 38), at least for a time. Third, for all intents and purposes, the brothers themselves treat Joseph as if he were "no more" (42:13, 32). Fourth, by ending with Joseph's consignment to slavery in Egypt (37:36) and transitioning to the Judah–Tamar narrative (ch. 38), the narrator has left the reader with the gnawing fear that Joseph – the one son who has not yet manifested a negative character (besides Benjamin) and who, therefore, remains the most likely candidate for the blessing – has been eliminated from the picture and is "no more"!' (ibid. 219–220).

[50] Sigmon posits that the brothers' 'jealousy' (Gen. 37:11; *wayqan'û*) may evoke the name of Cain (*qayin*), which itself is 'a pun on the Hebrew word for "jealousy" (*qin'â*)' even though the name formally comes from the verb *qānâ* (Sigmon 2013: 135).

(*dām*) is also prominent in both accounts (Gen. 4:11; 37:22, 26, 31–33; 42:22),[51] and in each account Moses 'portrays fratricide as the shedding of blood, and both [accounts] use blood as evidence that death has taken place'.[52]

These linguistic and thematic parallels tie the narrative threads of Genesis 37 to the Cain and Abel narrative, with the conflict between Joseph and his brothers becoming the climactic episode of sibling rivalry. The brothers recapitulate Cain's fratricide in their plot to murder Joseph, while Joseph undergoes metaphorical death in the pit, narrowly avoiding actual murder.[53]

The dramatic twist in the Joseph story is that Joseph's wise plan to 'test' his brothers (Gen. 42:15–16) coupled with Judah's repentance (Gen. 44:18–34) leads to a reversal of the Cain and Abel story. As Wilson notes, 'the unresolved brotherly strife of previous generations is finally overcome by Joseph's ruse in chapters 42–45, and by his refusal to exact vengeance on his brothers after Jacob's death (50:15–21)'.[54] In this way, the Joseph story reverses one of the primary literary motifs in Genesis. Sibling conflict has racked the covenant family and endangered the seed since Adam and Eve's first children. Joseph undoes this cycle of violence, but only by exercising forgiveness after his own humiliation and exaltation. In this way, Joseph is an anti-Cain. He is truly his brothers' keeper.

---

[51] *Dām* occurs only three other times in Genesis, all in Gen. 9:4–6. Pirson comments, 'An earlier account in Genesis told about fratricide. Hence it is hardly surprising to come across words like דם ("blood;" vv. 37.22, 26), נכה ("smite;" v. 37.21) and הרג ("kill;" vv. 37.20, 26), that were encountered before in Gen. 4, in which chapter the one who is described as רעה ("shepherd", 4.2) loses his life' (Pirson 2002: 61).

[52] Sigmon 2013: 137. Sigmon also posits that the Cain and Abel evocation explains the vexing episode in Gen. 37:15–17, where Joseph wanders in a field before being directed to his brothers by an unnamed man. In Sigmon's estimation, Moses' description of Joseph as 'in the field' (*baśśādeh*) echoes Cain's murder of Abel 'in the field' (Gen. 4:8; *baśśādeh*). Sigmon notes, 'This scene does not echo the murder of Abel directly, and Joseph's sale into slavery does not even take place at this location. The episode does, however, use the field to emphasize the fact that Joseph is alone and vulnerable . . . In this way, Joseph's wandering in the field just before finding his brothers resonates with the journey of Abel into the field with Cain, from which he never returned' (ibid. 137–138).

[53] In Ps. 30:4b [3b] David identifies the 'pit' with death. The word *bôr* is both the opposite of 'life' and parallel with 'sheol'. In addition 'pit' in the rest of the Hebrew Bible is often associated or synonymous with death (Isa. 14:15, 19; 38:18; Ezek. 26:20; 31:16; 32:18, 23–25, 29–30; Pss 28:1; 88:5[4], 7[6]; Prov. 1:12; 28:17). The word 'pit' is also associated with prisons (Gen. 41:14; Exod. 12:29; Isa. 24:22; Jer. 37:16; Zech. 9:11), which was also seen as a place of death in the ANE. Mitchell explains, 'ANE prisons were underground dungeons, and so there developed a widespread association between imprisonment and death' (D. C. Mitchell 2010: 7, n.). See also Keel 1978: 69–73.

[54] R. R. Wilson 1975: 222.

Moses beautifully portrays the theme of reconciliation by using clothing as symbolic of narrative developments. Throughout Genesis, and in the Joseph story in particular, clothing represents deception, stature and change of fortune (good or ill). Joseph's robe marks Jacob's special love for Joseph and incites the brothers' hatred (Gen. 37:3–4). Joseph's change of fortune for the worse is marked by two 'disrobing' episodes. The brothers' stripping Joseph of his robe accompanies his descent into the pit (Gen. 37:23–24). Next, Joseph's disrobing by Potiphar's wife marks his descent into the prison (Gen. 39:12). Joseph's fortunes change, however, when he receives a new robe at the hand of Pharaoh, once again marking a position of superiority and rank (Gen. 41:42). These clothing episodes form a chiasm in the life of Joseph:

A   Joseph receives robe
   B   Joseph disrobed
   B'   Joseph disrobed
A'   Joseph receives robe

Clothing marks more than a change of fortune for Joseph; it also serves the same function in the lives of his brothers. Joseph gives his brothers new clothes after the story's climactic reconciliation (Gen. 45:22). As Matthews notes:

Once they have been convinced of his true identity, Joseph gives . . . each [of his brothers] gifts of new garments as evidence of his forgiveness and favor toward them. This final step brings the story full circle and provides one final use of garments as a status marker. Joseph is now in a position to give clothing to his brothers.[55]

The result is the following chiasm:

A   Joseph receives robe
   B   Joseph disrobed
   B'   Joseph disrobed
A'   Joseph receives robe
      C   Joseph gives robes[56]

---

[55] V. Mathews 1995: 35.
[56] For more on the clothing motif in the Joseph narrative, see Huddlestun 2002: 47–62.

Joseph understands that their reconciliation has broader implications than mere family dynamics. The reconciliation of the seed serves the preservation of the seed. In both reconciliation episodes (Gen. 45:5–8; 50:19–21) Joseph affirms that God sent him to Egypt to 'preserve life' and thus save the covenant line. After Jacob's death, the brothers fear that Joseph may exact retribution by endangering their lives just as they endangered his (Gen. 50:15). Again, the implication is that if that family is not truly reconciled, the covenant seed cannot flourish. But Joseph again assures them of his forgiveness and his confidence that God sent him to protect the covenant line (Gen. 50:19–21). The Cain-like violence of the brothers is overcome by Joseph's kindness. As a result, the seed survives and the promise continues.

6

Joseph and covenant: land and blessing

The land theme in Genesis

The land theme in Genesis begins (like kingship and seed) in the first chapters of Genesis with the creation of Eden. Moses describes Eden, as we have seen, as a garden-sanctuary.[1] God commissions Adam to carry out his royal-priestly duties in Eden – an archetypal temple (cf. Ezek. 28:13's designation of Eden as the 'garden of God'). Thus, Adam's kingship not only includes the notion of 'reign' but also 'realm'. Adam's dominion includes cultivating and caring for the land, protecting it from evil and expanding the borders of God's dwelling.

Land is, therefore, a central component of God's creation enterprise. Adam is given 'a domain over which humans are to realize their humanity'.[2] As Martin states:

> The importance of Eden does not rest primarily on its being the dwelling place of humans, but on its being the place where God dwells on earth in a unique way and where he has fellowship with his image bearers.[3]

Additionally, Eden is a foretaste of the eschaton. If Adam remains faithful, in time the entire world will share the sacredness of the garden and be filled with God's presence.

King Adam's realm is the land of Eden, a sanctuary. The fall, however, disrupts the relationship between the king and his realm. God drives

---

[1] Beale 2004: 66–79; Fesko 2007: 57–75.
[2] Dempster 2003: 48.
[3] Martin 2015: 38.

Adam from the garden, away from his presence, and establishes angelic sentinels to bar him from returning (Gen. 3:24). Additionally, the land itself is cursed, no longer yielding produce with ease or regularity (3:17–19).

The ensuing narratives further develop the discordant relationship between man and land. Cain is a wanderer, living east of Eden (Gen. 4:12, 16). Lamech prophesies that Noah will be God's agent in providing relief from the cursed land (Gen. 5:29). Further, the land turns hostile in the 'de-creation' event of the flood. The world reverts to the primordial chaos of Genesis 1:2 and swallows humanity whole.[4]

God works to undo this discord in the Abrahamic covenant. He promises Abraham and his descendants the land of Canaan as an everlasting possession (Gen. 15:7, 18–21; 17:8), thus supplying 'a commodity that has been in short supply for human beings: a land to call [their] own'.[5] But this promise means more than mere real estate. The exile from Eden is being overturned. Canaan represents restoration to Eden and access, once again, to life in God's presence.[6]

For the most part the patriarchs live out their time within Canaan's boundaries (though acquiring only enough land for their burial plots).[7] This situation in the Joseph story changes abruptly when famine forces Jacob's sons to go to Egypt, as it had with Abraham three generations before (Gen. 12:10–20).

The Promised Land in the story of Joseph

With regard to the land promise, the Joseph story appears to be a retrogression in redemptive history. In fact, as Hamilton points out, Genesis is bookended by two major literary sections characterized by life outside the Promised Land.[8] Both famine and fraternal strife drive the covenant family away from Canaan – displacing, and thus apparently returning, them to a pre-Genesis 12 state of life 'east of Eden'. This migration reveals that threats to the seed also endanger the land promise. Thus, the covenant

---

[4] Dempster 2003: 73.

[5] Ibid. 48.

[6] 'The theology of land in the early part of the OT anticipates the final chapters of the Bible, where the apostle John describes the new heaven and earth in language taken from Genesis 1–3' (Millar 2000). Also Robertson 2000: 4; Williamson 2000b: 25.

[7] Dempster 2003: 78–80, 86–88.

[8] V. Hamilton 1990: 10.

family's sojourn in Egypt builds suspense. Will God be able to overturn these circumstances and fulfil the land promise?[9]

Due to the Egyptian setting of the story, Joseph's relevance to the land promise is not immediately clear. As Wilson observes, 'the promise of the land does not loom large in the Joseph narrative, since the story takes not only Joseph, but also Jacob and his other sons, out of Canaan and into Egypt'.[10] Yet, as with the seed theme, the reconciliation episode in Genesis 45 results in a resurfacing of the land theme. Explicit references to the land promise, for example, appear in Genesis 46:4 and 48:4. In the first instance, Yahweh promises to bring Jacob back to Canaan. In the second, Jacob recounts Yahweh's covenant promise to him at Luz (Gen. 35:9–15) as a way of transferring those covenant blessings to his children, which now include Joseph's own Ephraim and Manasseh.

Furthermore, the land theme is prominent in the final scene of the narrative, no doubt to transition to the story of the exodus. Moses, it appears, subtly identifies Joseph with the fulfilment of the land promise in the death narratives of Jacob and Joseph. As Lunn has argued, Genesis 49:29 – 50:26 is a concentric pattern that places the final words of Jacob and Joseph in parallel (see the chiasm below), with Jacob's funeral at the centre[11] – a surprising narrative progression given the prominence of Joseph in the story thus far.[12]

Lunn demonstrates linguistic and thematic correspondences as well as internal literary features that support his proposal.[13] The chiasm also

---

[9] While this sojourn outside Canaan creates tension for the covenantal promises, how the events unfold also highlights the fact that Abraham's family will be a blessing to the nations. Hamilton writes, 'The crucial center section of Genesis (chs. 12–36) is bracketed geographically by two sections of the Near Eastern world with whose history that of Israel would be constantly interlocked. The impact created by these broad geographical contours is that Genesis is a book about world history . . . The ultimate reason for the election of Abraham is that the nations of the earth (such as those falling within the geographical boundaries of chs. 1–11 and 37–50) might find the knowledge of God and his blessing' (V. Hamilton 1990: 10).

[10] Wilson 2004: 225.

[11] On the centre of the symmetrical pattern as the focal point of the structure, see Breck 1994; Dorsey 1999: 28; Walsh 2001: 14; Leithart 2009: 167–168.

As Lunn also notes, by word count alone, Moses highlights the death and burial of Jacob as the most significant event in this section of the Joseph story. This section has 220 words in 15 verses compared to just 11 words in one verse for the death of Joseph (Lunn 2008: 164).

[12] This proposed concentric structure appears unique to Lunn, who also recognizes this proposal as a 'previously undetected pattern' (Lunn 2008: 164). Ross similarly recognizes Gen. 49:29 – 50:26 as the last narrative unit of the Joseph story but does not argue, as does Lunn, for any concentric pattern (Ross 1996).

[13] Chiasm reproduced from Lunn 2008. For a complete accounting of the linguistic evidence, see ibid. 164–166.

follows a pattern of monologue » dialogue » narrative » dialogue » monologue.

A The last words and death of Jacob (49:29 – 50:3): *monologue*
  B Joseph's appeal to Pharaoh (50:4–6): *dialogue*
    C The funeral of Jacob (50:7–14): *narrative*
  B' The brothers' appeal to Joseph (50:15–21): *dialogue*
A' The last words and death of Joseph (50:22–26): *monologue*

Each A section records the final words of a dying man to his family (introduced by *wayyō'mer* . . . *'el*): 'I am about to be gathered to my people' (49:29); 'I am about to die' (50:24).[14] After these statements both Jacob and Joseph give instructions for their burial, 'invoking in each case the names of earlier Hebrew patriarchs and the promised land (49:30 and 50:25)'.[15] Finally each section records the death of the patriarch, also indicating that the body was embalmed (*wayyaḥanṭû*; Gen. 50:2, 26).

Lunn argues that in the B sections the correspondence is 'one of form more than content'.[16] Each section contains an indirect request that invokes a father's instructions. In Genesis 50:5 Joseph says, 'My father made me swear, saying' (*'ābî hišbî'anî lē'mōr*), whereas in Genesis 50:16 the brothers say, 'Your father gave instructions before his death, saying' (*'ābîkā ṣiwwāh lipnê môtô lē'mōr*). Additionally, after Jacob's instructions are relayed, both Joseph (Gen. 50:5) and his brothers (Gen. 50:17) introduce their appeal with *wĕ'attāh* with the particle *nā'*.[17]

At the centre of the chiasm is Jacob's funeral procession and burial in the land of Canaan. As others have noted, Moses probably highlights Jacob's burial for its typological significance. The removal of Jacob's body from Egypt foreshadows the exodus – an 'acted prophecy' of the nation's future deliverance.[18] Just as the beginning of the patriarchal narratives

---

[14] Ibid. 164.
[15] Ibid.
[16] Ibid.
[17] Ibid. 164–165.
[18] Wenham 1994a: 51. Lunn provides a thorough defence of the 'foreshadowing' character of Jacob's burial and a helpful summary of both his own arguments and the arguments of other scholars on this point. He summarizes the evidence:
  'Genesis 50 contains indicators which suggest that just as the earlier descent of Abraham into Egypt in 12:10–13:4 foreshadowed the later exodus event, so too the coming out of Egypt described in connection with the burial of Jacob is to be interpreted the same way. It looks both ways, back to the earlier Abrahamic account, and forwards towards the actual exodus

foreshadow the exodus with Abraham's journey to and from Egypt (Gen. 12:10–20), so now the end of the patriarchal narratives foreshadows the journey to the Promised Land with Jacob's removal. These two 'exodus episodes' form an inclusio around the entire patriarchal history.[19]

This structure indirectly associates Joseph with the fulfilment of the Abrahamic land promise. The symmetrical pattern places Jacob and Joseph's final wishes in parallel (A and A'). Both men ask to be buried in

---

itself. Here are the most noteworthy verbal connections and similarities in detail with the two other narratives:

(1) The use of the verb "go up" describing the journey out of Egypt. Genesis 13:1 states that "Abram went up from Egypt" (וַיַּעַל אַבְרָם מִמִּצְרַיִם). In the narrative of Genesis 50:7–14 this same verb is employed four times (vv. 7 [twice], 9, 14), also denoting the going up from Egypt. It occurs frequently with reference to the later exodus, such as in Exodus 13:18, "The sons of Israel went up from the land of Egypt" (עוֹלוּ בְנֵי־יִשְׂרָאֵל מֵאֶרֶץ מִצְרַיִם); cf. also 17:3; 32:1; 33:1, etc. The preposition אֶת "with" is joined to this verb when speaking of those foreigners who accompanied the Hebrews, as in Genesis 50:7 (אִתּוֹ·וַיַּעֲלוּ) and Exodus 12:38 (עָלָה אִתָּם).

(2) The phrase "very substantial" (כָּבֵד מְאֹד, literally "very heavy") occurs in all three accounts. In Genesis 13:2 Abraham came out of Egypt with much wealth, flocks and herds, silver and gold, which had been given him by Pharaoh (cf. 12:16). In 50:9 the same phrase describes the host of Egyptians who accompanied Joseph and his brothers in the funeral procession. The phrase also appears in Exodus 12:38 regarding the flocks and herds that the Hebrews brought with them out of Egypt.

(3) On the occasion of Abraham's descent into and ascent from Egypt, it is stressed that "the Canaanite was in the land" (Gen. 12:6, וְהַכְּנַעֲנִי אָז בָּאָרֶץ; cf. 13:7, "the Canaanite and the Perizzite were then living in the land", וְהַכְּנַעֲנִי וְהַפְּרִזִּי אָז יֹשֵׁב בָּאָרֶץ). At the time of Jacob's burial a similar phrase, "the Canaanite living in the land" (Gen. 50:11, הַכְּנַעֲנִי יוֹשֵׁב הָאָרֶץ) is found.

(4) It is in accordance with Jacob's command that his sons transported his body to Canaan, "His sons did for him as he commanded them" (Gen. 50:12, וַיַּעֲשׂוּ ... כַּאֲשֶׁר צִוָּם). The exodus was similarly a response of obedience. On that occasion it was Moses and Aaron who took the initiative in leading the people of Israel to Canaan "as Yahweh had commanded them" (Exod. 7:6, וַיַּעֲשׂ ... כַּאֲשֶׁר צִוָּה יְהוָה אֹתָם; cf. 6:13).

(5) The use of the noun "possession" (אֲחֻזָּה) in Genesis 50:13 referring to the plot purchased for burial points forward to the possession of the land of Canaan subsequent to the exodus (e.g. Lev. 14:34; 25:24; Deut. 32:49; Josh. 21:12; cf. Gen. 17:8; 48:4).

(6) Other common words and phrases include: "sheep and cattle" and "livestock" (Gen. 12:16; 13:2; 50:8; Exod. 10:26; 12:32, 38), "chariots and horsemen" (Gen. 50:9; Exod. 14:9, 17, 18, 23, 26, 28; 15:19), "infants" (Gen. 50:8; Exod. 10:24; 12:37), "camp" denoting the Egyptian army (Gen. 50:9; Exod. 14:20), "officials of Pharaoh" (Gen. 12:15; 50:7; Exod. 9:20; 10:7; 11:3, etc.), and Pharaoh's "house" (Gen. 12:15; 50:7; Exod. 8:24). It will be noted that some of these are used contrastively. At the time of the actual exodus, the Israelites took their children and animals with them, while on the occasion of Jacob's burial they remained in Egypt. Likewise, the Egyptian chariots and horsemen in the earlier account actually escorted the Hebrews, yet later were to pursue them.

(7) Finally, it has been noted that the procession in Genesis 50 takes the same approximate route as the later exodus, skirting round the southern end of the Dead Sea and approaching Canaan from the east side of the Jordan. It would seem then, in the light of these intertextual parallels, that this account in the last chapter of Genesis is intended by the author to be taken as a picture of "Israel" coming up out of Egypt to Canaan.' (Lunn 2008: 174–178). See also Sailhamer 1992: 239; Waltke 2001: 579, 616.

[19] Lunn 2008: 178.

the Promised Land (Gen. 49:29; 50:25). As a result, upon death Jacob (Israel) undergoes his own exodus to Canaan. The implication is that Joseph's death anticipates the same thing for the nation at large. Just as the death of Jacob led to an exodus from Egypt to the place of inheritance, so also Joseph's death is a harbinger of the real exodus to come. Joseph's own last words highlight this point: 'God will surely come to your aid,' he tells his brothers, 'and take you up out of this land to the land he promised on oath to Abraham, Isaac and Jacob' (Gen. 50:24b, 25b; cf. Heb. 11:22).

God uses Joseph to fulfil the other features of the Abrahamic covenant (kingship, seed, blessing). Joseph's role in securing the land is not as obvious. Yet, given that his story takes place almost entirely in Egypt and that he lives there until his death, the parallel between Jacob and Joseph's deaths and the resulting 'exodus' may be Moses' way of connecting the life of Joseph with the fulfilment of the land promise. Joseph's dying words look forward to life in the Promised Land. His death signals hope for a national exodus from Egypt.

Blessing in Genesis

Blessing, as Gentry and Wellum note, is most fundamentally 'connected with life'.[20] Blessing characterizes the fertility and vitality of the garden and is associated in Genesis 1:28 with the commission to 'be fruitful and multiply' (Gen. 1:28). Indeed, the entire creation project culminates in the 'blessed' Sabbath day, a foretaste of the blessing Adam was meant to experience in the eschaton (Gen. 2:3).

The fall shatters the Edenic state of blessing. Creation becomes characterized by the infertility and death of the curse (Gen. 3:14–19). The curse represents humiliation and eventual defeat for the serpent (Gen. 3:14), infertility and pain for the woman, marital discord and social disharmony for humanity (Gen. 3:16), toil for the man and the corruption of the cosmos (Gen. 3:17–19). The land will produce death with thorns and thistles. Indeed, the land originally meant to sustain an abundant life for humanity, will now swallow man up in death.

The same themes of humiliation and death characterize God's curse on Cain (Gen. 4:11) and Noah's curse on Canaan (Gen. 9:25). Gentry and Wellum summarize that 'cumulative deprivation and increasing loss is

---

[20] Gentry and Wellum 2012: 241.

therefore associated with the word "curse," bringing man from Eden to Babel'.[21] Further, and worst of all, these horizontal dimensions of the curse are all a result of the vertical dimension – alienation between God and humanity, as man now lives away from God's presence and under his judgment.

Again, God establishes the Abrahamic covenant in response to the corruption and decay of the curse. God's call of Abraham in Genesis 12:1–3 is bathed in the language of blessing, using the word 'bless' five times in response to the fivefold use of 'curse' in Genesis 1 – 11.[22] God will bless Abraham (Gen. 12:2) and thus begin to undo the curses of Genesis 3. As Waltke notes, blessing here 'connotes redemption, a relationship with God that transforms the beneficiary and provides security'.[23]

The blessing of Abraham is also characterized by the promise of divine presence and covenant access to God. As in Eden, blessing is not simply life itself, but life *with* God. As the covenant passes from one generation to the next, God promises to be 'with' each of the patriarchs. This promise of divine presence is always inextricably linked to the other covenantal promises of land and seed (cf. 26:3–5, 24; 28:13–15; 31:3; 46:3–4). Yahweh repeatedly implies that his presence should ground the patriarchs' assurance that he will fulfil his covenant obligations. In other words, only the presence of Yahweh can ensure the fulfilment of the promises – and his presence also guarantees that fulfilment.[24]

Yet Abraham is more than a recipient of blessing: he is a conduit. He is blessed to be a blessing (Gen. 12:3). Through Abraham, the families of the earth (*mišpĕḥōt*), last seen in the Table of Nations (Gen. 10:5; 18, 20, 31, 32), will also receive life. This 'blessing to the nations' is shown throughout the patriarchal accounts as those outside Abraham's immediate family benefit from their positive relationship with him or his children (cf. Gen. 18:16–33; 20:14, 17).

Blessing in the Joseph story

Genesis 39:2–3 provides the first mention of covenant blessing in the Joseph story. Yahweh is 'with Joseph', causing him to excel in his

---

[21] Ibid.
[22] Gen. 3:14, 17; 4:11; 5:29; 9:25. Wolff 1974: 54–55; Dempster 2013: 77.
[23] Waltke 2007: 316.
[24] See further J. M. Hamilton 2003: 113–133.

administration of Potiphar's house. The same phrase is repeated even when Joseph lands in prison: Yahweh is 'with Joseph', giving him favour with his superiors and success in his vocation (Gen. 39:21, 23).

These affirmations of divine presence are significant. Divine presence characterizes God's covenant relationship with the Abrahamic family. Yahweh's presence is the *sine qua non* of covenant fulfilment. Without Yahweh being 'with' the patriarchs, there is no hope of seeing the promise of seed and land come to fruition. After Yahweh's opposition to Judah in Genesis 38 (the only other time the narrator mentions Yahweh in the Joseph story), the prospects of seed and land appear to be on shaky ground. The reaffirmation of divine presence with Joseph re-establishes God's commitment to fulfil his promises but identifies Joseph as the conduit of those blessings. Like Isaac and Jacob before him, Joseph now, by virtue of God's presence, carries the hope for the fulfilment of God's promises.

In accord with the pattern established in Genesis 12:2–3, Joseph is blessed and a blessing. Potiphar appoints Joseph as a steward 'over his house' (*'al bêtô*) and as a result Yahweh blesses Potiphar 'for Joseph's sake' (Gen. 39:4–5). Even Arnold, who favours a minimalist approach to the relationship between Joseph and the patriarchal narratives, admits that here we find an 'allusion to the ancestral promises . . . Yahweh blessed Potiphar's household because of Joseph, who has no personal abilities to bless others'.[25] Later we again find Joseph established 'over a house' (*'al bêtô*) – the house of Pharaoh (Gen. 41:40).[26] The result is the same: Joseph blesses the nations by providing grain during a 'severe famine', first for Egypt (Gen. 41:56) and then for 'all the earth' (Gen. 41:57).

After the reconciliation episode, blessings emerge as a prominent feature of the story. Indeed, the final chapters are largely characterized by three blessing episodes, as Jacob blesses Pharaoh (Gen. 47:7–10), Ephraim and Manasseh (Gen. 48), and finally his twelve sons (Gen. 49). The most striking of these is Jacob's blessing of Pharaoh. Just prior to this encounter Pharaoh treats the covenant family well, giving them the 'best of the land' and hiring them to care for the royal court's livestock (Gen. 47:6). Given

---

[25] Arnold 2009: 331. See also Sailhamer: 'Joseph's sojourn in Egypt, like that of his father Jacob's (30:27), has resulted in an initial fulfilment of the Abrahamic promise . . . This is not a story of the success of Joseph, but rather of God's faithfulness to his promises' (Sailhamer 1992: 210–211).

[26] Stone argues that 'the term "house" is a strange way to refer to Pharaoh's kingdom and unique to this instance, inviting a comparison between Joseph's rule in the two houses' (Stone 2012: 68).

narrative patterns thus far, and given God's promise to bless those who bless Israel (Gen. 12:3), these events suggest that both Pharaoh and his nation will be blessed.

Genesis 47:7–10 narrates, with some emphasis, the giving of that blessing to Pharaoh. Jacob is brought before Pharaoh and blesses him (Gen. 47:7). The narrative sequence is quite startling. Jacob, though a sojourner and the father of a small band of seventy, takes the initiative and blesses Pharaoh before Pharaoh even speaks to him. This blessing is not a trifling detail in the narrative but a point Moses emphasizes through chiasm. The exterior sections of the chiasm (Gen. 47:7, 10) mention that 'Jacob blessed [bārak] Pharaoh', while the interior sections (Gen. 47:8–9) focus on Jacob's age. McKenzie summarizes the significance of these two features, noting that

> the reference to Jacob's age apparently serves to heighten the significance of this blessing. A man whose closeness to God and favor in God's eyes is attested by his attainment of an age greater than any Egyptian dared to hope for blesses Pharaoh.[27]

A   Then Joseph brought in Jacob his father and stood him   (7)
    before Pharaoh [lipnê parʿōh], and Jacob blessed Pharaoh
    [waybārek yaʿăqōb 'et parʿōh].

  B   And Pharaoh said to Jacob [wayyōʾmer parʿōh 'el   (8)
    yaʿăqōb], 'How many are the days of the years of your
    life [yĕmê šĕnê ḥayyêkā]?'

  B' And Jacob said to Pharaoh [wayyōʾmer yaʿăqōb 'el   (9)
    parʿōh], 'The days of the years [yĕmê šĕnê] of my
    sojourning are 130 years. Few and evil have been the
    days of the years of my life [yĕmê šĕnê ḥayyê], and they
    have not attained to the days of the years of the life
    [yĕmê šĕnê ḥayyê] of my fathers in the days of their
    sojourning.'

A' And Jacob blessed Pharaoh [waybārek yaʿăqōb 'et parʿōh]   (10)
    and went out from the presence of Pharaoh [millipnê parʿōh].

Ultimately, what Moses portrays is a narrative outworking of the Genesis 12:3 promise. Through the family of Abraham, the nations of

---

27 Ibid. 394.

the earth are blessed. Dempster notes, 'there are not just two individuals meeting here, but two nations, one of them embryonic and the other the most powerful nation on earth'.[28] Yet, in a shocking twist, Jacob twice blesses Pharaoh. Again, Dempster rightly notes, 'the irony is impossible to miss. The hope for the world comes from Israel and not from Egypt. Blessing comes from a decrepit and broken Israel and not from a dominant and strong Egypt.'[29] Joseph's role in this episode is indirect, but no less significant. Jacob is present only because of Joseph's administrative genius and favour with Pharaoh. In the context of Genesis 37 – 50, this account evinces Moses' view of Joseph as the one who triggers the fulfilment – at least initially – of the Abrahamic promises.

In this light, the following account in Genesis 47:13–26 describing Joseph's agrarian reforms ought also to be interpreted as an outworking of Jacob's blessing to Pharaoh. As McKenzie notes, 'there is no other adequate explanation for the inclusion of an extensive account of Joseph's land reforms'.[30] Given that blessing characterizes Joseph's interactions with Pharaoh and with Egypt, and given the blessing to Pharaoh in Genesis 47:7–10, it would seem far-fetched to interpret Joseph here as a corrupt 'tyrant' wielding power to oppress the less fortunate.[31] More likely, this narrative signals blessing to the nations along the lines of Genesis 12:3.[32] Contrary to the rather negative spin on these events by modern interpreters, the Egyptians themselves praised Joseph for employing his wisdom to save their lives (Gen. 47:25).

Ultimately, Joseph is both blessed and a blessing. As the one whom God is 'with', Joseph mediates blessing to the nations, bringing prosperity to Potiphar and Pharaoh's houses. Finally, Jacob (Israel) blesses Pharaoh and the nation he represents. As a result, through Joseph's wise administration, the Egyptians find life in the midst of the famine. Israel's purpose is coming to fruition. The covenant family, led by Joseph, both blesses and is blessed by the nations.[33]

---

[28] Dempster 2013: 89.
[29] Ibid.
[30] McKenzie 1983: 396.
[31] Watt 1995: 68–69.
[32] Kline et al. 1970: 112; McKenzie 1983: 395–398; Garrett 1991: 176.
[33] Wenham concurs, 'In Joseph . . . "the families of the earth found blessing" (cf. 12:3): in his career the promises to Abraham of universal blessing to all nations began to see fulfillment' (Wenham 1994a: 493).

Other possibly significant biblical-theological features of the Joseph story

This chapter and the previous two have focused on Joseph's relationship to the Abrahamic covenant and to the overall storyline of Genesis. I have attempted to demonstrate Joseph's biblical-theological significance by interpreting him according to his covenantal context, explaining his place in the Genesis story. There are, however, other plausible connections between Joseph and earlier episodes and figures in Genesis.

Beale sees the blessing of Jacob in Genesis 49:22–26 (a notoriously vexing passage) as a depiction of the 'career of Joseph and the destiny of his descendants' bathed in 'new creational-imagery' and derived from Genesis 1:28. In Beale's estimation the depiction of Joseph as a 'fruitful bough by a spring' (Gen. 49:22) recalls the idyllic situation of Genesis 1 – 2 when Eden was well-watered and characterized by prosperity and abundance.[34] He summarizes:

> The double use of the participial form of 'bear fruit' (*pārâ*) in verse 22 followed by the repeated mention of 'blessing' in verses 25–26 also reflects the close placement of 'bless' and 'bear fruit' in Gen. 1:28. There is even evocation of 'filling the earth' prosperously in the mention that 'the blessings of your father [Jacob's blessing on Joseph] have surpassed the blessings of my [Jacob's] ancestors [beginning with Adam] up to the utmost bound of the everlasting hills.' Although Adam had failed to possess full end-time blessings, Joseph received them at some point in the future. Although an end-time climax is not as clear here as in the Judah prophecy, the Joseph prophecy may overlap with its fulfillment in conjunction with the Judah prophecy because it is so saturated with new-creational motifs related also to Joseph's descendants that a culminating eschatological notion of a renewed creation is likely elicited. Furthermore, the reference to 'surpassing the blessings . . . up to the utmost bound of the everlasting hills' may suggest not some figuratively vague future condition but rather a zenith point of blessings beyond which no more blessing can be given and that will not be reversible.[35]

---

[34] Beale 2011: 96–97.
[35] Ibid. 97–98.

Whatever the eschatological implications of the prophecy may be, the association of Joseph with Edenic/new creation imagery discloses Moses' own interpretation of the life and career of Joseph as one intimately associated with the restoration of Edenic blessing. In this sense Joseph is an anti-Adam, restoring covenant blessing and marking fruitfulness of the people of Israel.

Joseph's faithful-Adam identity is also hinted at in Genesis 39. Joseph is given charge of everything in Potiphar's house except the food he eats (Gen. 39:6) – a possible euphemism for Potiphar's wife (cf. Gen. 39:9). Adam ate the forbidden food because he 'listened to the voice of his wife' (3:17). Intriguingly, Moses uses the same phrase in Abraham's own fall narrative in Genesis 16 when he 'listened to the voice of Sarai' and took Hagar. Joseph, however, resisted forbidden food and 'would not listen' to Potiphar's wife (39:10). The conclusion of each narrative is also inverted – Adam goes from naked to clothed as a sign of his guilt (Gen. 3:21), Joseph goes from clothed to naked (Gen. 39:12) – a sign of his innocence for readers, though evidence of his guilt in the eyes of Potiphar.[36]

Additionally, parallels between Genesis 3 and Genesis 50 contrast Joseph with the Serpent and with fallen Adam. In Genesis 3 the Serpent entices Eve with the words 'you will be like God, knowing good and evil'. The same sequence of being 'like God' followed by the coupling of 'good' and 'evil' (a prominent and unique feature of Genesis 2 – 3 [cf. Gen. 2:9, 17; 3:5, 22]) appears in Genesis 50, where Joseph refuses divine status and says, 'Am I in the place of God? You meant evil for me, but God meant it for good' (Gen. 50:20). Joseph is an anti-Adam: he refuses to count equality with God a thing to be grasped. Further, whereas the serpent promises that Eve 'surely will not die' (Gen. 3:4), Joseph works to keep 'many people . . . alive' (Gen. 50:20).[37]

Moses' use of 'good and evil' language nicely draws the book of Genesis to a close.[38] The language of 'good and evil' represented rebellion and chaos at the book's beginning;[39] by its end we find Moses employing the

---

[36] Stone 2012: 66–67; Sigmon 2013: 148–187.

[37] Dahlberg 1977: 363–364. Dahlberg also argues for an Adamic character to the Joseph story, noting that the only two instances of כתנת [kĕtōnet] in Genesis are when God gives Adam 'garments of skins' (Gen. 3:21) and when Jacob gives Joseph a coat with long sleeves (Gen. 37:3) (365).

[38] Interestingly, 'good and evil' also occurs in Moses' final charge to the Israelites at the close of the Pentateuch in Deut. 30:15.

[39] Clark 1969: 266–278.

language to signal that God sovereignly brings salvation out of chaos, light out of darkness, and even 'good' out of 'evil'. Ultimately, Genesis' solution to the problem of evil comes down to one thing: the glorious grace of a sovereign God who unfailingly keeps his covenantal promises.

Suffering, glory and the promise-keeping God: synthesizing the major themes of the Joseph story

At this point, we must synthesize these observations with the broader context of the Joseph story and with the whole Genesis narrative. This type of synthesis not only allows for potentially contradictory textual data to have its voice in shaping interpretation but also keeps us from running foul of myopia – a particular problem among biblical scholars who, as Doug Moo has asserted, often 'learn more and more about less and less – until they know everything about nothing'.[40]

This type of synthesis is also necessary to engage faithfully in the task of biblical theology with exegetical integrity. Biblical theology seeks to integrate the different themes and storylines of Scripture authentically into a cohesive narrative according to Scripture's own interpretive schema and literary development. If Joseph is indeed a typological royal figure who mediates blessing to the nations, how does this fact square with the other major themes of the Joseph narrative and with the larger story of Genesis? More specifically, how does Joseph's anticipatory fulfilment of the covenant fit with the themes of divine providence, preservation and the theme of the suffering of the righteous seed? This final theme poses a particular challenge since it seems incongruous with the notion of Joseph as both blessed and a conduit of blessing.[41]

Moses has intertwined both the theme of suffering and the theme of covenant blessings (kingship, seed and land) throughout Genesis. The Joseph story, the denouement of Genesis, provides the most explicit

---

[40] Moo 2013.

[41] As most scholars note, suffering is a major theme in Gen. 37 – 50. Later biblical summaries of the Joseph narrative underscore this point. Ps. 105, e.g., highlights that before Joseph is made 'Lord' and 'ruler' of Pharaoh's house, he was first 'sold as a slave. His feet were hurt with fetters; his neck was put in a collar of iron; until what he had said came to pass' (Ps. 105:17–19). Likewise, Stephen in Acts 7 emphasizes that the story of Joseph's rise to power and provision for his family emerges from slavery, imprisonment and 'afflictions' (Acts 7:9–10).

juxtaposition of these two themes. As Levenson summarizes, 'The story of humiliation and exaltation of the beloved son reverberates throughout the Bible because it is the story of the people about whom and to whom it is written.'[42]

The entrance of sin in Genesis does not undo God's teleological purposes for creation; it just reroutes the path to that end.[43] As Treat argues, the transformation of the command 'be fruitful and multiply' (Gen. 1:28) into the patriarchal promise unites God's purposes in redemption with those of creation. Thus, the goal of establishing God's global kingdom remains but, because of the fall, 'a new way of arriving at the consummation was introduced'.[44]

This 'new way' maintains the centrality of a king who mediates the reign and blessings of God, but it introduces the notion that this king will endure suffering on the path to the throne. Again, Treat observes, 'suffering will be a key ingredient in God's victorious plan of redeeming his people and their royal task'. This idea appears first in Genesis 3:15: the seed of the woman will engage in mortal combat with the seed of the serpent. The seed of the woman will emerge victorious, but wounded. His victory will come with a cost – a 'bruised heel' atop the 'bruised head' of the serpent.

As Alexander argues, Genesis traces the line of the seed of the woman through Noah to the patriarchs.[45] These seeds are royal, inheriting Adam's royal commission now in the form of covenantal promises. Yet each of these seeds endures suffering on the path to enjoy God's blessing. Genesis 22 particularly highlights these themes. God commands Abraham to sacrifice his only son – the promised seed. Isaac's near-death experience 'echoes the suffering of the seed of the woman' and is nothing less than a narrative portrayal of death and resurrection.[46] After God provides a substitutionary ram (with language that portends the Day of Atonement), he promises that Abraham's seed 'shall possess the gate of his enemies' (Gen. 22:17) – a promise of royal victory over the foes of Abraham's descendants. The portrait may be faint, but the elements of suffering, substitution and royalty all converge in the Akedah. Isaac, the promised

---

[42] Levenson 1993: 67.
[43] See Treat's excellent discussion of this entire point in Treat 2014: 53–67.
[44] Kline 1972: 155.
[45] Alexander 1993.
[46] Treat 2014: 61.

seed of Abraham, embodies the future generations. The offspring of Abraham will suffer like Isaac, but they are promised royal victory over their enemies and salvation by substitutionary sacrifice. Their story will play out like a riff on Genesis 22 – a story of death and resurrection.

Continuing the twin drumbeat of seed and suffering, Joseph rises to the highest seat in the land *through* the experience of suffering. If Genesis 22 shows that the suffering of the seed is akin to death and resurrection, the Joseph story clarifies that the 'death' of the seed comes at the hands of his own brothers.[47] Thus the suffering of Joseph develops a pattern visible since Genesis 3:15 and, in so doing, sets expectations for the new Joseph to emerge from the line of Judah (Gen. 49:8).

Joseph's royal administration fulfils the expectations set earlier in Genesis. He uses his position to bless and forgive the same brothers who threw him into the pit. 'Joseph's ascension to royalty is characterized by suffering and his reign is exercised over his brothers with forgiveness.'[48]

---

[47] As Dempster notes, the Old Testament's conception of death and resurrection is much more dynamic than modern Western notions: 'The ancient Israelite conception of death and life should not be viewed in a reductionistic manner as the mere termination of physical existence, a view associated more with notions in modern, western medicine. In my judgment this is the major problem with the predominant view of scholarship which argues that belief in resurrection was an extremely late development in the OT . . . The biblical view, however, is far more dynamic. Thus, there is a sense in which the world before the flood is a world filled with violence and curse, death and exile, and it is buried under the waters only to be reborn after its baptism by deluge (Gen. 6–8)' (Dempster 2014: 385).

Likewise, Levenson notes, 'Death and life in the Hebrew Bible are often best seen as relational events and are for the selfsame reason inseparable from the personal circumstances of those described as living or as dead. To be alive in this frequent biblical sense of the word inevitably entailed more than merely existing in a certain physical state. It also entailed having one's being within a flourishing and continuing kin group that dwelt in a productive and secure association with its land. Conversely, to be widowed, bereaved of children, or in exile was necessarily to experience death. Indeed, each of these states (even death) and others (notably, health or illness) could serve as a synecdoche for the condition brought about by any of the others' (Levenson 2006: 154–155). Thus, death and resurrection are often understood narratively through the suffering and salvation of individuals as they are brought from conditions characterized by the curse to conditions of blessing (i.e. life; see Dempster 2014: 385–386).

For further defence of reading OT narrative as types of death and resurrection, see Keel 1978: 61–176; Wheaton 2008: 245–253; Chase 2013; 2014b: 467–480; Lunn 2014: 523–535.

Evidence from within the Joseph narrative also supports reading the sufferings and glory of Joseph as a type of death and resurrection. The characters' experience from within the story is one in which Joseph appears to die and then rise again. Joseph's father believes Joseph to be dead (Gen. 37:33–34). Later in the story the brothers themselves think Joseph is dead (Gen. 42:21–22). Joseph's appearance, then, is a sort of resurrection. The brothers' shocking report to their father is not just that Joseph is reigning in Egypt, but first, and perhaps most surprising, 'Joseph is still alive!' (Gen. 45:26).

[48] Treat 2014: 62.

Joseph's story is one of glory through suffering, exaltation through humiliation, the cross and the crown.

Additionally, while Moses keeps Joseph centre stage in Genesis 37 – 50, the main actor is none other than Yahweh himself. Joseph makes that point clearly in Genesis 45. After reuniting with his brothers, Joseph comforts them by explaining God's larger purposes in their actions. No fewer than three times, Joseph says that 'God' sent him into Egypt (Gen. 45:5, 7, 8) to preserve life in the midst of the famine. Genesis 37 – 50 is not just about how Joseph fulfils Abrahamic expectations but also how Yahweh keeps his covenant and fulfils his promises *through* a rejected but royal seed. God's providence serves God's promises. The divine providence theme in Genesis 37 – 50 cannot be divorced from its covenantal context. Moses does not highlight God's providence to make an abstract point about God's sovereignty. Instead, he emphasizes that God's providence guarantees God will fulfil his promises. The covenant is secure in the hands of the God who can sovereignly orchestrate the actions of evil men for his good purposes (Gen. 50:20).

Ciampa rightly summarizes how all this shapes expectations for the reader of Genesis:

> That God will raise up a descendant of Abraham who will bring blessing to all the world, perhaps as God's own vice-regent reigning in the land promised to the patriarch, would be an easily imagined scenario, given what God had already done through Joseph while he was in a foreign land.[49]

The two apparent opposites of suffering and blessing merge in this single character. Joseph is both sufferer and saviour, the prisoner and the prince.

Joseph is the beloved son who suffers in exile before blessing the nations and being exalted. He is part of a pattern developed, at least in nascent form, in Genesis. The rest of the Old Testament continues this trajectory as other characters (David, Daniel, Esther) repeat the pattern. Further, as Gathercole notes, this is the story of Israel itself:

> A general pattern in the Old Testament [is that] God makes Israel as well as individuals go through exile, misery, and even death before

---

[49] Ciampa 2007: 267.

displaying his glory through saving them. The overarching pattern of Israel's history – sin, exile, return – is one case in point. Within that larger framework, the life story of Joseph is another.[50]

Joseph's experience is Israel's experience. He is thus, first and foremost, a type of Israel. His experiences of suffering and exile are shared by his kin and, in many ways, his righteousness and consequent covenant blessings exemplify what Israel *ought* to be in the world. If Joseph is indeed a type of the Messiah (as this book proposes) it is first because he is a type of the nation.

Implications for a canonical understanding of the Joseph narrative

In this chapter and the two that preceded, I have sought to interpret the story of Joseph according to its covenantal context. We have seen that Joseph is intimately related to the promises of Abraham. Through Joseph come the first major fulfilments of the covenantal promises.

This study yields three important implications. First, these observations illuminate the plot and literary character of Genesis as story. The Joseph story is not just the last item in Genesis but also the *resolution* of the Genesis story. Genesis takes readers on a journey from promise to fulfilment and from fratricide (Cain and Abel) to forgiveness (Joseph and his brothers).

Second, contrary to modern critical proposals, the Joseph story has strong connections to the preceding narratives. It develops the redemptive-historical storyline from Adam to Noah to the patriarchs. The full implications of the Joseph narrative are clear only in the light of the literary and theological relationship between Gen. 1 – 36 and 37 – 50.

Third, Genesis itself supplies textual warrant that Joseph is a type of the Messiah. If Joseph fulfils the Abrahamic hopes, he creates an expectation that other Joseph figures will do the same – though more completely – in the future. As a royal seed of Abraham, endowed with God's very presence (Gen. 39:2, 23), Joseph mediates blessing to the nations, preserves the offspring of Abraham, triggers the 'multiplication and fruitfulness' of Israel's seed, and is a harbinger of Israel's exodus from Egypt and

---

[50] Gathercole 2015: 60. Also Levenson 1993: 67.

inheritance of Canaan. Moses, through Jacob's prophecy, projects this Josephite pattern of covenantal fulfilment into the future by patterning Israel's 'last days' messianic king after the life of Joseph (Gen. 49:8). All these elements contribute to our understanding of Joseph according to his covenantal context, which in turn warrant a typological reading of the Joseph story.

Implications for a canonical understanding of the Joseph narrative

7

Joseph in the Old Testament

As noted in chapter 1, some scholars see the sparse references to Joseph in the Old Testament as indicating his relative unimportance in redemptive history. Again, as Westermann posits, 'the Joseph narrative has found a remarkably faint echo in the writings of the OT and the NT ... He received no promise from God and so has no direct significance for the later history.'[1]

This chapter argues that Old Testament authors do, in fact, see Joseph as having 'direct significance' for redemptive history. More fully, this chapter shows that later biblical authors interpreted Joseph's life as orchestrated by God to fulfil his promises to Abraham. They also see his life as a pattern anticipating later biblical characters and events.

In order to unpack this proposal, first, I consider some of the mentions of Joseph in the Old Testament, explaining the biblical-theological significance that biblical authors ascribe to the Joseph story. Second, I examine allusions to the Joseph story, particularly in the book of Daniel. Daniel saw himself as a new Joseph and composed his book in such a way as to help readers make that same link. After establishing the literary dependence of Daniel on the Joseph story, I consider the significance such allusions hold out for a biblical-theological understanding of Joseph. Third, I consider how Joseph fits into the pattern of the 'exalted Jew in a foreign court', which resurfaces throughout the canon.

Joseph and the exodus

Joseph is mentioned nine times in the Old Testament. These mentions fall into three categories. The first five mentions (found in Exodus and Joshua) all pertain to Joseph's relationship to the exodus, particularly the removal

---

[1] Westermann 1982: 252.

of his bones from Egypt and their burial in Canaan. Next, Joseph's life story is retold in Psalm 105's theocentric overview of Israel's history from the life of Abraham to the exodus. Finally, Joseph is mentioned in the Chronicles' genealogy in 1 Chronicles 2:2 and, most notably, in an annotation in 1 Chronicles 5:1–2. Since these final mentions do not hold out much significance for this project, this section and the next will instead focus on the mentions of Joseph in Exodus, Joshua and Psalm 105.

Genesis ends with Joseph forecasting Israel's return to Canaan (Gen. 50:24–26). Exodus begins on the same note. Exodus 1:1–6 lists the sons of Jacob who travelled to Egypt, relying on elements of similar genealogies in Genesis 46:8, 26–27 and 35:23–26. Exodus 1:7, alluding to Genesis 1:28, 9:7 and 12:2–3, is an escalated restatement of Genesis 47:27. Moses highlights that, under Joseph's protection, Israel fulfils the Adamic and Abrahamic commission. They are 'fruitful' (*pārâ*), 'increase greatly' (*šāraṣ*), 'multiply' (*rābâ*) and grow exceedingly strong. In a clear allusion to Genesis 1:28, Moses even states that they 'fill the land' (*wattimmālē' hā'āreṣ 'ōtām*).

Exodus 1:8 indicates that Israel flourished because of Joseph. Once the memory of Joseph is wiped from the royal court, Israel's fortune in Egypt transforms into persecution. A 'new king' who 'did not know Joseph' takes power and enslaves Israel (Exod. 1:8). This moment triggers the events of the exodus that Joseph foretold.

Joseph's part in Israel's story, however, is not yet over. The story of Joseph's bones frames the entire exodus episode. Moses makes good on Israel's promise to exhume Joseph's bones in the exodus (Exod. 13:19). At the end of the conquest, the Israelites bury Joseph's bones in Shechem (Josh. 24:32). Scripture never reveals the biblical-theological significance of this reburial. The author of Hebrews, however, does commend Joseph for believing that God would restore Israel to Canaan (Heb. 11:22).

Yet, the mention of Joseph's bones may hold out other implications as well. First, by reminding readers of Joseph at both the beginning and the end of Exodus, the biblical authors recall Joseph's significance in preparing the way for the exodus. Without Joseph, Israel would not have survived the famine. Additionally, as already noted, Joseph's death signalled the coming exodus. His final words reminded Israel to prepare for that event on the basis of God's covenant promise (Gen. 50:24–26).

Second, these mentions of Joseph's bones may further attest that Joseph's life is a miniature portrayal of Israel's story. Israel's history is bracketed by two exiles: Egypt and Babylon. In both cases, God rescues his people according to his covenantal promises. Joseph, like Israel, undergoes exile, persecution and even death in Egypt. In the face of death, Joseph trusts in God's promise to restore Israel after their sojourn in a foreign land. God then keeps those promises, restoring Joseph to his true home in Canaan – even to the inheritance of his children, the land of Shechem (Josh. 24:32). Joseph's post-mortem participation in the exodus shows that nothing, not even exile and death, can stop God from fulfilling his promise. Joseph, though dead, participates in the exodus and returns to Canaan.

At the same time, Joseph represents Israel at its finest. Unlike Israel, sin is not the cause for Joseph's exile. While in exile, Joseph blesses the nations. In captivity, he is unwaveringly faithful (Gen. 39). He trusts in God's promise of restoration to the land, even in the face of death (Gen. 50:24–26). Joseph not only anticipates Israel's future but also demonstrates the pattern of righteousness Israel ought to mimic. Joseph's life represents Israel par excellence – he establishes a pattern of faithfulness Israel can choose to follow in the face of its own 'death' in exile (cf. Ezek. 37:11–14).[2]

Joseph in Psalm 105

Psalm 105 is part of a series of psalms (Pss 104 – 106) that present an overview of redemptive history from creation to the exile, tracing God's faithfulness to his promises. As such, this psalm provides an opportunity to uncover the 'interpretive perspective' of a later biblical author on Joseph's role in Israel's history. Relying on earlier Old Testament texts, the psalmist rehearses Israel's history to uncover redemptive-historical patterns and their significance for his audience. This and other historical summaries in the Psalms placed audiences into the narrative to identify their situation with previous episodes in Israel's history. As Hamilton notes, past events

> were rehearsed in the Psalms to form a remnant in Israel that would look for God to save them in the future the way he had in the past.

---

[2] On exile as an experience of 'death' for Israel, see Chase 2013; 2014a: 9–29.

Worshippers enculturated by the Psalms would live in the scenes sung in the book's poetry.[3]

The anthologist's placement of these psalms is important. The psalms conclude Book IV, which focuses on God's sovereignty and commitment to re-establish the Davidic kingdom after its demise in the exile rehearsed at the end of Book III (cf. Ps. 89).[4] For the anthologist, the arrangement of these psalms, which trace God's faithfulness to his promises from creation to the exile, is meant to stimulate the post-exilic community's faith in Yahweh's commitment to those same promises. By emphasizing the sovereignty of God over redemptive history and reminding Israel of God's gracious acts of salvation throughout their existence, the psalmist assures his audience that just as God kept his promises to Abraham and Moses by exercising his sovereign power, so also he will keep his promises to David. He will bring Israel out of exile and re-establish David's throne. Additionally, rehearsing Israel's history at the end of Book IV prepares the way for the end of the exile – celebrated in Book V (Ps. 107) and ushered in by a new David (Ps. 110).

> The cumulative effect of these three psalms [104 – 106] is to present the restoration of Israel from exile under the Davidic king as the fulfillment of all salvation history. By bringing mankind back to Himself through the son of David and the kingdom of God, the Lord accomplishes his goal in creation, fulfills His oath to Abraham, realizes the vocation of Israel, and remembers the covenant He swore to David.[5]

In Psalm 105, then, Joseph is part of a larger picture meant to stimulate Israel's hope for a future based on God's faithfulness in the past. In this light, we can see three important features of the psalmist's interpretive perspective on Joseph. First, the psalmist confirms Joseph's interpretation of his life's significance found in Genesis 45:1–8 and 50:20. Both Joseph and the psalmist highlight God's providential orchestration of Joseph's rise to power in order to save the Abrahamic line. The psalmist, for

---

[3] J. M. Hamilton 2014b: 228; cf. P. House 2005: 229–245; Wenham 2012: 53.
[4] For a compelling defence of this position, as well as a survey of the debate on David's role in Book IV, see Grant 2004: 34–37; Gundersen 2015.
[5] Barber 2001: 125–126.

instance, indicates that God ordained the famine and sent Joseph to Egypt, downplaying the role of the brothers by using the passive *nimkar*.[6] This retelling adheres to Joseph's so closely that it is likely dependent on Genesis 45. The psalmist affirms that God 'sent' Joseph to Egypt (Ps. 105:17 [*šālaḥ lipnêhem 'îš*]), echoing Joseph's words when he recounts the same event to his brothers in Genesis 45:7 (*wayyišlāḥēnî 'ělōhîm lipnêkem*). Similarly, the statement 'he made him lord over his house and ruler over all his possessions' (Ps. 105:21 [*śāmô 'ādôn lěbêtô ûmōšēl běkol qinyānô*]) recalls Joseph's words in Genesis 45:8 (*wayśîmēnî lě'āb lěpar'ōh ûlě'ādôn lěkol bêtô ûmōšēl běkol 'ereṣ miṣrāyim*). This focus on divine providence and dependence on Joseph's interpretation of his life confirms the centrality of Genesis 45:4–8 and 50:20 for rightly understanding the Joseph story.

Second, like Genesis 37 – 50, Psalm 105 highlights God's providence not to make an abstract point about God's sovereignty but to show how God fulfils his covenantal promises. The psalmist includes Joseph, not ultimately to show that God is sovereign over human affairs but to demonstrate how God exercises his sovereignty to fulfil his covenant in seemingly impossible situations.

This focus on the Abrahamic covenant is evident at both the beginning and end of the psalm. The psalmist calls on Israel to praise God because 'he remembers his covenant forever . . . the covenant that he made with Abraham . . . an everlasting covenant, saying "To you I will give the land of Canaan as your portion for an inheritance"' (Ps. 105:8–11).[7] The rest of the psalm records how God makes good on his covenant promise by exercising his sovereign power. The end of the psalm makes this same point. God's saving acts in the exodus were rooted in his commitment to his promises to Abraham (Ps. 105:42).

Why does the psalmist mention Joseph? In the light of this theme, the reason is clear. The psalmist sees Joseph, like Moses, as an agent used by God to fulfil his covenantal promises. Sometimes God intervenes in history, without human instruments, to protect his people (Ps. 105:14–15). More often, though, God employs specific people from Israel to mediate blessing to the nation, fulfil his covenantal promises and deliver the nation

---

[6] Compare use of the qal *wěnimkěrennû* in Gen. 37:27.

[7] The psalmist's emphasis on the Abrahamic covenant is also revealed by his mentions of the patriarch. Excluding the mention of the 'God of Abraham' in Ps. 47:10, Ps. 105 is the only psalm that mentions Abraham, which it does on three occasions (Ps. 105:6, 9, 42).

from destruction. In this psalm, Joseph and Moses are singled out as two men employed by God for those purposes.

Joseph's life, therefore, is an expression of God's covenant faithfulness. God sends Joseph to preserve the Abrahamic line, deliver the people of Israel and mediate blessing to the nations. In other words, the psalmist sees the Joseph story as a provisional and anticipatory fulfilment of the Abrahamic promises. Joseph's place in biblical theology is not merely to bridge readers 'from Canaan to Egypt'.[8] His life is an expression of God's faithfulness to his covenant with Abraham. God saves Israel through Joseph, like Moses, because 'he remembered his holy promise and Abraham, his servant' (Ps. 105: 42).

Third, the psalmist indirectly presents Joseph as a 'messianic' figure. He portrays him as a figure in a line of messiahs God uses to deliver the covenant line. As already mentioned, this psalm's summary of Israel's story is not merely to instruct Israel about its past. The psalmist is extolling God's covenant faithfulness (Ps. 105:1–8) by documenting how he keeps his covenant with his people, delivering them from danger. This pattern begins as early as Abraham and Isaac. God delivers them from the oppression of foreign kings on account of their being 'prophets' and 'messiahs' (*bimšîḥāi* [Ps. 105:14–15]).[9]

The psalmist's designation of Abraham and Isaac as 'anointed ones' or 'messiahs' is striking for three reasons. First, this verse, along with the parallel verse in 1 Chronicles 16:22, is the only instance where the term *māšîaḥ* is plural. Second, the term *māšîaḥ* is generally reserved for Israel's priests (Lev. 4:3, 5, 16; 6:15) or kings (1 Sam. 2:10, 35; 12:3, 5; 16:6; 24:7, 11; 26:9, 11, 16, 23; 2 Sam. 1:14, 16, 21; 19:22; 22:51; 23:1; Lam. 4:20; Dan. 9:25, 26; 2 Chr. 6:42; Hab. 3:13) and is only here applied to the patriarchs. Third, elsewhere in the Psalms, *māšîaḥ* is used only to refer to David or his eschatological heir (Pss 2:2; 18:51; 20:7; 28:8; 84:10; 89:39, 52; 132:10, 17).[10]

---

[8] Coats 1976.

[9] The episodes in view in vv. 14–15 are clearly the wife/sister stories of Gen. 12, 20 and 26 (cf. *nāgaʿ* in Gen. 12:17; 20:6; 26:11, 29; Ps. 105:15). While Moses never applies 'messiah' to Abraham, Abraham is called a 'prophet' in Gen. 20:7. Rolfson (Declaissé-Walford, Jacobson and Tanner 2014: 790) posits that the textual warrant for seeing Abraham as a messiah may reside in his being cast as a prophet (Gen. 20:7), priest (Gen. 12:7–8) and king (Gen. 17:6). He also posits that the 'more likely' explanation is that 'the special status of anointed ones and prophets is extended to the entire people' (cf. v. 6) (790).

[10] The term 'messiah' occurs only two other times in the OT, where the term is not applied to an Israelite priest or king: (1) in 1 Chr. 16:22, the parallel passage to Ps. 105:15, and (2) in Isa. 45:1, which refers to Cyrus as God's 'Messiah'.

While Abraham and Isaac were never literally anointed with oil, the psalmist likely applies the term to them since they typologically anticipate the role later embodied by messiahs such as David. These messiahs functioned as covenant mediators, represented the nation and were used by God to fulfil his promises. The plural 'messiahs' (as opposed to the more traditional 'messiah') further demonstrates the psalmist's understanding that the Old Testament witnesses to multiple messianic figures prior to the Davidic monarchy. These men fulfilled a messianic role in the nation's history.

The psalmist never calls Joseph or Moses 'prophets' or 'messiahs', but presents them as continuing in the same vein as the patriarchs. Just as God protected Abraham and Isaac, so too he protected Joseph and Moses and thus delivered Israel through their ministries. The implication of continuing in the patriarchal pattern is that they have a share in the prophetic and messianic identity. God saves Joseph (and Israel) from the famine and Moses (and Israel) from Pharaoh because of his commitment to them as his messiahs. The same verdict spoken over Abraham and Isaac's lives applies to them: 'touch not my anointed ones, do my prophets no harm' (Ps. 105:15).

By implication, the psalter's post-exilic community is meant to see themselves in the line of Abraham, Joseph and Moses. Like Israel's fathers and the nation at the time of the exodus, the post-exilic Israelites are called God's 'servants' and 'chosen ones' (Ps. 105:6; cf. vv. 17, 26, 43). Like their father Abraham, they know what it is like to 'wander about from nation to nation, from one kingdom to another people' (Ps. 105:13). Through this identification, the psalmist encourages Israel to see itself as part of a pattern of suffering and deliverance reiterated through Israel's history and orchestrated by God's sovereignty. The psalmist's emphasis on divine providence anticipates God's future work of redemption. The stories of Abraham, Joseph, Moses and Israel all forecast the type of salvation in which post-exilic Israel can hope.

The psalmist's perspective on Joseph, therefore, confirms a covenantal understanding of Joseph's role in Genesis. The psalmist adheres to Joseph's interpretation of his life as one sovereignly orchestrated to fulfil the Abrahamic covenant. The psalmist further implies that Joseph, like Moses, is in a line of messianic figures, beginning with Abraham and Isaac, whom God employs to deliver the nation from danger and foreign hostility. The psalmist hints that Joseph's story is a microcosm of Israel's.

Joseph's life is, at the very least, part of a pattern that re-emerges through-out Israel's story – one that stimulates hope for post-exilic Israel. Joseph's story reminds them not only that God is sovereign but also that God's providence often entails suffering before deliverance and glory.

Joseph and Daniel

Of all the books in the Old Testament, Daniel has the highest concentration of allusions to the Joseph narrative. The exegetical evidence suggests that Daniel, noting the parallels between his own life as a dream-interpreting exile and Joseph's, saw himself as a new Joseph and interpreted his own experiences in the light of Joseph's story. As a result, Daniel crafted his narrative to highlight these correspondences as a way of signalling his redemptive-historical significance for exilic Israelites.

Establishing Daniel's literary dependence on Joseph

In many respects, the Daniel narrative appears to be modelled on Joseph, particularly Daniel 2. We will examine these textual links below. But correspondences between Joseph and Daniel occur outside Daniel 2 as well. Many features of Daniel's narrative attest to historical correspond-ences between these two characters.[11]

First, both characters are Jews living in exile. Second, both are enlisted to serve government officials. Joseph serves Potiphar (the captain of the guard) and eventually Pharaoh, while Daniel serves in the royal court of Babylon (Dan. 1:3–6, 17–20) and, eventually, Nebuchadnezzar

---

[11] While scholars differ on how Daniel used the Joseph story, most recognize some sort of literary dependence. Collins notes, 'Though some of these similarities derive from the common setting in a Near Eastern court and the common concern for dream interpretation, the verbal correspondences make it highly likely that the author of Daniel knew and was influenced by the story of Joseph' (J. J. Collins 1993: 39). For a small sampling of authors who discuss or affirm a literary relationship between Joseph and Daniel see Rosenthal 1895: 278–284; Gan 1961: 144–149; J. J. Collins 1975: 218–234; Meinhold 1975: 306–324; Davies 1976: 392–401; Hartman 1978: 56, 145; Goldingay 1989: 36–41, 43; Frieden 1990: 193–203; Gnuse 1990: 29–53; Wesselius 1999: 24–77; Wahl 2000: 59–74; Bezalel 2002: 10–16; Nel 2002: 780–798; 2005: 241–283; Segal 2009: 123–149; Shepherd 2009: 71, 78, 87, 115; Rindge 2010: 85–104; Greidanus 2012: 56–57; Henze 2012; Olojede 2012: 351–368; Milán 2013: 335–362; Widder 2014: 1112–1128; J. M. Hamilton 2014b: 221–235; Philpot 2018: 681–696. Commentary on the corres-pondence between Daniel and Joseph is also found among pre-modern exegetes. For a sampling of patristic interpreters who see correspondences between Daniel and Joseph, see Stevenson and Glerup 2008: 161–173. Some scholars posit that the similarities are not a product of literary dependence but shared genre (Redford 1970: 96; Labonté 1993: 284; Morris 1994: 69–85).

(Dan. 2:46–49). Third, though dreams are widespread throughout the Old Testament, Joseph and Daniel are the only Jews able to interpret dreams. This fact, coupled with the reality that both characters exercise their gift as exiles in a foreign court for kings creates a close association between the two. Fourth, Scripture describes both characters as handsome. Joseph is 'handsome in form and appearance [*wîpēh mar'eh*]' (Gen. 39:6). Daniel is 'of good appearance [*wĕṭôbê mar'eh*]' (Dan. 1:4).[12] Fifth, both are given new names by their captors (Gen. 41:45; Dan. 1:7). Sixth, both characters are presented as models of faithfulness and piety. Joseph resists the advances of Potiphar's wife by recalling that adultery was a 'sin against God' (Gen. 39:9). Similarly, Daniel is characterized by 'faithfulness', such that even his enemies 'could find no ground for complaint or any fault' with him (Dan. 1:4). He is also marked by his careful observance of the law. He refuses to 'defile himself' with the king's food (Dan. 1:8–16) and continues in prayer even when it may cost his life (Dan. 6:10). Seventh, both find favour before their superiors (Gen. 39:21; Dan. 1:9).[13] Eighth, both are characterized by great wisdom, which is recognized by their captors (Gen. 41:39; Dan. 1:4, 17; 5:11). Ninth, both men serve in a foreign court for ninety-three years.[14]

These thematic similarities between Daniel and Joseph are joined by a host of linguistic correspondences. Philpot, who has provided the most in-depth assessment of the relationship between Genesis 41 and Daniel 2, adeptly summarizes these linguistic and sequential event correspondences in table form (see Table 3 on pp. 110–111).[15]

Philpot's assessment of these linguistic correspondences is worth summarizing here.[16] For instance, he notes that while *ḥālam* is not a rare

---

[12] See also 1 Sam. 16:12, 18, which describes David as having a 'good appearance' or 'form', as well as Esth. 2:7, which describes the beauty of Esther in similar terms.

[13] The word *ḥesed* is used in both accounts. In Genesis, God gives Joseph *ḥesed*, resulting in his receiving favour from the keeper of the prison. In Daniel, God gives Daniel *ḥesed* before the chief of the eunuchs.

[14] Philpot (2018: 685–686) and Wesselius (2005: 250–251) each provide a similar list of historical correspondences.

[15] The following table has been taken, with slight modification, from Philpot 2018: 688–689. I am indebted to Philpot for summarizing these points of contact so capably and for sharing his research with me before his article was published. For similar lists of correspondences between Gen. 41 and Dan. 2, see Gnuse 1990: 29–53; Labonté 1993: 271–284; Rindge 2010: 88–90; J. M. Hamilton 2014b: 230–231.

[16] While a number of scholars have commented on these correspondences, in the following three paragraphs I have closely followed Philpot's excellent assessment of the linguistic data. See Philpot 2018: 689–693.

Table 3 Verbal correspondences between Genesis 41 and Daniel 2

	Genesis 41	*Daniel 2*
1	Pharaoh's dream occurs two years after Joseph's incarceration (41:1) – *šĕnātayim yāmîm*	Nebuchadnezzar's dream occurs two years into his reign (Dan. 2:1) – *ûbišnat šĕtayim*
2	'Pharaoh had a dream' (41:1) – *ûparʿōh ḥōlēm*	'Nebuchadnezzar dreamed dreams' (2:1) – *ḥālam nĕbukadneṣṣar ḥălōmôt*[17]
3	Pharaoh's spirit was troubled (41:8) – *wattippāʿem rûḥô*	Nebuchadnezzar's spirit was troubled (2:1) – *wattitpāʿem rûḥô*; (2:3) – *wattippāʿem rûḥî*
4	Pharaoh calls for his magicians (41:8) – *ḥarṭōmim* – and Egypt's wise men – *ḥăkāmêh* – to interpret – *pātar* – his dream	Nebuchadnezzar calls for his magicians (2:2) – *ḥarṭōmim* – satraps, and enchanters, who are later called 'wise ones of Babel' – *ḥakkîmê bābel* – (2:12) – to interpret – *pĕšar* – his dream
5	'Pharaoh recounted to them his dreams' (41:8)	'The king gave orders . . . to tell the king his dreams' (2:2)
6	Professionals are unable to interpret Pharaoh's dream (41:8)	Professionals are unable either to declare or interpret Nebuchadnezzar's dream (2:4–11)
7	[New character introduction] Captain of the guard – *śar haṭṭabbāḥîm* – is aware of a captive Jew with dream-interpreting abilities (41:10–12)	[New character introduction] Captain of the guard – *rab ṭabbāḥayyāʾ* – is aware of a captive Jew with dream-interpreting abilities (2:14)
8	Joseph introduced to Pharaoh by his ethnicity – a 'Hebrew youth' (41:12).	Daniel introduced to Nebuchadnezzar by his ethnicity – 'a man among the exiles of Judah' (2:25)
9	'Pharaoh sent and called for Joseph' (41:14)	'Daniel went in and requested of the king' (2:16)
10	'They hurriedly – *wayrîṣuḥû* – brought [Joseph]' (41:14)	'Arioch, in haste – *bĕhitbĕhālāh* – brought Daniel' (2:25)
11	Joseph is asked if he can interpret the dream (41:15)	Daniel is asked if he can declare *and* interpret the dream (2:26)

---

[17] Goldingay notes that the plural 'dreams' may echo the 'double dream in Gen. 41' (Goldingay 1989: 30).

	Genesis 41	Daniel 2
12	Joseph downplays his abilities and attributes dream interpretations to God (41:16)	Daniel downplays his abilities and attributes dream interpretations to God (2:28–30)
13	The dream is recounted by Pharaoh to Joseph (41:17–24)	The dream is recounted by Daniel to Nebuchadnezzar (2:31–35)
14	Joseph tells Pharaoh that his dream is about what God will do in the future (41:25)	The *interpretation* is recounted by Daniel to Nebuchadnezzar (2:37–44)
15	The *interpretation* is recounted by Joseph to Pharaoh (41:26–31)	Daniel tells Nebuchadnezzar that his dream is about what God will do in the future (2:45)
16	The dream is 'determined by God, and God will quickly bring it about' (41:32)	'The dream is true; and its interpretation is trustworthy' (2:45)
17	Joseph is worshipped as a result of his dream reporting (Gen. 41:40, 43), receiving homage – *'abrēk* ('Kneel!') – from the people (41:40)	Daniel is worshipped as a result of his dream reporting (Dan. 2:46), receiving homage – *sĕgid* – from Nebuchadnezzar (2:46)
18	Joseph is given gifts (41:42)	Daniel is given gifts (2:48; cf. 5:16, 29)
19	Joseph is promoted to being a ruler in a foreign land 'over all the land of Egypt' – *'al kol 'ereṣ miṣrāyim* (41:41)	Daniel is promoted to being a ruler in a foreign land – *'al kol mĕdînat bābel* (2:48; cf. 5:16, 29)

word, its prominence in both passages is significant. The word *ḥālam* and its cognates occur 121 times in the Old Testament. Forty-two of these occurrences appear in Genesis 37 – 50 and another twenty-eight in Daniel.

Perhaps even more significantly, the dreams 'trouble' (*pā'am*) the kings. This word is far less common in the Old Testament, occurring only five times. Three are in Genesis 41 and Daniel 2 (Gen. 41:8; Dan. 2:1, 3).[18] Additionally, only Genesis 41:8 and Daniel 2:1, 3 employ *rûaḥ* as the subject of *pā'am*. These are the only instances in the Old Testament where dreams function as the agent of trouble.

Other rare vocabulary also links the two passages, demonstrating Daniel's literary dependence on Genesis 41. After their dreams, both Pharaoh and Nebuchadnezzar summon their 'magicians' (Gen. 41:8 [*ḥartummê*]; Dan. 2:2 [*ḥarṭōmim*]) and 'wise men' (Gen. 41:8 [*ḥăkāmêhā*];

---

18 Compare the other instances of *pā'am* in Judg. 13:25 and Ps. 77:5.

Dan. 2:12 [*ḥakkîmê bābel*]) to interpret the dream. The word *ḥarṭōm* is rare in the Old Testament, occurring eleven times and only with reference to the royal court magicians in Egypt and Babylon (Gen. 41:8, 24; Exod. 7:11, 22; 8:3, 14, 15; 9:11 [×2]; Dan. 1:20; 2:2). Both Pharaoh and Nebuchadnezzar require the magicians to 'interpret' (Hebr. *pātar*; Aram. *pĕšar*) the dreams. These cognates, along with their nominal forms *pitrôn* and *pišrāʾ*, occur forty-nine times in the Old Testament. Forty-seven of those occurrences are in Genesis 40 – 41 or Daniel 2 – 5.[19] Just like Pharaoh's magicians (Gen. 41:8), Nebuchadnezzar's magicians are incapable of interpreting the dream (Dan. 2:1–11). Joseph and Daniel, however, succeed where the magicians fail (Gen. 41:25–37; Dan. 2:31–45). They are recognized by the pagan court officials as having the 'spirit of God(s)' (Gen. 41:38; cf. Dan. 4:8, 9, 18; 5:11, 14).

Some elements in Genesis 41 have linguistic and thematic connections not only to Daniel 2 but elsewhere in Daniel as well. For instance, Daniel 5 records a set of gifts given to Daniel (by the Babylonian king) that resemble the gifts given to Joseph (Dan. 5:16, 29). In Genesis 41:42, Pharaoh gives Joseph his signet ring, 'clothes' (*wayyalbēš*) Joseph in fine linen and places 'a gold chain around his neck' (*hazzāhāb ʿal ṣawwāʾrô*). Excluding the signet ring, Belshazzar gives Daniel the same gifts. Daniel 'was clothed' (*wĕhalbîšû*) with a purple robe and 'a chain of gold was put around his neck' (*dî dahābāʾ ʿal ṣawwĕʾrēh*).[20]

The evidence listed above demonstrates Joseph's literary influence on Daniel. Daniel, understanding his life through the lens of Joseph, writes his narrative so as to evoke the Joseph story. By doing so, Daniel identifies himself as a new Joseph. Like Joseph, Daniel is exiled, interprets dreams and rises to the highest ranks in the royal court. The question still remains, however, what significance would this identification have for Daniel and his readers?

Biblical-theological significance

As I argued in chapter 3, Joseph embodies hope for the nation in the midst of exile and famine. Just when the covenantal promises seemed most imperilled by the prospect of starvation, Joseph's authority in a foreign court secures salvation for the nation. Additionally, Moses indicates that

---

[19] The two other occurrences are in Dan. 7:16 and Eccl. 8:1.
[20] See also the discussion in Rindge 2010: 89.

Joseph's life signals the coming of the exodus. At his death, Joseph reminds the nation of God's promise to return them to Canaan, asking that his bones be taken back to the land (Gen. 50:24–25) – evoking the anticipatory 'exodus' of Jacob's bones back to Canaan in Genesis 50:7–14. In sum, the story of Joseph is a story of hope for exiles.

In this light, we can see why Daniel might have interpreted his own life through the lens of Joseph. We can also see the theological significance this interpretation would have for Daniel's audience. As Joseph was 'sent ahead' of the nation (Ps. 105:17) to preserve them from harm, so too Daniel went to the royal court of Babylon in the first wave of exiles (605 BC) and served there before the other exiles arrived in 597 and 586 BC. Just as Joseph cared for the nation during its stay in Egypt, so too Daniel likely leveraged influence for his Jewish brothers during their exile in Babylon.[21] With Daniel in the royal court, Jewish exiles could maintain hope that God would somehow fulfil his promises to the nation and preserve them through trial, just as he had through Joseph in the first years of Israel's history.

Furthermore, Daniel's depiction of himself as a new Joseph also stimulates hope for a new exodus. Joseph embodied the hope of returning to the Promised Land (Gen. 50:24–25). Indeed, as seen above, the exodus account mentions Joseph's post-mortem participation in the journey to Canaan (Exod. 13:19). Even the conquest narrative concludes with Joseph's burial in the hill country of Ephraim (Josh. 24:32). Joseph's life and death intersect closely with the exodus and conquest. If Joseph teaches Israel anything about God's purposes, it is that God will restore his people to Canaan. Joseph died in exile, but was laid to rest in Canaan. Israel's exile is a death, but they too will come through it into the land of promise.

Hamilton strikes these same notes in his analysis of Daniel's reliance on Joseph. He writes:

> To highlight correspondences between Joseph and Daniel was to fuel the flames of Israel's expectation. To invoke Joseph was to invoke the

---

[21] As is clear from Ezekiel, Daniel was known by fellow Jews outside the royal court as a man of great piety and wisdom (Ezek. 14:14, 20; 28:3). Furthermore, if indeed Darius is Cyrus, as some scholars have posited, then it might be the case that Daniel leveraged his influence as one of Cyrus's three chief advisers (Dan. 6:1–3) to bring about Cyrus's decree to release the Jews and rebuild the temple (Ezra 1:1–11). On Cyrus's and Darius's possibly being the same person, see Lucas 2002: 136–137; Steinmann 2008: 293–296. See also J. M. Hamilton 2014b: 232, who posits the same argument.

paradigm of which Joseph was a part, a paradigm that proceeded to the exodus, the Sinai covenant and the conquest of Canaan, and to invoke that procession was to point to the new exodus, the new covenant and the new conquest of the new Eden. Pointing to an Israelite figure with characteristics reminiscent of Joseph meant drawing attention to the Lord setting events in motion to bring about the fulfillment of his promises.[22]

Joseph and Daniel stand at the two poles of Israel's Old Testament history. Joseph and his brothers (the eponymous tribal heads) are the first generation of the Israelite nation. As such, they foreshadow the history of the nation they will sire – just as events in Abraham's life did the same (Gen. 12:10–20; 22). As Genesis indicates, this tribal family did not blossom into a nation in Canaan, but in exile in Egypt (Gen. 46:3; 47:27; Exod. 1:8). And the family blossomed only because Joseph secured their well-being by advancing into the highest ranks of a foreign court. Joseph achieved his rank by interpreting the dreams of the king and being a man of recognizable wisdom. When famine forced them to Egypt, Joseph provided for them, and the nation multiplied from seventy to a great multitude (Gen. 46:3; 47:27). Thus, Israel was born in exile (Gen. 46:3). Yet, as Joseph predicts, they will not die in exile (Gen. 50:24–25). God will rescue his people (even Joseph) and take them back to Canaan. Joseph's ministry to his family, therefore, was not ultimately to settle them in Egypt but to prepare them for the exodus.

Daniel stands at the opposite pole of Israel's Old Testament history. In Daniel the story of Israel 'comes full circle'.[23] If Jacob's sojourn in Egypt is the birth of the nation (Gen. 46:3), then the exile, by all appearances, is its death (cf. Ezek. 37:1–14). Yet, Daniel's Joseph-like story suggests life after death – a new birth in exile. Daniel, like Joseph, is a young man sent ahead of the nation, who secures its well-being by advancing into the highest ranks of a foreign court. Daniel achieves his rank by interpreting the dreams of the king and being a man of recognizable wisdom.

In some sense, the stakes are even higher for Daniel. His task is more difficult than Joseph's. Whereas Joseph only needed to interpret Pharaoh's

---

[22] J. M. Hamilton 2014b: 225.
[23] Philpot 2018: 694.

dream, Daniel had to know the content of the dream without being told. Whereas Joseph's life was never in peril, Daniel risks his life and the lives of his friends (Dan. 2:13). Whereas Pharaoh enjoined his servants to honour Joseph (Gen. 41:40, 43), Nebuchadnezzar himself bows to Daniel (Dan. 2:46).[24]

Daniel himself understands rescue from captivity as a new exodus. He draws this parallel when he appeals to God's 'mighty hand', which delivered Israel in the first exodus, to act on Israel's behalf in Babylon (Dan. 9:15; cf. vv. 1–2, 16–19). Further, as both Hamilton and Gentry have noted, the vision Daniel has next is developed within the framework of the prophetic expectation for a new exodus (cf. Isa. 40:3–5; Hos. 2:14–15).[25]

These literary parallels between Joseph and Daniel ignite hope among exiled Jews for Israel's future. If the nation was birthed in exile in Egypt, then, despite all appearances to the contrary, it can experience new birth in exile in Babylon. If Joseph was a forerunner of the exodus, then Daniel, a new and better Joseph, portends a new exodus – one even greater than before. Philpot summarizes the evidence well:

> Thus, the Hebrew canon is supported on two sides by two great exodus events, each of which is advanced by a dream-interpreting prophet. On one side stands Joseph, an exile in Egypt who saves the people of God, and who grounds his dying hope in God's covenantal promises. On the other side stands Daniel, an exile in Babylon who desires to save the people of God, and who grounds his hope on those same promises. Both envisage an exodus in the near future. Both make provisions to see it through.[26]

The exalted Jew in a foreign court

While only Daniel exhibits strong linguistic correspondences with Joseph, other stories of exiled Jews in foreign courts also share similarities with

---

[24] Other scholars also see escalation or intensification from Joseph to Daniel. See Goldingay 1989: 43; Rindge 2010: 90–98; Widder 2014: 1123–1125. Rindge largely overstates his case and argues that the discontinuities between Daniel and Joseph reveal disagreement on how to interact with foreign powers. For Rindge, Joseph's approach to foreign interaction is one of assimilation, whereas Daniel's story promotes 'moderate resistance' (Rindge 2010: 98–103).

[25] J. M. Hamilton 2014b: 26–44.

[26] Philpot 2018: 695.

Joseph's story. For instance, Esther and Mordecai resemble Joseph. While there are only a few linguistic correspondences between the stories, Esther and Genesis 37 – 50 share a number of similar themes and narrative features. Like Joseph, Esther is essentially a slave in a foreign land. She is also 'handsome in form and appearance' (*wĕhanna'ărāh yĕpat tō'ar wĕṭōbat mar'eh* [Esth. 2:7]; cf. *yôsēp yĕpēh tō'ar wîpēh mar'eh* [Gen. 39:6]).[27] She is cleaned up, presented to the king, 'finds favour' before him (Esth. 2:17; cf. Gen. 39:3–4; Dan. 1:9) and makes requests that result in the salvation of her people.[28]

Similarly, the description of Mordecai's daily refusal to bow to Haman resembles Joseph's repudiation of Potiphar's wife (*wayhî bĕ'omrām 'ēlāyw yôm wāyôm wĕlō' šāma' 'ălêhem* [Esth. 3:4]; cf. *wayhî kĕdabbĕrāh 'el yôsēp yôm yôm wĕlō' šāma' 'ēlêhā* [Gen. 39:10]). Also, Mordecai's life shares the same trajectory as Joseph's. Mordecai is an exiled Jew in a foreign court who rises to second in command over the nation (Esth. 10:3). Even the account of Mordecai's exaltation shows some verbal correspondence to Pharaoh's promotion of Joseph (Esth. 6:11 [cf. 3:10; 8:2]; cf. Gen. 41:42–43).[29]

Jehoiachin also shows some similarity to Joseph.[30] Jehoiachin is an exiled Jew shown favour by a foreign king. Like Joseph, Jehoiachin is rescued from prison by the king (Evil-Merodach), given a change of clothes (2 Kgs 25:29; cf. Gen. 41:14, 43) and granted a privileged place in the royal court (2 Kgs 25:28, 30).[31] Additionally, some scholars posit that Evil-Merodach's 'lifting the head' (*nāśā' . . . 'et rō'š*) of Jehoiachin echoes

---

[27] Cf. 1 Sam. 16:12, 18; Dan. 1:4.

[28] Some scholars also assert a correspondence between Esther's words in Esth. 4:16 and Jacob's in Gen. 43:14 (Van Seters 1965: 160; Berg 1979: 125; Levenson 1997: 85). Given the lack of specific verbal correspondence between the two texts, Esther's 'if I perish, I perish' and Jacob's 'if I am bereaved of my children, I am bereaved' most likely merely reflect an idiomatic way of speaking.

[29] Scholars have posited a number of other verbal correspondences between Esther and Joseph. For instance, Gen. 40:2, cf. Esth. 2:21; Gen. 40:20, cf. Esth. 1:3; 2:18; Gen. 41:34–37, cf. Esth. 1:21; 2:3–4; Gen. 41:46, cf. Esth. 8:15; Gen. 44:24, cf. Esth. 8:6; Gen. 44:34, cf. Esth. 8:6; Gen. 43:31; 45:1, cf. Esth. 5:10; Gen. 50:3, cf. Esth. 2:12 (Rosenthal 1895: 278–284; Gan 1961: 144–149; Van Seters 1965: 158–160; Berg 1979: 125; Levenson 1997: 54–65, 72, 97; Link and Emerson 2017: 132–137).

[30] Granowski 1992: 173–188; Römer 1997: 10–11; Schmid 1999: 142–143; Harvey 2010: 54–55; Chan 2013: 566–577; Patton 2014: 63–64, 302–304.

[31] Sarna and Dempster both note that the open-ended conclusions of Kings and Chronicles foreshadow Israel's hope for a future beyond exile. In the case of Chronicles (cf. 2 Chr. 36:23), this hope is suggested by the use of 'key verbs' *'ālâ* and *pāqad*, which appear to draw from Joseph's dying words anticipating the exodus (Gen. 50:24–25). See Sarna 1972: 831; Dempster 1997: 210–211.

Pharoah's lifting of the cupbearer's head (*yiśśā'* ... *'et rō'šekā* [Gen. 40:13]). Chan contends that the idiom *nāśā'* + *rō'š* occurs only with the connotation 'review a case and release from prison' with Joseph (Gen. 40:13) and Jehoiachin (2 Kgs 25:27; and the synoptic account in Jer. 52:31).[32]

Traditionally, scholars have accounted for the resemblances between the Joseph, Esther, Mordecai and Jehoiachin stories in one of two ways. First, some posit direct literary dependence. They believe the authors of Esther and the Jehoiachin narrative intentionally model their stories on Joseph's, even borrowing the language of Genesis 37 – 50 where possible. Berg, for instance, notes that

> the striking linguistic similarities between [Esther and Joseph], when taken with the quantity of more general correspondences, remain explained best by the thesis that the story of Joseph, in some sense, provides a literary model for the Book of Esther.[33]

Additionally, Harvey and Chan argue that Jehoiachin's similarities to Joseph are a result of a 'deliberate incorporation' of material from the Joseph story.[34]

Second, critical scholars have generally opted for the notion that the similarities between Joseph, Daniel, Esther and the others are a function of their shared genre as court tales[35] – stories that 'deal with the exploits of a godly exile in a foreign court whose piety and wisdom enable him to emerge triumphantly from various tests and rise to personal prominence'.[36] Ascribing resemblances purely to shared genre, however, also has its problems.[37] This approach generally de-historicizes these texts, positing that these characters and their stories are fictional – 'history-like' rather than actual history.[38] The problems with de-historicizing are too numerous to mention here and are beyond the scope of this project. More to the

---

[32] Chan 2013: 566–577; cf. Harvey 2010: 54. Additionally, in the synoptic account in Jer. 52:31, Codex Vaticanus includes the phrase *kai ekeiren auton*, which the *BHS* editors see as a possible allusion to Gen. 41:14.

[33] Berg 1979: 151; cf. Rosenthal 1895: 278–284.

[34] Harvey 2010: 53–54; Chan 2013: 569.

[35] Humphreys 1973: 211–223; J. J. Collins 1975: 218–324; 1993: 38–52; Müller 1976: 338–350; Niditch and Doran 1977: 179–193; Wills 1990.

[36] Patterson 1993: 447.

[37] Morris 1994: 82.

[38] Berg 1979: 15.

point, simply classifying these narratives as court-tales or ascribing similarities to shared genre does little to unpack the biblical-theological significance of these texts.

To whatever degree the authors of Esther and Chronicles utilized the Joseph story, at the very least what we find is that the lives of Joseph, Daniel, Esther, Mordecai and Jehoiachin represent a divinely ordained pattern in redemptive history – the pattern of the exalted Jew in the foreign court. Joseph is the first instantiation of this pattern. Daniel, perceiving his life as fitting a mould first established by Joseph, models his narrative on Joseph's. Daniel's account reveals his interpretive perspective on the Joseph story. For Daniel, Joseph's experiences are prototypical.

Later, Esther, Mordecai and Jehoiachin, resembling Joseph and Daniel, further establish the pattern of the exalted Jew in the foreign court. Once all of these figures emerge on to the scene, readers can retrospectively discover the thematic and narrative correspondences. The repetition in their accounts 'add[s] to the impression that this is the kind of thing God does for his people. Each installment in the pattern builds escalating anticipation'.[39]

In this light, the correspondences discussed above are not primarily a function of literary dependence (with the exception of Daniel) or shared genre. Instead, they reveal a providentially ordered pattern within redemptive history. Whenever Israel finds itself in exile, God works in a way paradigmatically exhibited in Joseph. He sends a representative into exile. That representative suffers, is exalted and then delivers the nation or signals the hope of deliverance.

What is the significance of this pattern? In addition to the similarities mentioned above, the primary feature shared by each story is that each takes place while Israel is in exile. This fact may explain why no Joseph-like characters emerge between the exodus and the exile – and the apparent clustering of Joseph-like characters in narratives after 586 BC. As already argued, Joseph and Daniel, who first establish the pattern of the exalted Jew in the foreign court, signal hope for return from exile. Like Joseph and Daniel, then, Esther, Mordecai and Jehoiachin likely reiterate that hope in their own narratives. Their privileged place in foreign courts reminds readers that Israel has been in similar circumstances before. Just

---

[39] J. M. Hamilton 2014b: 224.

as Joseph embodied the hope of return to the land, so also these later counterparts do the same.[40]

What does this pattern contribute to a canonical understanding of the Joseph story? First, it solidifies Joseph's role as one embodying the hope of exodus and signalling God's coming redemption and fulfilment of the Abrahamic promises. Genesis 50:24–25 makes this point from within the Joseph story itself. These later figures point to that same reality.

Second, these correspondences may reveal Joseph as part of a typological pattern anticipating some form of new-covenant fulfilment. As Beale notes, one criterion for discerning types within the Old Testament is whether a person, event or institution is part of a cyclic pattern in redemptive history.[41] Beale, relying on von Rad, illustrates this point by appealing to the cyclic pattern of charismatic Israelite leaders being called, commissioned and achieving some victory for Israel, before finally failing to bring about eschatological fulfilment of God's promises.[42] This pattern portends some future fulfilment.

If this is the case, then Joseph's place as the first in a pattern of exiled Jews who deliver the nation hints at something greater to come. Viewed through the lens of later exiles such as Esther, Mordecai and especially Daniel, Joseph is a prototype in a pattern expecting resolution. Daniel himself appears to acknowledge this by modelling his own narrative after Joseph's story so as to inculcate in his readers hope for a new exodus. Daniel suggests that the type of work God did through Joseph will be repeated in his own life. Esther and the others witness to this same theme. The presence of this pattern in the canon, then, intimates a typological character of the Joseph story. Joseph is a prototype in a pattern of exiled Jews who either deliver the nation or function as signposts of God's future redemptive work.

---

[40] As Chan notes, 'Hope lies in the fact that the Book of Kings ends as Genesis does – with some of Israel in Egypt and with an impending new exodus that is signaled by the benevolent treatment of Jehoiachin . . . The Book of Kings achieves its denouement on a note of hope that, at some point in the future, Israel would again experience a second exodus and a new opportunity to live in the land . . . [2 Kgs 25:27–30 is] not meant to describe the end of an era. In fact, quite the opposite is true: [these verses] open the possibility of a new one' (Chan 2013: 575–576). Cf. Granowski 1992: 185.

[41] Beale 2012: 20–21; cf. von Rad 1963: 372–374.

[42] Beale 2012: 20–21.

Implications for a canonical understanding of the Joseph narrative

This chapter has explored the use of the Joseph story by later Old Testament authors in order to understand their interpretive perspective on his life. This study has yielded several important points for a canonical understanding of the Joseph narrative.

First, Psalm 105 clearly interprets Joseph within the framework of the Abrahamic promises. The author sees Joseph, like Moses, as Yahweh's instrument for fulfilling his covenantal promises. God fulfils (partially and temporarily) his covenant with Israel by preserving the seed through Joseph. Joseph's ministry, therefore, provides an anticipatory fulfilment of the promises. Furthermore, Joseph is identified as part of a line of deliverers called 'messiahs'. This designation further signifies the anticipatory and typological nature of the Joseph story. Joseph, along with Moses, is part of a biblical-theological trajectory of men through whom Yahweh delivers his people and keeps covenant with Israel.

Second, Joseph's post-mortem participation in the exodus, later uses of the Joseph story by Daniel and the similarities between Joseph and later exilic figures all tie Joseph closely to the exodus. Joseph embodies Israel's hope for deliverance. His life is a signpost of Israel's redemption. Further, the story of Joseph's bones and the canonical pattern of exiled Jews in a foreign court all suggest that Joseph's story is typological. Joseph's experiences in exile anticipate Israel's later exilic experiences in Babylon and Medo-Persia. The journey of Joseph's bones echoes Israel's journey from exile in Egypt to rest in Canaan. Joseph is a prototype of God's work with his people in exile.

8

Joseph in the New Testament

This chapter examines the two significant, explicit mentions of the Joseph story in the New Testament, Acts 7:9–16 and Hebrews 11:22, as well as other possible allusions to Joseph in the New Testament. In my analysis of Acts 7, I show that Stephen (and, by implication, Luke) understands Joseph in the same terms presented in chapter 4–6: (1) as a figure employed by God to fulfil the Abrahamic covenant and mediate blessing, and (2) as a type of Christ. In my analysis of Hebrews 11, I show that the text presents Joseph as an example of faith in the covenantal promises in the face of death.[1] Finally, I consider the most probable allusion to Joseph in the New Testament in the parable of the tenants and its significance for a canonical understanding of the Joseph story.

Joseph in Acts 7

Acts 7 is a pivotal chapter in the book of Acts. Stephen's speech relativizes the temple and establishes Jesus as the new locus of God's presence, which provides the theological grounds for the advance of the gospel in Samaria and beyond. Further, his death catalyses the dispersion of the church beyond Jerusalem.[2]

---

[1] While a good deal of literature from Second Temple Judaism comments on the Joseph story, much of it is beyond the scope of this book. Most of it is either commentary on Gen. 37 – 50 or retellings of the Joseph story that portray Joseph as a model of piety and virtue. Interestingly, these Second Temple texts also attest to a 'Messiah ben Joseph' tradition. 'Messiah ben Joseph' is an eschatological figure, marked by suffering, whose death immediately precedes the advent of the victorious 'Messiah ben David'. It is noteworthy that a 'Messiah ben Joseph' tradition exists in the theological milieu that surrounded the NT authors. Yet, the NT authors clearly never appropriate or even interact with that tradition. For literature on Joseph in Second Temple Judaism, see C. W. Mitchell 1987: 304–350; 2005a: 545–553; 2005b: 77–90, 166–191; 2006a: 211–228; 2006b: 221–241; 2009: 181–205; Hollander 1998: 237–263; 1975.

[2] For more on Acts 7 as a major turning point in the narrative, see Thompson 2011: 165.

In this chapter, Stephen defends himself against false accusations of disparaging the temple and the law (Acts 6:13–14). He does this by rehearsing Israel's history, selectively highlighting parts that challenge his audience's understanding of the temple and the law. His defence is one of the earliest instances of biblical theology in the life of the church – a biblical theology that devotes significant attention to Joseph (Acts 7:9–16). Thus, Acts 7 reveals not only how Stephen and Luke (and by implication the other apostles) understood the Joseph story but also how they understood it to fit within the broader biblical storyline. Stephen's speech gives us a glimpse of how the apostolic community understood Joseph's significance in redemptive history.

In order to unpack the theological significance of Stephen's use of Joseph, I examine Stephen's speech in four stages. First, I consider the form and structure of the chapter, highlighting features that help to shed light on Stephen's seemingly unusual method of defence and on his interpretive method. Second, I briefly explain Stephen's argument, tracing it through each section of his speech. Third, I uncover Stephen's interpretive perspective on the Joseph story by exegeting Acts 7:9–16 and then considering how this section contributes to Stephen's argument. Finally, I establish the biblical-theological significance of Stephen's use of the Joseph story, particularly focusing on whether Stephen presents Joseph as a type of Christ.

Stephen's speech as a 'summary of Israel's story'

Stephen's defence rehearses Israel's history from Abraham to the exile. For many readers, this historical survey is odd given that Stephen never counteracts the charges levelled against him. As a result, some scholars posit that much of his speech is a largely irrelevant rehearsal of the past. This sentiment is represented by Conzelmann, who argues that 'the content of the speech (with the exception of the closing remarks) has no connection with the charges against Stephen' and condemns any attempt to understand the speech as polemical or as 'artificial'.[3] Haenchen, apparently exasperated with the speech, exclaims, 'Stephen is supposed to be answering the question of whether he is guilty of the charges, but a very large part of his speech has no bearing on this at all!'[4]

---

[3] Conzelmann 1987: 57.
[4] Haenchen 1971: 286.

Yet, while Stephen's speech does not directly refute the accusations against him, it does posit an alternative reading of the Old Testament that flies in the face of his accusers' theological convictions. As his own audience understood, Stephen's sharp condemnation of Israel was not merely a tacked-on conclusion to an otherwise innocuous history lesson. It was the climax of a biblical-theological argument that unravelled his opponents' perception of the temple and of themselves.

Recent literature on the ancient genre of 'Rewritten Bible' (RB) and its literary cousin 'Summaries of Israel's Story' (SIS) sheds some light on the paraenetic and polemic function of speeches such as Stephen's that, to modern ears, may seem like dispassionate history lessons.[5] SIS are, as their names imply, theologically interpreted recitals of Israel's history and were fairly common forms of literature in the Old Testament (cf. Ps. 105), New Testament (Matt. 1:1–17; Acts 7, 13; Heb. 11), Second Temple Judaism (1 Macc. 2.50–61; 1QS 1.21 – 2.6), and early Christian communities (1 Clem. 4–6, 9–12; 17.1 – 19.2; 31.1 – 32.4).[6]

As Hood explains, authors employ SIS to bring the patterns of Israel's past to bear on present circumstances and to affirm or condemn the behaviour of the community by association. Thus, the paraenetic function is to provide 'moral instruction through positive and negative examples . . . Stephen intends for his audience to see the Jewish rejection of Jesus, God's chosen agent, in line with the Israelites who rejected God's chosen agents Joseph and Moses.'[7] Ultimately, this point strengthens the idea that the original audience would themselves have understood that Joseph's and Moses' lives anticipated some facet of that audience's experience. The crowd is enraged, however, when they unexpectedly find themselves on the side of the 'bad guys' in the speech, with Jesus (and eventually Stephen) on the side of the 'good guys', Joseph and Moses. These heroes of the faith do indeed anticipate events in first-century Israel, Stephen claims, but they anticipate the life and death of Jesus, not the Jewish people. This explains the form of Stephen's defence. By appealing to patterns from Israel's history, Stephen shows that it was his detractors, not he, who had dishonoured the law and the temple.

---

[5] For a survey of recent research on RB and SIS, see Hood and Emerson 2013. Also see Hood 2011: 35–62.

[6] For a complete list, see Hood and Emerson 2013: 340–344.

[7] Ibid. 56.

Yet, the speech contains more than moral judgment – quite a bit more, in fact. Stephen makes claims about the identity of Christ that are rooted in Scripture's unfolding of redemptive history. This, too, is a common characteristic of Christian SIS, particularly in the New Testament. For instance, Mark 12:1–12, Acts 13:16–41 and Revelation 12 all focus on the culmination of Israel's story in Jesus and the implications of this culmination for his people.[8] We should expect, then (as would Stephen's audience), some sort of typological interpretation of the characters, institutions or events Stephen mentions. Again, as Hood mentions, in SIS 'ancient interpreters use *ancient characters and events to adumbrate or guide the salvation-historical present and future*'.[9] If Stephen's speech does not exhibit typological exegesis of Joseph and Moses, we must ask why it breaks with the pattern so firmly established in similar summaries throughout the New Testament and early Christian literature.

With regard to its literary structure, Bruno, Compton and McFadden have shown that Stephen structures his speech according to the major covenants in the Old Testament.[10] Specifically, Stephen traces through three covenants (Abrahamic, 7:2–16; Mosaic, 7:17–45a; and Davidic, 7:45b–50) the themes of (1) God's presence and (2) the rejection of leaders by their people. As we will see, Stephen shows that each figure he considers is intimately associated with God's presence, is rejected by the people and, ultimately, is a vehicle through whom God fulfils his promises to the nation.

Surveying the argument: an overview of Stephen's speech

In Acts 6, the synagogue of the Freedmen makes a number of false accusations against Stephen (Acts 6:9). First, they accuse him of speaking 'blasphemous words against Moses and God' (Acts 6:11). Next, they claim he speaks against 'this holy place and the law', arguing that he said 'Jesus of Nazareth will destroy this place and will change the customs that Moses delivered to us' (Acts 6:13–14). Ultimately, then, the accusations primarily focus on Stephen's teaching regarding (1) the temple

---

[8] 'Providing a Christian spin on the "restorationist tendency" noted by [N. T.] Wright, the canonical Christian SIS are all clearly messianic in nature, focusing Israel's story on Christ and his mission (vocation)' (Hood 2011: 59).

[9] Ibid.; emphasis original.

[10] Bruno et al. 2020: 55–66.

('God' [6:11], 'this holy place' [6:13], 'this place' [6:14]) and (2) the law ('Moses' [6:11], 'the law' [6:13], and 'customs that Moses delivered' [6:14]).

Stephen answers each accusation by (1) tracing the theme of God's mobile presence across biblical history and (2) highlighting Israel's regular rejection of covenant mediators, particularly Moses. First, with regard to God's presence, Stephen shows that the Old Testament never confines God's presence to a particular location, not even the temple. Instead, God's special presence is dynamic. Stephen highlights this dynamism, showing how it anticipates something greater than the localized Solomonic temple. Second, with regard to Moses, Stephen shows that both Moses and the law point beyond themselves to a figure who will fulfil the law. Like the temple, both Moses and the law are anticipatory. They were never intended to be an end in themselves.

Stephen begins his speech by showing that the Old Testament never limited God's presence to the temple or even to Canaan. Instead, God appears to Abraham outside the Promised Land in Mesopotamia as 'the God of glory' (Acts 7:2), a phrase intimately associated throughout the Old Testament with the temple (1 Kgs 8:10–13; Isa. 6:1–3; Ezek. 1:4–28; 8:1–4; 10:1–22). At the same time, God promises to bring Abraham's descendants to Canaan to 'worship' him – an anticipation of temple worship (7:7).[11] This promise thus suggests that the story of God's presence will develop across redemptive history. The 'God of glory' may appear to Abraham in Mesopotamia, but he will not be present there for ever. Readers should expect redemptive-historical development as well as eschatological resolution.[12]

Verses 6 and 7 anticipate Israel's journey into and exodus from Egypt. God promises Abraham that after the exodus Israel will worship him in 'this place' (*topos* [7:7]), likely a reference to Horeb (Exod. 3:12), while at the same time alluding to the charges that Stephen spoke against 'this place' (the temple) in Acts 6:13.[13] Thus, Stephen shows that while he might have spoken against the temple, God's supposedly unique *topos* in 6:13, God himself speaks of other dwelling places (*topoi* [7:7]) in the Old Testament.

Continuing the patriarchal story, verse 8 traces the family line from Abraham through Isaac and Jacob to the twelve 'patriarchs', who all share

---

[11] Beale 2004: 216.

[12] Ibid. 216–217.

[13] Thompson 2011: 168–169.

in the 'covenant of circumcision' given to Abraham. Yet, unlike their great-grandfather, these patriarchs fail to experience God's presence because they reject Joseph, the one with whom God dwells (v. 9). Verse 9, then, introduces the theme of the Israelite leader rejected by a rebellious Israel. Joseph's brothers were 'jealous' of Joseph and sold him into Egypt (v. 9). God, however, rescued Joseph from his 'afflictions' and exalted him over Egypt (7:9–10).

Stephen illustrates that even when the fledgling nation of Israel consisted of only twelve representative patriarchs, it spurned the blessings of the covenant by rejecting a divinely appointed, Spirit-endowed leader. Additionally, the notion that God was 'with Joseph' in Egypt advances the theme of the dynamism of God's presence. First God appears to Abraham in Mesopotamia; now he is 'with' Joseph in Egypt (v. 9). He is not confined to one location – or even to the land of Canaan.

Stephen identifies a major redemptive-historical development from Abraham and Joseph to Moses by indicating that, with the birth of Moses, 'the time of the promise drew near, which God had granted to Abraham' (v. 7:17). The promise in view is likely the promise of the exodus in the Abrahamic covenant of Genesis 15, mentioned in Acts 7:6–7. The Abrahamic era is coming to a close as the fulfilment of those promises begins to emerge in the inauguration of the covenant at Sinai.

Stephen dedicates the majority of his speech to Moses, as might be expected given the accusation that Stephen blasphemed Moses and spoke against the law, and develops many of the themes from 7:2–16 at length in 7:17–45a. He treats Moses' life in three forty-year blocks (vv. 23, 30, 36), each of which contains some element of rejection by the people of Israel (vv. 27, 35, 39). As Stephen summarizes, 'Our fathers refused to obey him, but thrust him aside, and in their hearts they turned to Egypt' (v. 39). Moses might have taken the people out of Egypt, but could not get Egypt out of the people. The covenant community rejected their God-appointed leader and thus also rejected God.

Finally, Stephen mentions the next stage in the story of God's presence: the tabernacle (v. 44). Notably, he depicts the tabernacle as transient, moving from the wilderness with Moses, to Canaan with Joshua (v. 45). Even after the construction of the tabernacle, God's presence is mobile. Further, the tabernacle reveals yet again that the story of God's presence in the Old Testament progressively unfolds across redemptive history, thus demanding eschatological resolution.

Acts 7:45b marks the transition to the Davidic covenant and another major step forwards in redemptive history (2 Sam. 7, alluded to in v. 46). Stephen shows God's dwelling place is not fixed until Solomon finishes the temple (7:47). Yet even then, the Israelites fail to understand that God's presence cannot be limited to a single building, since 'the Most High does not dwell in houses made by hands [*cheiropoiētois*]' (7:48). With these words Stephen again emphasizes Israel's pattern of rejecting God by rejecting his covenant leaders and institutions. The word *cheiropoiētois* is, without exception, used with reference to idolatry in the LXX (Lev. 26:1, 30; Isa. 10:11; 16:12; 19:1; 21:9; 31:7; 46:6).[14] By using *cheiropoiētois*, Stephen is accusing the Israelites of idolizing the temple; thus associating them with the idolaters of Moses' day (cf. 7:41 [*tois ergois tōn cheirōn autōn*]). Just as Israel rejected Joseph and Moses, so also they rejected God's purpose for the temple.

At this point, Stephen's speech finally turns to a direct condemnation of his audience. Like their unfaithful fathers, Stephen's audience is stiff-necked, uncircumcised in heart and ears, and resisting the Holy Spirit (Acts 7:51; cf. Exod. 33:3, 5; Neh. 9:16–17; Jer. 6:10; 9:26; Isa. 63:10). Stephen makes explicit the connection between his audience and the Old Testament Israelites: 'As your fathers did, so do you' (Acts 7:51b). Just as the patriarchs rejected God's righteous deliverers, so too Israel rejected Jesus, 'the Righteous One' who was 'announced beforehand' throughout the Old Testament (7:52–53). Like fathers, like sons.

Thus, as Stephen concludes (vv. 51–53, 56),[15] the themes of divine presence and rejection of deliverers converge. Israel has rejected Jesus, 'the Righteous one' (7:52), whom Luke and Stephen identify as the new locus of God's presence (7:55–56).[16] Stephen exposes Israel's rejection of Jesus as a rejection of the one who fulfils the purpose of the temple. The irony is thick. Those who accused Stephen of maligning the temple and the law have themselves maligned the law by rejecting Jesus, the true temple 'announced beforehand' by the law (7:52). Thompson summarizes the argument well:

---

[14] Pao 2000: 195; Thompson 2011: 169.

[15] On 7:56 as the proper conclusion to the Stephen speech, see Sleeman 2009: 141; Schnabel 2012: 361–362.

[16] Thompson 2011: 170. While Luke and Stephen highlight that God's presence centres around Jesus in heaven (as opposed to on earth), Luke also describes Stephen as 'full of the Holy Spirit' (7:55). This phrase indicates that God mediates his presence to his people such that they are now his dwelling place on earth.

Thus Stephen shows that he is not *against* Moses or the temple because (1) in proclaiming the suffering Lord Jesus, he proclaims the One whom God's suffering messengers, such as Moses, have always pointed to (and his accusers therefore belong to those who have always been the cause of that suffering and are the ones who are opposed to Moses); and (2) in proclaiming the ascended Lord Jesus as the One with universal authority and the One who is in God's presence and who provides access to God's presence, he proclaims the culmination and fulfilment of the various locations for meeting God throughout Israel's history, including the temple (and his accusers belong to those who have been characterized by the idolatry of false worship in Israel's history) ... In response to both charges, Stephen points beyond Moses and the temple to Jesus, the One whom Moses and the temple anticipated.[17]

Stephen's interpretive perspective on the Joseph narrative

In the light of this survey of Stephen's defence, we are now in a position to consider more thoroughly how Stephen's use of the Joseph story integrates with the rest of his argument. In this section I will first consider Stephen's use of Genesis 37 – 50 by providing an exegesis of Acts 7:9–16. Then, based on that exegesis, I will examine how the Joseph section (7:9–16) contributes to Stephen's argument.

Exegesis of Acts 7:9–16. As already noted, verse 9 continues the patriarchal story – the story of the Abrahamic covenant. Verse 8 indicates that Abraham has only one son, Isaac, who in turn fathers Jacob. Jacob fathers the first Israelite community. His twelve sons represent the nation and share in the 'covenant of circumcision' (7:8). This first generation, however, characterizes the nation they will sire by establishing a pattern of disobedience. They are introduced as 'jealous' (*zēlōsantes*) of Joseph and sell (*apedonto*) him into slavery (7:9a). Stephen's language is nearly identical to Genesis 37:11, except he substitutes *hoi patriarchai* for *hoi adelphoi autou*. Notably, the LXX never uses *hoi patriarchai* for Joseph's brothers; thus Stephen's edit likely anticipates his identification of his audience with their 'fathers' (7:51), who reject their

---

17 Thompson 2011: 171–172; emphasis original.

leaders.[18] From the first moment it is even possible to speak of Israel as a nation, its corporate life is characterized by rebellion and rejection of God's leaders. Israel's earliest 'fathers' reject their divinely appointed leader, in turn, spurning the very presence of God (7:9).

In 7:9b, Stephen quotes, with slight modification, Genesis 39:2, 3 (cf. 39:21, 23), 'God was with [Joseph]'.[19] This key phrase develops the theme of God's presence, highlighting two facts. First, God approves of Joseph, a point further emphasized in verse 10. Second, God's presence extends beyond the temple and even Canaan. Stephen drives this point home by repeatedly emphasizing that God was with Joseph *in Egypt*. As Stott notes:

> if Mesopotamia was the surprising context in which God appeared to Abraham (7:2), Egypt was the equally surprising scene of God's dealings with Joseph. Six times in seven verses Stephen repeats the word 'Egypt,' as if to make sure that his hearers have grasped its significance.[20]

Verse 10 continues to focus on God's presence with Joseph. God is not only with Joseph; he also 'rescues' him (*exeilato*), 'gives' him favour with Pharaoh (*edōken*) and 'appoints' him (*katestēsen*) as ruler over Egypt and the whole house of Pharaoh. God's commendation of Joseph (vv. 9b–10) starkly contrasts with the patriarchs' rejection of him (v. 9a). The implication is clear. God gifts his presence to those he favours, not to the nation irrespective of their faithfulness. In fact, the contrast highlights that God often fulfils his promises through people the nation has rejected.

In verse 10, Stephen also mentions that God gave Joseph 'grace and wisdom' (*charin kai sophian*) before Pharaoh. The attribution 'grace' derives from Genesis 39. In fact, Acts 7:9b–10 shows remarkable similarity to Genesis 39:21. Both passages indicate that 'God was with Joseph' (*ēn kyrios meta Iōsēph* [Gen. 39:21] // *ēn ho theos met autou* [Acts 7:9b]) and,

---

[18] The phrase *apedonto eis Aigypton* is a telescoped summary of the events of Gen. 37:28, 36, which reports the selling of Joseph first into the hands of the Midianites/Ishmaelites and then into Egypt. Stephen's telescoped version of the events matches Joseph's own retelling of his story in Gen. 45:4, *Ego eimi Iōseph ho adelphos hymōn, hon apedosthe eis Aigypton*.

[19] Genesis uses *kyrios* instead of *theos*. Stephen/Luke may have modified the passage given how in the early Christian community, as evidenced by the NT, *theos* was regularly used for the Father, whereas *kyrios* was a title typically reserved for the Son.

[20] Stott 1990: 133.

as a result, God 'gave him favour' (*kai ēdōken autō charin enantion* + genitive [Gen. 39:21; Acts 7:10]) before his superior. Consistent with Stephen's telescoped retelling of the story, he applies the language to Joseph's favour before Pharaoh, rather than to events in Potiphar's house described in 39:21.

Stephen adds that God bestows 'wisdom' (*sophia*) on Joseph (v. 10). As many scholars note, wisdom is a major theme in Genesis 37 – 50.[21] Yet, strangely, *sophia* occurs nowhere in LXX Genesis 37 – 50. The translator instead uses *phronimos* for *bîn* and *synetos* for *ḥākam* (cf. Gen. 41:33, 39). Some scholars have asserted that Stephen's inclusion of 'wisdom' reflects his interpretive dependence on Second Temple traditions.[22] Yet Stephen's use of *sophia* may merely reflect Psalm 105:22 (104:22 LXX), which indicates that Joseph taught Pharaoh's elders 'wisdom' (*sophisai* [Ps. 104:22 LXX]).

More importantly, Stephen's use of *sophia* is probably a rhetorical device meant to associate the protagonists of the story. As others note (and as we will see), Luke and Stephen describe Joseph, Moses, Stephen and Jesus in ways that parallel one another. Stephen attributes 'grace and wisdom' to Joseph, recalling Luke's own description of Stephen's 'grace' (Acts 6:8) and 'wisdom' (Acts 6:10), while also anticipating the 'wisdom' of Moses (Acts 7:22) or the 'grace' given to David. As Burns notes, that wisdom is 'attributed by Luke to Joseph, Moses, Stephen, and Jesus is not likely coincidental'.[23] Indeed, these similarities between the 'protagonists' enhance Stephen's argument that Israel always rejects their righteous prophets (Acts 7:51–52).

Further, Stephen's description of Joseph as having *charis* and *sophia* recalls Luke's own depiction of Jesus in Luke 2:40, 52. These verses are the only other times Luke uses this word pair.[24] Furthermore, while divine presence is a major theme of Stephen's speech, Joseph is the only person Stephen describes God as 'with'. Luke, however, uses that language once elsewhere: in Acts 10:38, when God is 'with Jesus' (*ho theos ēn met autou*). In fact, the New Testament rarely speaks of God's being 'with' a particular

---

[21] See Alter 2011: 159; Sigmon 2013: 188–300; chiefly Wilson 2004.

[22] See Whitenton 2012.

[23] Burns 2006: 150.

[24] Pervo 2009: 182; Whitenton comments, 'The inclusion of σοφίαν in Acts 7:10 allows the Lukan Stephen to use an encomiastic σύγκρισις between Joseph and Jesus' (Whitenton 2012: 165; cf. Parsons 2008: 94; Braun 2010: 209–210.

person – Acts 7:9 and 10:38 are the only instances when God is 'with' an individual in the Synoptic Gospels and Acts.[25]

The remainder of Acts 7:9–16 focuses on Joseph's deliverance of his family. Whereas God delivered Joseph from all his 'afflictions' (*thlipsis*; 7:10), he now uses Joseph to deliver his family from their 'afflictions' (*thlipsis*; 7:11). This deliverance comes when famine sends Joseph's brothers to Egypt on two separate occasions (7:11–13). Stephen concludes with a summary of the reconciliation episode in Genesis 45.

Because Acts 7:9–16 lacks 'deliverance' language, some scholars believe that Stephen does not see Joseph as a saviour figure in Israel's history.[26] This claim missteps by demanding that Stephen mention 'deliverance'. In reality, Stephen's commitment to his source material leads him to communicate that idea more subtly. As demonstrated in chapters 4–6, the focus of Genesis 42 – 45 (summarized by Stephen in vv. 11–13) is not that Joseph saves his brothers from the famine per se. Rather, these chapters focus on how he reconciles with his estranged family. Moses then shows how *through* reconciliation Joseph saves the family and preserves the covenant line. For Joseph's family, reconciliation is the means of salvation. Stephen's summary adheres closely to Genesis – highlighting, not glossing over, the centrality of reconciliation. At the same time, Stephen mentions the 'affliction' of the patriarchs and says that 'our fathers could find no food' (v. 11), establishing that he sees the reconciliation episode as an act of deliverance for the patriarchs. Further, Stephen surely has deliverance from famine in view as he recounts what follows the reconciliation: the patriarchs become 'known to Pharaoh' (v. 13) and Joseph summons his father's seventy-five-member clan to Egypt (v. 14, summarizing Gen. 46).

Verses 14–16 record the descent of Jacob and his family into Egypt. Jacob, Joseph and his brothers all die in Egypt but are eventually 'carried back' to Shechem to be buried. As Schnabel notes, the mention of Shechem 'seems to underline the point that God's fulfillment of his promises is not focused exclusively on Jerusalem or Judah; rather, the place where the Samaritans live is part of God's history with his people'.[27]

---

[25] Lunn 2012: 31; cf. D. G. Peterson 2009: 251, n.; Braun 2010: 209–210.

[26] Bock 1987: 217–218. For a reading more sympathetic to the notion that Stephen portrays Joseph as a deliverer, see Schnabel 2012: 370–371.

[27] Schnabel 2012: 372. Schnabel later writes, 'There may be a "negative" typology at work as well: while the patriarchs died and were buried in a grave whose location is known, Jesus died and was buried but did not remain in the grave.'

Remarkably, Stephen tells the entire Joseph story without making Joseph the agent of a single verb. In fact, Joseph is the subject of only two finite verbs, the passive *anegnōristhē* in 7:13 and the middle *metekalesato* in 7:14. Instead, Stephen focuses on God's actions, particularly the way God accomplishes his purposes through his appointed leader.[28] Stephen uses this focus to contrast the story's two agents, God and the patriarchs. The patriarchs are jealous of Joseph and sell him into slavery. On the other hand, God is 'with' Joseph, delivers him from suffering and exalts him in Egypt. As a result, Joseph saves his family. In sum, Stephen sees in Joseph's story (as in Moses') that God primarily works not through Abraham's family at large (who are characterized as rebels) but through rejected, Spirit-endowed covenant mediators such as Joseph.

Acts 7:9–16 in the context of Stephen's argument. Stephen's interpretive perspective on Genesis 37 – 50 is that Joseph is the foremost example of the rejected prophet in the Abrahamic era. Similarly, Stephen sees Joseph, the appointed deliverer of his brothers, as the locus of God's presence and, as such, the mediator of blessing. Joseph's life is thus representative of a pattern repeatedly played out in Israel's history. God employs a covenant representative, distinguished by exemplary character and an experience of God's personal presence, to bring about his purposes for Israel, despite Israel's rejection of that representative.

As Stephen notes, Moses' life repeats this pattern. Moses, like Joseph, is distinguished by remarkable character (7:20, 22, 35–36; cf. 7:10), unique access to God's presence (7:30–33, 35, 38, 44) and deliverance of the nation (7:24–25, 35), yet he is rejected by the 'fathers' (7:25, 27–28, 35, 39). The pattern of Moses' and Joseph's lives plays out like a motif across the pages of the Old Testament. Their favour with God, deliverance of Israel and rejection by their brothers is the *type* of thing that happens throughout Israel's history. The nation at large is rebellious, while God works to keep his promises through covenant representatives.

Stephen makes this point explicit in the final verses of his speech. 'You stiff-necked people, uncircumcised in heart and ears, you always resist the Holy Spirit. As your fathers did, so do you' (v. 51). The phrase 'your fathers' (*hoi pateres hymōn*) recalls the rebellious 'fathers' (*patēr* // *patriarchēs*) already mentioned throughout Stephen's speech (vv. 9, 11, 12,

---

[28] Martín-Asensio 1999: 245–246.

15, 19, 39). As noted earlier, Stephen likely designates Joseph's eleven brothers as *patēr* (vv. 11, 14, 15) or *patriarchēs* (vv. 8, 9), as opposed to the typical LXX designation *adelphoi*, in order to make the connection between them, the fathers of Moses' era and Israel in his own day, abundantly clear. Stephen concludes that modern Israel is just like the brothers of Joseph and the idolatrous Israelites in the time of Moses. They have rejected the one whom the prophets anticipated, 'the righteous one', Jesus Christ.

As Stephen goes on to explain, Israel 'resists the Holy Spirit' by 'persecuting the prophets' (7:52). With these words Stephen shows how both themes of rejection and divine presence are connected throughout Israel's history. Stephen saw that agents of God such as Joseph and Moses had a unique experience of God's Spirit. Rejecting them was tantamount to rejecting God. This pattern culminates with Jesus. Jesus is in the line of Joseph and Moses, while Israel behaves like Joseph's brothers and the idolaters at Sinai. Like Joseph and Moses, Jesus is distinguished by remarkable character (7:52), divine presence (7:55–56) and salvation, yet Israel rejects him (7:52).

Thus, Stephen shows that Joseph's story is not just *part* of Israel's story; in some sense it *is* Israel's story. Joseph and his brothers, the first generation of the nation, represent the nation's story in miniature. Israel's rebellion against covenant representatives and Spirit-endowed deliverers is not just a story that repeats throughout Israel's history; it is a story that develops and climaxes with the nation's ultimate rejection of *the* deliverer, Jesus. In the light of this, Stephen's interpretive perspective on Genesis 37 – 50 is that Joseph's life and the actions of his brothers are a miniature portrayal of the history of the nation. As Stephen indicates in 7:51–53, Joseph and Moses are not just single episodes in Israel's story, they are small-scale, anticipatory reproductions of Israel's story.

Biblical-theological significance

The most significant biblical-theological implication of Stephen's argument is that Joseph is a type of Christ. The story of Joseph and his brothers represents a pattern through Israel's history, anticipating the culmination of that history in Israel's rejection of Jesus. Several scholars affirm that Stephen interprets Joseph typologically. For instance, Fitzmyer comments, 'The enslaving of Joseph connotes the rejection of him by his own kin, by "patriarchs" of Israel itself. Joseph thus becomes the type of Jesus, the rejected one, in Stephen's argument.'[29] Even scholars who prefer not to speak of Joseph as a type in Acts 7, understand him to be in a prospective, pattern-fulfilment relationship with Jesus. Schreiner, for instance, notes, 'the rejection both Joseph and Moses experienced from their contemporaries . . . anticipated the rejection of Jesus by Stephen's contemporaries'.[30]

Other scholars, however, deny a typological significance to the Joseph story in Acts 7. Bock, for instance, demurs that 'no thorough typology is present . . . Whether a more complete Joseph typology existed in the pre-Lucan stage of this speech cannot be determined, but if it did, Luke made no use of it.'[31] Likewise, Marshall comments, 'It is possible for the reader to see where the characters in the story can be regarded as "types" . . . but despite strong hints . . . the possibility is not followed up.'[32]

Bock and Marshall's reasoning, however, largely misses the mark. Marshall, on the one hand, seems to dismiss the possibility of typology unless the author employs typological language. This, however, makes demands of the biblical authors that they would not have placed on themselves. It assumes that they cannot *show* a type without *telling* their audience about it. Bock, on the other hand, is merely dissatisfied (and perhaps for good reason) with the arguments he has encountered that affirm a Joseph typology. For instance, Bock indicates that scholars generally posit 'three elements' which point to a Joseph typology: Joseph's deliverance of the patriarchs, his innocent suffering and the two comings of Joseph that parallel two comings of Christ.[33]

---

[29] Fitzmyer 1998: 373. Schnabel sees here a typological relationship between Joseph and Jesus' disciples, between Joseph and Stephen, and between Joseph and Jesus. 'Even though Stephen (Luke) does not make such connections explicit, the jealous patriarchs can be seen as prototypes of the contemporary Jewish leaders who plotted to eliminate Jesus (Acts 2:23, 36; 3:13–15; 4:10–11; 5:30), and Joseph as a prototype of Jesus' followers, whom the Jewish leaders oppose out of jealousy (5:17; cf. 13:45; 17:5) . . . Joseph is a prototype of the righteous and wise person who suffers and is thus a prototype of Stephen (cf. Acts 6:3, 8, 10); being eventually vindicated, Joseph becomes a prototype of Jesus, who was vindicated by God (2:24, 36; 3:15; 4:10–11; 5:31) because "God was with him" (10:38; cf. Luke 2:40) . . . The patriarchs' emigration to Egypt participates in the dual aspect of the fulfillment of God's promise and of the typological foreshadowing of the story of Jesus, which characterizes in particular the Joseph section of Stephen's speech . . . The role of Joseph, who rescues Israel from affliction, corresponds to the role of Moses (cf. v. 36) and especially Jesus' (Schnabel 2012: 370).

[30] Schreiner 2008: 298.

[31] Bock 1987: 217–218. Also, 'Thus it seems the question of a thorough Joseph typology here must be answered negatively' (218).

[32] Marshall 2007: 571. So also Conzelmann: 'The emphasis [in the Joseph section] does not fall on typological significance, but on the notion that God carries through his saving work contrary to human probability' (Conzelmann 1987: 53).

[33] Bock 1987: 217–218.

Bock correctly asserts that building an argument on those grounds would be a fool's errand. They have nothing to do with the content of Stephen's speech. Bock, however, overlooks that typology need not be based on any of these features. Further, he seems to assume that the deliverance theme is necessary for the presence of a type. He writes, 'If the deliverance of the Patriarchs had been intended typologically, some type of deliverance terminology like that used in Luke or the New Testament would surely have been used.'[34] Yet, other Old Testament persons, events and institutions affirmed as types in the New Testament do not employ deliverance language either. Adam, for instance, is a type on account of his federal headship (Rom. 5:12–21), not because he is a deliverer, an innocent sufferer or associated with 'two comings'. As Hamilton rightly concludes, 'If these broader questions are not the author's agenda in Acts 7, it does not seem fair to reject the possibility of typology because Acts 7 does not address these broader questions.'[35]

As I have argued, Stephen presents Joseph as a type by showing how his life anticipates Israel's history, which culminates in the nation's rejection of Jesus. As Bock mentions:

> There can be little doubt that Joseph fits into the general pattern of this speech which seeks to show that the Jews, beginning as far back as the Patriarchs, rejected the very men through whom God was working or revealing himself. This point is acknowledged by virtually every exegete of this passage. [Joseph] is mentioned because his history exposes the pattern of disobedience that began with the earliest Israelites, the Patriarchs ... This pattern is Stephen's only concern.[36]

In this, Bock is precisely right, though he misses that this 'pattern of disobedience' is the foundation for Stephen's typological conclusion: 'As your fathers did, so do you!' (7:51). Joseph is a type because, like Moses and like Jesus, he is a spirit-endowed covenant representative who is rejected by the nation through which God fulfils his promises. Joseph's life is,

---

[34] Ibid. 217.
[35] J. M. Hamilton 2008: 75.
[36] Bock 1987: 218.

therefore, a pattern – an event that prophetically forecasts later events in Israel's history; particularly the climactic rejection of Jesus.[37]

As already noted, other features of the speech have hinted at the typological character of these figures. Stephen, citing Deuteronomy 18:15, reminds his audience of Moses' typological role in redemptive history, 'This is the Moses who said to the Israelites, "God will raise up for you a prophet like me from your brothers"' (Acts 7:37) – a judgment that, given his argument, appears to apply as equally to Joseph as it does to Moses.

Additionally, linguistic similarities between Joseph, Moses, Jesus and Stephen abound. We have already seen how Joseph, Moses, Stephen and Jesus share the attributes of grace and wisdom (6:8, 10; 7:22; cf. Luke 2:40, 52). Stephen refers to Moses as 'ruler and redeemer' (*archonta kai lytrōtēn* [7:35]), echoing Peter's description of Jesus as 'Ruler and Saviour' (*archēgon kai sōtēra* [5:31]). The fathers' 'rejection' (*arneomai* [7:35]) mirrors Israel's own 'rejection' of Jesus (*arneomai* [3:13–14]).[38] Likewise, Luke associates Moses with Stephen, characterizing both by 'wonders and signs' (6:8; 7:36). The similarities between characters are so numerous that Schnabel sees Joseph corresponding to Jesus' followers, to Moses, to Stephen and to Jesus.[39] Finally, numerous scholars point out the many similarities between the martyrdom of Stephen and the crucifixion of Jesus, such as Jesus' petition for the Lord to receive his spirit (7:59; cf. Luke 23:46), his crying out with a 'loud voice' and his intercessory prayer for his persecutors (7:60; cf. Luke 23:34).[40]

With this web of linguistic connections, Luke hints at the typological relationship the characters share with one another.[41] The rejection of Joseph and Moses foreshadow Israel's rejection of Jesus, while Stephen's martyrdom recalls Jesus' death, marking Stephen as a true disciple – one who shares in the Spirt but is also a partaker of Jesus' suffering. Thus, for those who have been monitoring the speech, Stephen's typological

---

[37] Bock may now be slightly more open to a typological reading of Joseph in Acts 7. In his more recent commentary he states, 'One can sense a parallel to Jesus in Stephen's view [of Joseph]' (Bock 2007: 286–287).

[38] Thompson 2011: 167.

[39] Schnabel 2012: 370–371.

[40] For a complete account of scholarly conversation on these points and a thorough exploration of these linguistic and thematic similarities, see Chase 2008.

[41] Even Marshall, who ultimately rejects a typological reading, suggests that these connections (particularly the parallel between Joseph and Jesus with regard to divine presence [7:9; cf. 10:38]) are 'strong hints' in the direction of typology (Marshall 2007: 571).

conclusion ('As your fathers did, so do you') is nothing unexpected. As Thompson correctly notes, Stephen's prophetic indictment of his audience 'is only making more explicit what he has developed throughout his speech'.[42]

In sum, two things may be said of Stephen's interpretive perspective on the Joseph story. First, Stephen interprets Joseph within the framework of the Abrahamic covenant. Joseph is an archetype of the rejected prophet during the Abrahamic epoch. He is both blessed with God's presence (even outside Canaan) and is a blessing to others. He even blesses Abraham's seed, whom he saves from the famine.

Second, Stephen's speech reveals how the apostolic community interpreted the Joseph narrative: a miniature portrayal of Israel's history culminating in the rejection of Jesus. They saw in Joseph a prophetic forecasting of the life of the Messiah. Joseph, like Jesus, is a Spirit-endowed prophet who fulfils God's covenantal promises in spite of (even through) rejection by his brothers. Johnson summarizes this point well:

> In the case of both Joseph and Moses, Luke has edited his account in such fashion as to show how each fits into a pattern of twofold sending and rejection, so that these biblical exempla point forward to the twofold sending and rejection of the prophet Jesus. By this editing of the biblical narrative, Luke not only reinforces the fundamentally prophetic character of Scripture and its heroes, but by doing this supports the ideological position of his community that Scripture is best understood when read as pointing toward the risen prophet Jesus . . . And he does all this within the tight limits set by the text of the LXX itself, whose wording he consistently employs.[43]

Joseph in Hebrews 11

Hebrews 11:22, though very brief, is the only other substantive comment on the Joseph story in the New Testament. The author writes, 'by faith Joseph, at the end of his life, made mention of the exodus of the Israelites and gave directions concerning his bones'. In this section, I will consider the author of Hebrews' use of the Joseph story and how it functions in the

---

42 Thompson 2011: 167–168.
43 L. T. Johnson 2002: 29.

argument of Hebrews 11. I will also examine whether, as some scholars claim, this verse reveals a typological understanding of the Joseph story.

Joseph appears in Hebrews in yet another overview of the Old Testament. Like the other characters mentioned in the chapter, Joseph is upheld as an exemplar of faith. The author of Hebrews commends Joseph for believing God's promise to bring the Israelites out of Egypt. The author could have appealed to any number of more dramatic moments in Joseph's life. Yet, since death is a major theme throughout Hebrews 11, he likely highlighted this one because it occurred at the time of Joseph's death.[44] This event also nicely rounds out the author's attention to the patriarchs (11:8–16), ending not only with Joseph but also with Joseph's death at the end of Genesis.

Drawing on Genesis 50:24–26, as well as Exodus 13:19 and Joshua 24:32, the author highlights two features of Joseph's faith. First, Joseph 'mentioned' the exodus. Second, he 'gave directions concerning his bones', requesting his family exhume them and rebury them in Canaan. The author places these lines in parallel by using *peri* + genitive to introduce both:

A   *Iōseph emnēmoneusen*
  B   *peri tēs exodou tōn huiōn Israēl kai*
  B'   *peri tōn osteōn autou*
A'   *eneteilato.*

This parallel emphasizes the relationship between the two clauses. In the first, Joseph expresses his confidence in God's promise. In the second, he expresses his desire to participate in it. As M. O'Brien comments, 'Despite his position of prominence in the Egyptian court, Joseph regarded himself as a resident alien in Egypt. His true home lay elsewhere.'[45]

Joseph's confidence is likely rooted in the covenant promise of Genesis 15:13–16. There, God indicated that he would bring the Israelites back to Canaan after a time of sojourning in a foreign land. Thus, Joseph 'could speak of the exodus, not because he had experienced it, but because God had promised it'.[46] His faith, rooted in God's covenant promise, was exactly the type the author of Hebrews commends to his audience. It was 'the assurance of things hoped for, the conviction of things not seen' (11:1).

---

[44] Easter 2014: 85; Schreiner 2015: 359.
[45] M. O'Brien 2010: 427; cf. Lane 1991: 366; Ellingworth 1993: 608.
[46] Koester 2001: 186.

In sum, the author holds up Joseph as an exemplar because he expressed confidence in an unseen land of rest based on God's covenant promise and, even after his death, desired to be a partaker in those blessings.

Additionally, Chris Richardson argues that Hebrews 11 makes redemptive-historical claims. He posits that the figures of Hebrews 11 (and, by implication, Joseph) are not merely paraenetic exemplars but also types of the Messiah. As he argues, Hebrews 11 is an 'encomium' on Jesus such that the 'main purpose for including these examples' is not to commend their faith to the readers but to present 'these ancestors as typological anticipations of Christ'.[47] 'Simply put,' he explains,

> when Hebrews 11 is properly integrated with the rest of the epistle [particularly Heb. 12:1–3], it is clear that Jesus is the $\tau\acute{\epsilon}\lambda o\varsigma$ or climax of Israel's history and that the Old Testament exemplars of faith anticipate and prefigure his person and work.[48]

Certainly, Hebrews 12:1–3 does treat Jesus as the supreme exemplar of the faith demonstrated in Old Testament saints. But this does not necessarily make *them* types of *him*. The author of Hebrews is not developing a redemptive-historical argument that traces patterns in Old Testament history that prophetically foreshadow new-covenant realities. Instead, he is showing Jesus as the supreme exemplar of faith, just as Jesus is the supreme exemplar of all virtues in Scripture. In other words, Hebrews 12:1–3 does indicate a Christological *telos* for Hebrews 11. Not all Christological claims, however, are necessarily redemptive-historical.

In sum, then, the author's interpretive perspective on the Joseph story is that he is an exemplar of faith. In life and in death he trusted God to fulfil his covenantal promises to Abraham – particularly the promise of future rest in a place of inheritance.

Allusions to the Joseph story in the parable of the tenants

While the New Testament mentions Joseph only four times, scholars have proposed a number of possible allusions to the Joseph story in the

---

[47] Richardson 2012: 109.
[48] Ibid. 110. For Richardson's complete argument, see ibid. 109–224.

Gospels.[49] The parable of the tenants, however, does contain the most probable allusion to Joseph – a point well attested by scholarly literature. Thus, the following section will examine the validity of this allusion in the parable of the tenants and its interpretive significance for both the parable and the Joseph story. I will focus on the Matthean account, noting any important departures in meaning or phraseology in the other Synoptics.

---

[49] Many of these suggested allusions are so passing or small that it is difficult to determine whether the correspondence is intentional or coincidental. One of the most promising suggestions is Luke 2:51, which describes Mary's reaction to the boy Jesus in the temple episode with language reminiscent of Jacob's reaction to Joseph's dreams in Gen. 37. The phrase *diatēreō . . . to rēma* occurs only in Gen. 37:11 and Luke 2:51. In each instance a parent (*patēr autou // mētēr autou*) takes an acute interest in the activities of the life of his or her son given the son's apparent unique relationship with divine activity. For discussions on Gen. 37:11 and Luke 2:51, see Meyer 1964: 43; J. M. Hamilton 2008: 66–67; Lunn 2012: 36–37. Meyer points out that Targum Pseudo-Jonathan on Gen. 37:11 includes the phrase 'in his heart'.

Lunn argues that Stephen's reference to God's making Joseph a ruler over Egypt (*katestēsen auton ēgoumenon ep Aigypton*) in Acts 7:10 echoes the language of Gen. 41:43 (*katestēsen auton eph holēs gēs Aigyptou*). The language of Gen. 45:8–9 (*epoiēsen kyrion*) is used only one other time in Luke's writings (Acts 2:36) in reference to God's 'making' (*epoiēsen*) Jesus 'Lord' (*kyrion*) and Christ. Lunn argues the connection between Gen. 45 and Acts 2 is further strengthened by the fact that 'these are the only texts in both Testaments where precisely this phrase is found' (Lunn 2012: 32).

Some scholars also see an allusion to Joseph in Luke's passing statement in the genealogy that Jesus was 'about thirty years of age' when he began his ministry (Luke 3:23; cf. Gen. 41:46). The OT and NT identify only three thirty-year-old characters: Joseph, David and Jesus. Hamilton comments, 'In each case the age is noted at the beginning of the figure's public service: Joseph as he begins to serve Pharaoh, David as he begins to reign over Israel and Judah, and Jesus as he begins to bring in the kingdom' (J. M. Hamilton 2008: 67).

Others see the thief's request to Jesus 'Remember me' (*mnēsthēti mou + hotan*) as an allusion to Joseph's request to the cupbearer when he foretells his future deliverance (Gen. 40:14). See Brown 1993: 1002–1003; Lunn 2012: 33. For a host of other proposed allusions in Luke–Acts (few of which are compelling), see Lunn 2012: 27–41.

Other scholars see allusions to Joseph in the Gospel of Matthew. For instance, though there are few linguistic parallels between the Matthean infancy narrative, there are quite a few narrative and thematic similarities between the patriarchal Joseph of Genesis and Joseph of the first Gospel; (1) Both Josephs have a father named Jacob, (2) both Josephs experienced revelation through dreams, (3) both Josephs went to Egypt because of their dreams, (4) both Josephs were subject to persecution and the threat of death, (5) both Josephs preserved their families – the foundation of the community of (the new) Israel, (6) both Josephs are associated with the character Rachel (Matt. 2:18). See Brown 1993: 111–112.

Another possible parallel between Joseph and Jesus in the Gospel of Matthew is the selling of Jesus for thirty pieces of silver. In the Genesis narrative, *Ioudas* (Judah) encourages his brothers to sell (*apodidōmi*) Joseph to the passing Ishmaelites (Gen. 37:26–27). In return the patriarchs receive twenty pieces of gold (*eikosi chrysōn*) for the life of their brother (Gen. 37:28). In the Matthean account another character by the name *Ioudas* (Judah) betrays (*paradidōmi*) Jesus for thirty pieces of silver (*triakonta argyria* [Matt. 26:14–15]). This passage also alludes to Zech. 11:12–13. See Murmelstein 1932: 51–55. For other proposed allusions or further defences of those mentioned above, see Sprinkle 2007: 193–205; Römer and Rückl 2009; Bronn 2010: 207–214.

In general, the parable of the tenants furthers one of the main goals of Matthew: to show how Jesus 'fulfils' the Old Testament by successfully recapitulating Israel's history. Matthew displays this goal repeatedly in the first chapters of the Gospel. He demonstrates that Jesus 'fulfils' Israel's history by embodying their corporate experiences, such as the exodus and exile (Matt. 1:22; 2:15, 17, 23; 4:14; etc.). These fulfilment formulas anticipate the rest of the book, which, in the whole and in its parts, constantly witnesses to Jesus as the summation of redemptive history.[50]

In order to retell Israel's history creatively while presenting Jesus as that history's fulfilment, the parable of the tenants draws from the well of Old Testament imagery. As Wright notes, parables such as this one 'are Israel's-story-in-miniature, Jesus' telling of the Israel-story in order to undermine the present way of understanding the nation's identity'.[51]

In this parable, the owner of a vineyard sends his servants to harvest the fruit, but they are beaten, killed and stoned by the tenants. Then the master sends his son – thinking the tenants will respect him – but he is thrown out of the vineyard and killed. In response to the tenants' treachery, the owner removes and destroys them, giving their positions to others (Matt. 21:41, 43–44). After the parable, Jesus adds that the rejected son becomes the 'chief cornerstone' of God's work (21:42). After Jesus tells the parable, the chief priests and Pharisees rightly discern that Jesus is speaking about them (Matt. 21:45). They are in league with the tenants. Their forefathers persecuted the servants (the prophets), and they now conspire against Jesus (Matt. 21:46).

The main Old Testament background to the parable is Isaiah 5. In that passage, Isaiah, similarly, refers to planting a vineyard, putting up a fence, digging a winepress and building a tower (Isa. 5:1–2). In Isaiah, the vineyard imagery hearkens back to Eden, conjuring up notions of God's presence and his covenant relationship with his people. God's purpose for Israel is to revivify the Edenic paradise. He wants them to produce the fruit of righteousness and be the locus of his presence in the world. Isaiah records, however, that the vineyard fails to respond to God's mercies and produce a good crop. Instead of fresh fruit, it produces 'wild grapes' (Isa. 5:4). In response, God judges and destroys the nation (Isa. 5:5–6). The story of the vineyard in Isaiah is the story of Israel: it is disobedience and exile.

---

[50] France 1989: 166–205; Gubler 2005: 15–19; Kennedy 2008.
[51] C. J. H. Wright 1997: 179.

Like Isaiah, Jesus uses vineyard imagery to recount Israel's unfaithfulness and coming destruction.[52] In Matthew, however, the vineyard is unfruitful because of its corrupt stewards – Israel's leaders. The repeated sending and rejection of servants (Matt. 21:34–36) reveals that their corruption has marked Israel throughout its history. The final element in the parable, the sending of the son, reveals a new phase of Israel's history. Jesus' obvious reference to himself with the parabolic 'son' (Matt. 3:17; 4:3, 6; 8:29; 14:33; 17:5; 28:19; Mark 1:1, 11; 3:11; 5:7; 9:7; 14:61; 15:39; Luke 1:32, 35; 3:22; 8:28; 9:35; 10:22) shows that his ultimate aim in retelling Israel's history is Christological. Israel's pattern of disobedience towards God and obstinacy towards the prophets culminates in their rejection of Jesus.

Jesus makes this point even more clearly when quoting Psalm 118:22–23 at the conclusion of the parable (Matt. 21:42).[53] Psalm 118 celebrates God's deliverance of Israel from foreign oppression, though the psalmist does not provide any specific historical details. This deliverance is summarized in verses 22–23, which speak of a rejected stone that becomes the cornerstone in God's temple community. Jesus interprets the words of the psalm as being fulfilled in himself, the rejected son (i.e. the rejected stone) at the centre of God's saving agenda.

Ultimately, then, the parable is a retreading of Israel's history with a Christological focus. The patterns of Israel's unfaithfulness and the rejection of God's appointed spokesmen and leaders anticipate Israel's rejection of Christ. Jesus' death is the climactic episode of Israel's sordid tale of repeated unfaithfulness.

The question is whether the language and imagery of the parable of the tenants also alludes to Joseph. If so, how does this allusion contribute to (1) our interpretation of the parable and (2) our understanding of Joseph in redemptive history? As scholars have noted, aspects of the parable seem to echo the story of Joseph[54] – particularly the mention of the owner's 'son' (Matt. 21:37) or, as Mark and Luke have it, the 'beloved son' (*huion*

---

[52] Blomberg notes, 'The account in Isaiah is remarkably similar to Jesus' story' (Blomberg 2007: 71.

[53] For a defence of the quotation's authenticity, see Lanier 2013: 733–751.

[54] For a sample of scholars who affirm or discuss a possible allusion to the Joseph story in the parable of the tenants, see Pesch 1976: 219; Gnilka 1979: 147; Evans 1988: 236; Davies and Allison Jr 1997: 183; Weihs 2000: 5–29; Luz 2005: 40–41; Kloppenborg 2006: 231–235; Blomberg 2007: 71; J. M. Hamilton 2008: 66; Ahearne-Kroll 2012: 37–38; Lunn 2012: 35–37; Pennington 2012: 201; Hays 2014: 9–11; 2016: 43. Snodgrass asks 'Is Gen. 37:20 relevant?' (Snodgrass 2008: 277).

agapēton [Mark 12:16]; *ton huion mou ton agapēton* [Luke 20:13]; cf. Gen. 37:3–4). Of course, Joseph does not have a monopoly on 'beloved son' language in the Old Testament (cf. Gen. 22:2; 2 Sam. 7:14; Ps. 2:7; Hos. 11:1). Yet, the son's description (and the surrounding details) in the parable make an allusion to Joseph likely.

The description of the master sending his son (*apesteilen pros autous ton huion autou* [Matt. 21:37; cf. Mark 12:6; Luke 20:13]) is similar to Jacob's own 'sending' of Joseph in Genesis 37:13 (*aposteilō se pros autous*). While the vocabulary is not particularly unique, other factors bolster the connection. In both instances a father (the subject) 'sends' (*apostellō*) a son (the object) to a people ('to them', *pros autous*) who will reject him. Only in Genesis 37 and the parable of tenants do we see this exact pattern of events in this language.[55] The responses of the tenants and Joseph's brothers to the arrivals of the beloved sons are also strikingly similar. The brothers of Joseph 'see' (*proeidon*) him from a distance and then 'speak' (*eipan*) about how they can destroy him (Gen. 37:18–19). The same sequence is followed by the tenants who 'see' (*idontes*) the son coming and 'speak' about his destruction (*eipon* [Matt. 21:38; cf. Mark 12:7; Luke 20:14]).[56] Further – and perhaps most striking – in both instances the hostile company uses the exact same phrase in their deliberation: 'Come, let us kill him' (*deute apokteinōmen auton* [Gen. 37:20; Matt. 21:38; Mark 12:7; Luke 20:14[57]]) – a phrase that occurs only in Genesis 37:20 and in the parable of the tenants.[58] Finally, as the brothers take Joseph (*kai labontes auton* [Gen. 37:24]) and throw him into the pit – a metaphorical murder – so the tenants take the son (*kai labontes auton* [Matt. 21:39; cf. Mark 12:8), throw him out of the vineyard, and murder him.

Donahue and Harrington posit that the verbal connections hint at a Joseph–Jesus typology, 'especially with regard to the theme of two innocent sufferers' or with regard to the jealousy motif seen both in Joseph's brothers and in the vineyard tenants.[59] This interpretation, however, does

---

[55] Lunn 2012: 36.

[56] Mark does not mention the tenants 'seeing' the son. Also Luke uses *dialogizomai* as opposed to *eipon* (Luke 20:14).

[57] Some manuscripts of Luke include *deute*. See ℵ C D L Θ *f*[13] 33 𝔐 *e sy*[s.c.p.h**] *sa*[ms] *bo*. This inclusion, however, is likely the result of synoptic harmonization.

[58] The phrase *apokteinōmen auton* does occur in Judg. 16:2. This passage, however, lacks both *deute* and conceptual similarities with the Joseph story and thus should not be taken into consideration.

[59] Donahue and Harrington 2002: 339.

not take into account the parable's primary significance as a retelling of Israel's history, focusing particularly on its regular rejection of God's prophets.[60] The point of the allusion is not to make a generic typological association between Joseph and Jesus. Instead, Jesus is retelling Israel's history as refracted through the Joseph story, Isaiah 5 and Psalm 118, among other possible Old Testament sources, as a way of showing himself as the culmination of a pattern deeply embedded in Israel's history. Jesus likely draws on Genesis 37, Isaiah 5 and Psalm 118 since they each witness, in their own contexts, to this pattern. An allusion to Joseph, therefore, further witnesses to this pattern. Like Isaiah 5 and Psalm 118, the Joseph story is the story of Israel in miniature. Their rejection of 'beloved sons', anointed leaders and deliverers of the nation begins as early as Joseph. As Hays summarizes:

> the parable thereby places the story of Jesus within the unfolding story of Israel and presents his death as the climax of a pattern of unfaithfulness and judgment familiar to any reader of Israel's prophetic literature. The pattern is as old as the story of Joseph's resentful brothers.[61]

In this light, Jesus, in fact, is suggesting a typological reading of the Joseph story. The foundation of this type, however, is not simply the verbal correspondence between the parable's 'beloved son' and Joseph. Instead, Jesus alludes to the Joseph story as part of a larger pattern in Israel's history of rejected prophets – a pattern that witnesses to Israel's rejection of Jesus (much like Stephen's argument in Acts 7).[62]

The use of 'beloved son' language may also intimate a soteriological facet to the parable. As Hays notes:

---

[60] Kloppenborg, similarly, protests Weihs' analysis of the Joseph allusion since 'he neglects the more obvious typological function of the figure of Joseph, representing the persecuted and vindicated one' (Kloppenborg 2006: 233).

[61] Hays 2014: 11.

[62] Hamilton writes, 'This parable, with its linguistic connection to the Joseph story, with the event sequence correspondence of the father sending the son, who is then rejected, and with the redemptive historical import of Jesus as the last of a long line of figures whom the owner of the vineyard has sent to his tenants, indicates that Jesus understood himself as the typological fulfillment of this pattern, which means that Jesus understood himself as the typological fulfillment of a pattern to which the Joseph story made a key contribution' (J. M. Hamilton 2008: 66).

the identification of Jesus as the 'beloved son' (Mark 12.6; Luke 20.13) – linking him both to Isaac and to the Davidic king [and, I would add, Joseph] – hints that his death is to be understood not merely as a tragic episode of violence but as an event of saving significance for Israel.[63]

This point is also attested to in the quotation of Psalm 118 where the rejected stone becomes the cornerstone of God's renewed work in the temple. The allusion to Joseph, therefore, coupled with the quotation of Psalm 118:22–23, witnesses not only to the pattern of the rejection of God's prophets, which culminates in Christ, but also to a pattern of vindication. Both Joseph and the stone are rejected and then made a centrepiece in God's redemptive plan. This pattern forecasts the destiny of the Christ himself.

In summary, the parable of the tenants contains a probable allusion to the Joseph narrative. This allusion reinforces Jesus' notion that Israel has always rejected its prophets. Like Israel in Isaiah 5, they are faithless and unrighteous. The allusion also reveals part of the interpretive perspective of Jesus and the Gospel writers on the Joseph story: they see Joseph as part of a typological pattern in Israel's history – which reaches its zenith in Israel's rejection of Jesus. This parable, then, witnesses to a 'Joseph typology', not merely on account of a few verbal parallels, but because Joseph is part of a pattern played out numerous times in Israel's history that ultimately comes to fulfilment in the Messiah.

Implications for a canonical understanding of the Joseph narrative

The preceding analysis yields some significant biblical-theological conclusions. First, contrary to much modern scholarship, both Acts and Hebrews speak well of Joseph's character. In Hebrews, Joseph is an example of faith worthy of imitation. In Acts, Joseph is favoured by God and mediates blessing to the nations. Second, both authors interpret Joseph within the framework of the Abrahamic covenant. Hebrews focuses on Joseph's faith in the Abrahamic promises, specifically the land promise. In Acts, Joseph is the archetypal covenant mediator rejected by

---

[63] Hays 2006: 54.

the nation. Finally, Acts and the parable of the tenants reveal that the apostolic community saw Joseph's life as a prospective pattern of Israel's history. In Acts, Joseph, like Moses and Jesus, is a Spirit-endowed prophet who fulfils God's covenantal promises despite (even through) rejection by his brothers. In the parable of the tenants, Jesus alludes to Joseph as part of a pattern in Israel's history that anticipates the rejection of the Messiah, Israel's true 'beloved son'. Thus, according to Acts 7 and the parable of the tenants, Joseph is a type of the Messiah.

9

Conclusion

In the first chapter I noted that Brevard Childs once asked:

> What is the shape of the final chapters [of Genesis] and what is their
> function within the book as a whole? . . . If Joseph is not the bearer
> of the promise in the same way as his forefathers, what then is his
> role in Genesis?[1]

This book has sought not only to answer Childs's question about the
role of Joseph in Genesis but also to account for Joseph's redemptive-
historical contribution to the entire canon of Scripture. Contrary to
much historical-critical scholarship, I have argued that the Joseph
story functions as the resolution to the plot of Genesis. In the Joseph story,
Moses continues to focus on the Abrahamic promises and describes how
those promises are fulfilled through Joseph – the rejected, royal deliverer.
Moses portrays Joseph as an anticipatory fulfilment of the promises.
Joseph's ministry multiplies the seed of Israel, blesses the nations and
prepares Israel to inherit Canaan. In the light of these features of the story,
Moses suggests that Joseph's life is typological – one that points to a future
and more complete fulfilment of God's promises. Later Old Testament
authors confirm this interpretation in their own discussions of or allusions to the Joseph narrative. Finally, New Testament authors also confirm
these same features and explicitly indicate the typological character of the
Joseph story.

For many Christians, Old Testament historical narrative remains a
locked box – an enormous but enigmatic section of Scripture regrettably
ignored by both preachers and laypeople. This work is a small effort in
unlocking for the church just one aspect of the biblical-theological riches

---

[1] Childs 1979: 156.

inherent in the Joseph story. I have sought to interpret the Joseph narrative according to the intent of the original author and according to the interpretive perspective of later biblical authors. I have also sought to interpret the Joseph story according to Scripture's covenantal framework. Applying the same interpretive principles to other portions of the Old Testament, particularly Old Testament historical narratives, would go a long way in constructing a truly 'biblical' theology for the benefit of Christ's church.[2]

What I hope to have demonstrated is that a commitment to authorial intent and confessional orthodoxy on the character of Scripture yields significant biblical-theological results. Many other sections of the Old Testament need a fresh examination that eschews historical-critical presuppositions and instead reads these narratives on their own terms. Further, the idea that typology must be grounded within Scripture's covenantal framework (and not merely on verbal correspondences or thematic similarities) may be of some value for arbitrating other disputed issues in biblical theology or typology.

John Owen noted that 'the only unique, public, authentic, and infallible interpreter of Scripture is none other than the Author of Scripture Himself . . . that is, God the Holy Spirit'.[3] I have sought to be faithful to that interpretive principle by allowing the covenantal structure of Scripture and the interpretive perspective of later biblical authors to shape my reading of the Joseph story. My hope is that this project has constructed a truly 'biblical' account of Joseph's place in Christian theology built on those theological and hermeneutical principles.

I began this work by puzzling over Joseph's prominence in Genesis. My contention is that Moses focuses on Joseph to highlight God's sovereign faithfulness to his covenantal promises. God uses Joseph to turn back the effects of the curse and accomplish, in part, his promises to Abraham. God stacks the odds against himself and then demonstrates his power by using an imprisoned slave exiled by his own family to keep his promises.

Perhaps Moses spends so much time on Joseph to show us that God can pull off the impossible – even through a seemingly insignificant Jew rejected by his own brothers. Perhaps Moses spends so much time on

---

2 For a helpful discussion on what it means to be truly 'biblical', see Gentry and Wellum 2012: 81–126.

3 Owen 1994: 797. See also Coxe's comments 'The best interpreter of the Old Testament is the Holy Spirit speaking to us in the new' (Coxe and Owen 2005: 36).

Joseph so his people will anticipate a coming Joseph who will finally reverse the curse and fulfil the promises.

Joseph's story is the story of the whole Bible. It is the story of glory through suffering, exaltation through humiliation. It is the story of the cross and the crown.

Bibliography

Ackerman, J. S. (1982), 'Joseph, Judah, and Jacob', in K. R. R. Gros Louis, J. S. Ackerman and T. Warshaw (eds.), *Literary Interpretations of Biblical Narratives*, Nashville: Abingdon, 2: 85–113.

Ages, A. (1993), 'Why Didn't Joseph Call Home?', *BRev* 9.4: 42–46.

—— (1998), 'Dreamer, Schemer, Slave and Prince: Understanding Joseph's Dreams', *BRev* 14.2: 46–52.

Ahearne-Kroll, S. P. (2012), 'Genesis in Mark's Gospel', in M. Menken and S. Moyise (eds.), *Genesis in the New Testament*, LNTS 466, London: T&T Clark, 27–41.

Albright, W. F. (1918), 'Historical and Mythological Elements in the Story of Joseph', *JBL* 37.3–4: 111–143.

—— (2006), *Archaeology and the Religion of Israel*, Louisville: Westminster John Knox.

Alexander, T. D. (1989), 'From Adam to Judah: The Significance of the Family Tree in Genesis', *EvQ* 61.1: 5–19.

—— (1993), 'Genealogies, Seed and the Compositional Unity of Genesis', *TynBul* 44.2: 255–270.

—— (1994), 'Abraham Re-Assessed Theologically: The Abraham Narrative and the New Testament Understanding of Justification by Faith', in R. S. Hess, G. J. Wenham and P. E. Satterthwaite (eds.), *He Swore an Oath: Biblical Themes from Genesis 12–50*, Cambridge: Tyndale House, 7–28.

—— (1995), 'Messianic Ideology in the Book of Genesis', in P. E. Satterthwaite, R. S. Hess and G. J. Wenham (eds.), *The Lord's Anointed: Interpretation of Old Testament Messianic Texts*, Grand Rapids: Baker, 19–39.

—— (1997), 'Further Observations on the Term "Seed" in Genesis', *TynBul* 48.2: 363–367.

—— (1998a), 'Royal Expectations in Genesis to Kings', *TynBul* 49.2: 191–212.

—— (1998b), *The Servant King: The Bible's Portrait of the Messiah*, Leicester: Regent College Publishing.

—— (2007), 'The Regal Dimension of the תולדותיעקב: Recovering the Literary Context of Genesis 37–50', in J. G. McConville and K. Möller (eds.), *Reading the Law: Studies in Honour of Gordon J. Wenham*, New York: T&T Clark, 196–212.

—— (2008), *From Eden to the New Jerusalem: An Introduction to Biblical Theology*, Grand Rapids: Kregel.

Alles, T. (2008), 'The Narrative Meaning and Function of the Parable of the Prodigal Son (Luke 15:11–32)', PhD diss., The Catholic University of America.

Allis, O. T. (1945), *Prophecy and the Church*, Philadelphia: P&R.

Allison Jr, D. C. (1994), *The New Moses: A Matthean Typology*, Minneapolis: Fortress.

Alter, R. (1990), 'Putting Together Biblical Narrative', in M. Griffith and D. Mastronarde (eds.), *Cabinet of the Muses: Essays on Classical and Comparative Literature in Honor of Thomas G. Rosenmeyer*, Atlanta: Scholars Press, 117–129.

—— (1996), *Genesis: Translation and Commentary*, New York: Norton.

—— (1999), *The David Story: A Translation with Commentary of 1 and 2 Samuel*, New York: Norton.

—— (2011), *The Art of the Biblical Narrative*, rev. edn, New York: Basic.

Andersen, F. I. (1970), *The Hebrew Verbless Clause in the Pentateuch*, JBLMS 14, Nashville: Abingdon.

—— (1974), *The Sentence in Biblical Hebrew*, Janua Linguarum. Series Practica 231, New York: Mouton.

Anderson, G. A. (2001), 'The Garments of Skin in Apocryphal Narrative and Biblical Commentary', in J. L. Kugel (ed.), *Studies in Ancient Midrash*, Cambridge: Harvard University Center for Jewish Studies, 101–143.

—— (2003), 'Joseph and the Passion of Our Lord', in E. F. Davis and R. Hays (eds.), *The Art of Reading Scripture*, Grand Rapids: Eerdmans, 198–215.

Argyle, A. W. (1956), 'Joseph the Patriarch in Patristic Teaching', *ExpTim* 67.7: 199–201.

Arnold, B. T. (2009), *Genesis*, NCBC, Cambridge: Cambridge University Press.

Aus, R. (1988), *Weihnachtsgeschichte, barmherziger Samariter, verlorener Sohn: Studien zu ihrem jüdischen Hintergrund*, ANTZ 2, Berlin: Institut Kirche und Judentum.

Baden, J. S. (2012), *The Composition of the Pentateuch: Renewing the Documentary Hypothesis*. ABRL, New Haven: Yale University Press.

Bailey, N. A. (1994), 'Some Literary and Grammatical Aspects of Genealogies in Genesis', in R. D. Bergen (ed.), *Biblical Hebrew and Discourse Linguistics*, Winona Lake: Eisenbrauns, 267–282.

Baker, D. (2014), *Genesis 37–50: A Handbook on the Hebrew Text*, Waco: Baylor University Press.

Baker, D. L. (2010), *Two Testaments, One Bible: The Theological Relationship Between the Old and New Testaments*, 3rd edn, Nottingham: Apollos; Downers Grove: InterVarsity Press.

Baker, D. W. (1980), 'Diversity and Unity in the Literary Structure of Genesis', in A. R. Millard and D. J. Wiseman (eds.), *Essays on the Patriarchal Narratives*, Leicester: Inter-Varsity Press, 189–206.

Bangsund, J. C. (2005), 'Am I in the Place of God? Theme and Variations in Genesis 50:17', *Africa Theological Journal* 28: 57–71.

Barber, M. (2001), *Singing in the Reign: The Psalms and the Liturgy of God's People*, Steubenville: Emmaus Road.

Barrett, C. K. (1994), *A Critical and Exegetical Commentary on the Acts of the Apostles*, vol. 1, ICC, Edinburgh: T&T Clark.

Baucham Jr, V. (2013), *Joseph and the Gospel of Many Colors: Reading an Old Story in a New Way*, Wheaton: Crossway.

Beale, G. K. (1989), 'Did Jesus and His Followers Preach the Right Doctrine from the Wrong Texts?', *Them* 14.3: 89–96.

—— (2004), *The Temple and the Church's Mission: A Biblical Theology of the Dwelling Place of God*, NSBT 17, Leicester: Apollos; Downers Grove: InterVarsity Press.

—— (2011), *A New Testament Biblical Theology: The Unfolding of the Old Testament in the New*, Grand Rapids: Baker Academic.

—— (2012), *Handbook on the New Testament Use of the Old Testament: Exegesis and Interpretation*, Grand Rapids: Baker Academic.

Beckerleg, C. (2009), 'The "Image of God" in Eden: The Creation of Mankind in Genesis 2:5–3:24 in Light of the Mīs Pî Pît Pî and Wpt-R Rituals of Mesopotamia and Ancient Egypt', PhD diss., Harvard University.

Beetham, C. (2013), 'From Creation to New Creation: The Biblical Epic of King, Human Vicegerency, and Kingdom', in D. M. Gurtner and B. L. Gladd (eds.), *From Creation to New Creation: Biblical Theology and Exegesis*, Peabody: Hendrickson, 327–354.

Berg, S. B. (1979), *The Book of Esther: Motifs, Themes and Structure*, Missoula: Society of Biblical Literature.

Berkhof, L. (1952), *Principles of Biblical Interpretation: Sacred Hermeneutics*, 2nd edn, Grand Rapids: Baker.

Bezalel, N. (2002), 'Joseph and Daniel: Court Jews and Dreamers', *JBQ* 30.1: 10–16.

Blomberg, C. L. (2007), 'Matthew', in G. K. Beale and D. A. Carson (eds.), *Commentary on the New Testament Use of the Old*, Grand Rapids: Baker, 1–109.

Bock, D. (1982), 'Proclamation from Prophecy and Pattern: Lucan Old Testament Christology', PhD diss., University of Aberdeen.

—— (1987), *Proclamation from Prophecy and Pattern: Lucan Old Testament Christology*, LNTS, Sheffield: Sheffield Academic Press.

—— (2007), *Acts*, BECNT, Grand Rapids: Baker.

Boersma, H., and M. Levering (eds.) (2013), *Heaven on Earth: Theological Interpretation in Ecumenical Dialogue*, Oxford: Wiley-Blackwell.

Braun, H. (2010), *Geschichte des Gottesvolkes und christliche Identität*, WUNT 279, Tübingen: Mohr Siebeck.

Breck, J. (1994), *The Shape of Biblical Language: Chiasmus in the Scriptures and Beyond*, Crestwood: St Vladimir's Seminary Press.

Brodie, T. (2001), *Genesis as Dialogue: A Literary, Historical, and Theological Commentary*, Oxford: Oxford University Press.

Bronn, W. (2010), 'Forgiveness in "My Brothers" of Matthew 28:10 and Its Significance for the Matthean Climax (28:16–20)', *BTB* 40.4: 207–214.

Brown, R. (1993), *The Birth of the Messiah: A Commentary on the Infancy Narratives in the Gospels of Matthew and Luke*, 2nd edn, ABRL, New York: Doubleday.

Brueggemann, W. (1982), *Genesis: A Biblical Commentary for Teaching and Preaching*, Interpretation, Louisville: Westminster John Knox.

Bruno, C. (2015), 'Biblical Theology According to the Earliest Christians: Stephen's Speech as a Model for OT Biblical Theology', paper presented at the Evangelical Theological Society, Atlanta.

Bruno, C., J. Compton and K. McFadden (2020), *Biblical Theology According to the Apostles: How the Earliest Christians Told the Story of Israel*, NSBT 52, London: Apollos; Downers Grove: InterVarsity Press.

Burns, D. G. (2006), 'Evoking Israel's History in Acts 7:2–53 and 13:16–41: The Hermeneutics of Luke's Retelling the Story of God's People', PhD diss., Westminster Theological Seminary.

Bush, F. W. (1996), *Ruth, Esther*, WBC 9, Dallas: Word.

Calvin, J. (1996), *Commentaries on the First Book of Moses Called Genesis*, tr. John King, CC, Grand Rapids: Baker.

Caneday, A. B. (2010), 'Covenant Lineage Allegorically Prefigured: "Which Things Are Written Allegorically" (Galatians 4:21–31)', *SBJT* 14.3: 50–77.

Carmichael, C. M. (2000), 'The Story of Joseph and the Book of Jubilees', in T. H. Lim and L. Hurtado (eds.), *The Dead Sea Scrolls in Their Historical Context*, Edinburgh: T&T Clark, 143–158.

Carr, D. (1996), *Reading the Fractures of Genesis: Historical and Literary Approaches*, Louisville: Westminster John Knox.

Carroll R., M. D. (2000), 'Blessing the Nations: Toward a Biblical Theology of Mission from Genesis', *BBR* 10.1: 17–34.

Carson, D. A. (2004), 'Mystery and Fulfillment: Toward a More Comprehensive Paradigm of Paul's Understanding of the Old and the New', in D. A. Carson, P. T. O'Brien and M. A. Seifrid (eds.), *Justification and Variegated Nomism*, WUNT 181, Grand Rapids: Baker, 2: 393–436.

—— (2007), review of *Judgment and Justification in Early Judaism and the Apostle Paul* by C. VanLandingham, *RBL* 12.

—— (2011), 'Theological Interpretation of Scripture: Yes, But . . .', in R. M. Allen (ed.), *Theological Commentary: Evangelical Perspectives*, London: T&T Clark, 187–207.

Carson, D. A., and G. K. Beale (eds.) (2007), *The Commentary on the New Testament Use of the Old Testament*, Grand Rapids: Baker.

Cassuto, U. (1964), *A Commentary on the Book of Genesis, Part 2: From Noah to Abraham*, tr. I. Abrahams, Jerusalem: Magnes.

—— (1973), 'The Story of Tamar and Judah', in *Biblical and Oriental Studies*, vol. 1: *The Bible*, tr. I. Abrahams, Jerusalem: Magnes, 29–40.

Chan, M. (2013), 'Joseph and Jehoiachin: On the Edge of the Exodus', *ZAW* 125.4: 566–577.

Chase, M. (2008), 'Luke-Acts Parallels Between Jesus and Stephen', ThM thesis, Southwestern Baptist Theological Seminary.

—— (2013), 'Resurrection Hope in Daniel 12:2: An Exercise in Biblical Theology', PhD diss., The Southern Baptist Theological Seminary.

—— (2014a), '"From Dust You Shall Arise:" Resurrection Hope in the Old Testament', *SBJT* 18.4: 9–29.

—— (2014b), 'The Genesis of Resurrection Hope: Exploring Its Early Presence and Deep Roots', *JETS* 57.3: 467–480.

Childs, B. S. (1979), *Introduction to the Old Testament as Scripture*, Philadelphia: Fortress.

Christensen, D. L. (1983), 'Anticipatory Paronomasia in Jonah 3:7–8 and Genesis 37:2', *RB* 90.2: 261–263.

Ciampa, R. E. (2007), 'The History of Redemption', in S. Hafemann and P. R. House (eds.), *Central Themes in Biblical Theology: Mapping Unity in Diversity*, Grand Rapids: Baker, 254–308.

Clark, W. M. (1969), 'A Legal Background to the Yahwist's Use of "Good and Evil" in Genesis 2–3', *JBL* 88: 266–278.

Clines, D. (1995), *Interested Parties: The Ideology of Writers and Readers of the Hebrew Bible*, JSOTsup 205, Sheffield: Sheffield Academic Press.

Clowney, E. P. (2002), *Preaching and Biblical Theology*, Phillipsburg, NJ: P&R.

Coats, G. W. (1972), 'Widow's Rights: A Crux in the Structure of Genesis 38', *CBQ* 34: 461–466.

—— (1976), *From Canaan to Egypt: Structural and Theological Context of the Joseph Story*, CBQMS 4, Washington, D.C.: Catholic Biblical Association of America.

—— (1980), 'Strife and Reconciliation: Themes of a Biblical Theology in the Book of Genesis', *HBT* 2: 15–37.

Cohen, N. J. (1983), 'Two That Are One – Sibling Rivalry in Genesis', *Judaism* 32: 331–342.

Cole, R. (2002), 'In Death, Larger than Life: Joshua 24:29–33 and the Rhetorics of Obituary', paper presented at the Evangelical Theological Society, Toronto.

Collins, J. (1997), 'A Syntactical Note (Genesis 3:15): Is the Woman's Seed Singular or Plural?', *TynBul* 48.1: 139–148.

Collins, J. J. (1975), 'The Court-Tales in Daniel and the Development of Apocalyptic', *JBL* 94.2: 218–234.

—— (1993), *Daniel*, Hermeneia, Minneapolis: Augsburg.

Conzelmann, H. (1987), *Acts of the Apostles*, Hermeneia, Philadelphia: Fortress.

Coxe, N., and J. Owen (2005), *Covenant Theology from Adam to Christ*, Owensboro: RBAP.

Craig, K. (2001), *Hebrews*, AB, New York: Doubleday.

Creach, J. (2008), *The Destiny of the Righteous in the Psalms*, St Louis: Chalice, 2008.

Currid, J. D. (1994), 'Recognition and Use of Typology in Preaching', *RTR* 53.3: 115–129.

—— (2003), *A Study Commentary on Genesis*, vol. 2, Darlington: Evangelical Press.

Currid, J. D., and L. K. Larson (2013), 'Narrative Repetition in 1 Samuel 24 and 26: Saul's Descent and David's Ascent', in *From Creation to New Creation: Biblical Theology and Exegesis, Essays in Honor of G. K. Beale*, Peabody: Hendrickson, 51–62.

Curtis, E. (1991), 'Genesis 38: Its Context(s) and Function', *CTR* 5: 247–257.

Dahlberg, B. T. (1977), 'On Recognizing the Unity of Genesis', *TD* 24: 360–367.

—— (1982), 'The Unity of Genesis', in K. R. R. Gros Louis (ed.), *Literary Interpretations of Biblical Narratives*, Nashville: Abingdon, 2: 126–133.

Davidson, R. (1981), *Typology in Scripture: A Study of Hermeneutical ΤΥΠΟΣ Structures*, AUSDDS, Berrien Springs: Andrews University Press.

Davies, P. R. (1976), 'Daniel Chapter Two', *JTS* 27.2: 392–401.

Davies, W. D., and D. C. Allison Jr (1997), *Matthew 19–28*, vol. 3, ICC, Edinburgh: T&T Clark.

Declaissé-Walford, N., R. A. Jacobson and B. L. Tanner (2014), *The Book of Psalms*, NICOT, Grand Rapids: Eerdmans.

Delcor, M. (1971), *Le Livre de Daniel*, Paris: J. Gabalda.

Dempster, S. G. (2003), *Dominion and Dynasty: A Biblical Theology of the Hebrew Bible*, Leicester: Apollos; Downers Grove: InterVarsity Press.

—— (2007), 'The Servant of the Lord', in S. Hafemann and P. R. House (eds.), *Central Themes in Biblical Theology: Mapping Unity in Diversity*, Grand Rapids: Baker, 128–178.

—— (2014), 'From Slight Peg to Cornerstone to Capstone: The Resurrection of Christ on "The Third Day" According to the Scriptures', *WTJ* 76: 371–409.

DeRouchie, J. (2013), 'The Blessing-Commission, the Promised Offspring, and the Toledot Structure of Genesis', *JETS* 56.2: 219–247.

Dibelius, M. (1956), *Studies in the Acts of the Apostles*, London: SCM Press.

Diffey, D. S. (2011), 'The Royal Promise in Genesis: The Often Underestimated Importance of Genesis 17:6, 17:16 and 35:11', *TynBul* 62.2: 313–316.

Dillard, R. B., and T. Longman III (1994), *An Introduction to the Old Testament*, Grand Rapids: Zondervan.

Donahue, J. R., and D. J. Harrington (2002), *The Gospel of Mark*, SP 2, Collegeville: Liturgical Press.

Dorsey, D. A. (1999), *The Literary Structure of the Old Testament: A Commentary on Genesis–Malachi*, Grand Rapids: Baker.

Drury, J. (1976), *Tradition and Design in Luke's Gospel: A Study in Early Christian Historiography*, London: Darton, Longman & Todd.

Dumbrell, W. J. (1993), *Covenant and Creation: A Theology of the Old Testament Covenants*, Grand Rapids: Baker.

—— (1994), *The Search for Order: Biblical Eschatology in Focus*, Grand Rapids: Baker.

Dunne, J. A. (2014), *Esther and Her Elusive God: How a Secular Story Functions as Scripture*, Eugene: Wipf & Stock.

Dupont, J. (1985), 'La Structure Oratorire du discourse d'Étienne (Actes 7)', *Bib* 66: 153–167.

Easter, M. (2014), *Faith and the Faithfulness of Jesus in Hebrews*, SNTSMS 160, Cambridge: Cambridge University Press.

Edwards, J. (2005), *The Works of Jonathan Edwards*, vol. 2: *Types of the Messiah*, Peabody: Hendrickson, 642–675.

Eisenbaum, P. (1997), *The Jewish Heroes of Christian History: Hebrews 11 in Literary Context*, SBLDS 156, Atlanta: Scholars Press.

Ellingworth, P. (1993), *The Epistle to the Hebrews*, NIGTC, Grand Rapids: Eerdmans.

Emadi, M. H. (2016), 'The Royal Priest: Psalm 110 in Biblical-Theological Perspective', PhD diss., The Southern Baptist Theological Seminary.

Emadi, S. (2018), 'Covenant, Typology, and the Story of Joseph', *TynBul* 69.1: 1–24.

Emanuel, D. (2012), *From Bards to Biblical Exegetes: A Close Reading and Intertextual Analysis of Selected Exodus Psalms*, Eugene: Pickwick.

Emerton, J. A. (1975), 'Some Problems in Genesis XXXVIII', *VT* 29: 338–361.

—— (1979), 'Judah and Tamar', *VT* 29: 403–415.

Evans, C. (1988), *Mark 8:27–16:20*, WBC 34B, Grand Rapids: Zondervan.

Fairbairn, P. (1900), *The Typology of Scripture*, London: Funk & Wagnalls.

Feinberg, J. S. (ed.) (1988), *Continuity and Discontinuity: Perspectives on the Relationship Between the Old and New Testaments*, Wheaton: Crossway.

Fesko, J. V. (2007), *Last Things First: Unlocking Genesis 1–3 with the Christ of Eschatology*, Fearn, Ross-shire: Christian Focus.

Fischer, G. (2001), 'Die Josefsgeschichte als Modell für Versöhnung', in A. Wénin (ed.), *Studies in the Book of Genesis: Literature, Redaction and History*, BETL 155, Leuven: Leuven University Press, 242–271.

Fishbane, M. (1985), *Biblical Interpretation in Ancient Israel*, New York: Clarendon.

—— (1998), *Biblical Text and Texture: A Literary Reading of Selected Texts*, Oxford: Oneworld.

Fitzmyer, J. A. (1998), *The Acts of the Apostles*, AB 31, New York: Doubleday.

Fokkelman, J. P. (1991), *Narrative Art in Genesis: Specimens of Stylistic and Structural Analysis*, 2nd edn, Eugene: Wipf & Stock.

—— (1996), 'Genesis 37 and Genesis 38 as the Interface of Structural Analysis and Hermeneutics', in L. J. de Regt, J. de Waard and J. P. Fokkelman (eds.), *Literary Structure and Rhetorical Strategies in the Hebrew Bible*, Leiden: Brill, 152–187.

Fortner, J. L. (2004), '"Much More Ours Than Yours": The Figure of Joseph the Patriarch in the New Testament and the Early Church', MA thesis, Miami University.

France, R. T. (1989), *Matthew: Evangelist and Teacher*, Eugene: Wipf & Stock.

—— (1998), *Jesus and the Old Testament: His Application of Old Testament Passages to Himself and His Mission*, Vancouver: Regent College Publishing.

Frei, H. (1974), *The Eclipse of the Biblical Narrative: A Study in Eighteenth and Nineteenth Century Hermeneutics*, New Haven: Yale University Press.

Fretheim, T. E. (1994), *The Book of Genesis*, The New Interpreters Bible, vol. 1, Nashville: Abingdon.

Frieden, K. (1990), 'Dream Interpreters in Exile: Joseph, Daniel, and Sigmund (Solomon)', in *Mappings of the Biblical Terrain*, Lewisburg: Bucknell University Press, 193–203.

Fuller, A. (1988), *The Complete Works of Andrew Fuller*, vol. 3, Harrisonburg: Sprinkle.

Fung, Y. (2000), *Victim and Victimizer: Joseph's Interpretation of His Destiny*, JSOTSup 308, Sheffield: Sheffield Academic Press.

Gan, M. (1961), 'Megillat 'Esther Be'aspaqlariyat Qorot Yoseph Be'misrayim', *Tarbiz* 31: 144–149.

Garrett, D. (1991), *Rethinking Genesis*, Grand Rapids: Baker.

—— (1996), 'Genesis, Theology of', *EDBT*, Grand Rapids: Baker.

—— (2001), 'The Undead Hypothesis: Why the Documentary Hypothesis Is the Frankenstein of Biblical Studies', *SBJT* 5.3: 28–41.

Gathercole, S. (2015), *Defending Substitution: An Essay on Atonement in Paul*, Grand Rapids: Baker.

Gentry, P. J. (2010), 'Daniel's Seventy Weeks and the New Exodus', *SBJT* 14.1: 26–44.

—— (2016), 'The Significance of Covenants in Biblical Theology,' *SBJT* 20.1: 9–33.

Gentry, P. J., and S. Wellum (2012), *Kingdom Through Covenant: A Biblical Theological Understanding of the Covenants*, Wheaton: Crossway.

George, S. (2013), 'Daniel', in *Esther and Daniel*, Brazos Theological Commentary on the Bible, Grand Rapids: Brazos, 95–222.

Gesenius, W. (1910), *Gesenius' Hebrew Grammar*, ed. E. Kautzsch, tr. A. E. Cowley, 2nd English edn, Oxford: Clarendon.

Gignilliat, M. (2008), 'Paul, Allegory, and the Plain Sense of Scripture: Galatians 3:21–23', *JTI* 2: 135–146.

Glenny, W. E. (1997), 'Typology: A Summary of the Present Evangelical Discussion', *JETS* 40.4: 627–638.

Gnilka, J. (1979), *Das Evangelium Nach Markus*, vol. 2, Zurich: Benziger Verlag.

Gnuse, R. (1990), 'The Jewish Dream Interpreter in a Foreign Court: The Recurring Use of a Theme in Jewish Literature', *JSP* 7: 29–53.

Goldin, J. (1977), 'The Youngest Son; Or, Where Does Genesis 38 Belong?', *JBL* 96: 27–44.

Goldingay, J. (1989), *Daniel*, WBC 30, Dallas: Word.

Goldsworthy, G. (2006), *Gospel-Centered Hermeneutics: Foundations and Principles of Evangelical Biblical Interpretation*, Nottingham: Apollos; Downers Grove: InterVarsity Press.

Goligher, L. (2008), *Joseph: The Hidden Hand of God*, Fearn, Ross-shire: Christian Focus.

Gonzales Jr, R. R. (2009), *Where Sin Abounds: The Spread of Sin and the Curse in Genesis with Special Focus on the Patriarchal Narratives*, Eugene: Wipf & Stock.

Goodwin, T. (1996), *The Works of Thomas Goodwin*, vol. 5: *Of Christ the Mediator*, Eureka: Tanski.

Goppelt, L. (1939), *Typos: Die typologische Deutung des Alten Testaments im Neuen*, Gütersloh: C. Bertelsmann.

—— (1982), *Typos: The Typological Interpretation of the Old Testament in the New*, tr. D. Madvig, Grand Rapids: Eerdmans.

Granowski, J. (1992), 'Jehoiachin at the King's Table: A Reading of the Ending of the Second Book of Kings', in D. N. Fewell (ed.), *Reading Between Texts: Intertextuality and the Hebrew Bible*, Literary Currents in Biblical Interpretation, Louisville: Westminster John Knox, 173–188.

Grant, J. (2004), *The King as Exemplar: The Function of Deuteronomy's Kingship Law in the Shaping of the Book of Psalms*, 17, Atlanta: Society of Biblical Literature, 34–37.

Green, B. (1996), *'What Profit for Us?'*, *Remembering the Story of Joseph*, Lanham: University Press of America.

Greidanus, S. (2007), *Preaching Christ from Genesis: Foundations for Expository Sermons*, Grand Rapids: Eerdmans.

—— (2012), *Preaching Christ from Daniel: Foundations for Expository Sermons*, Grand Rapids: Eerdmans.

Gubler, M. (2005), 'Vom Hunger in der Wüste zum Mahl im Namen Jesu : Essen und Trinken in der Bibel', *Diakonia* 36: 15–19.

Gundersen, D. A. (2015), 'Davidic Hope in Book IV of the Psalter (Psalms 90–106)', PhD diss., The Southern Baptist Theological Seminary.

Gunkel, H. (1901), *The Legends of Genesis*, tr. W. H. Carruth, Chicago: Open Court.

Haenchen, E. (1971), *The Acts of the Apostles*, Louisville: Westminster John Knox.

Hahn, S. W. (2009), *Kinship by Covenant: A Canonical Approach to the Fulfillment of God's Saving Promises*, New Haven: Yale University Press.

Hamilton, J. M. (2003), 'God with Men in the Torah', *WTJ* 65: 113–133.

—— (2006a), *God's Indwelling Presence: The Holy Spirit in the Old and New Testaments*, NAC Studies in Bible and Theology, Nashville: B&H Academic.

—— (2006b), 'The Skull Crushing Seed of the Woman: Inner-Biblical Interpretation of Genesis 3:15', *SBJT* 10.2: 30–54.

—— (2007), 'The Seed of the Woman and the Blessing of Abraham', *TynBul* 58.2: 253–273.

—— (2008), 'Was Joseph a Type of the Messiah? Tracing the Typological Identification between Joseph, David, and Jesus', *SBJT* 12.4: 52–77.

—— (2010), *God's Glory in Salvation Through Judgment: A Biblical Theology*, Wheaton: Crossway.

—— (2012a), 'A Biblical Theology of Motherhood', *Journal of Discipleship and Family Ministry* 2.2: 6–13.

—— (2012b), 'The Typology of David's Rise to Power: Messianic Patterns in the Book of Samuel', *SBJT* 16.2: 4–25.

—— (2014a), *What Is Biblical Theology? A Guide to the Bible's Story, Symbolism, and Patterns*, Wheaton: Crossway.

—— (2014b), *With the Clouds of Heaven*, NSBT 32, Nottingham: Apollos; Downers Grove: InterVarsity Press.

Hamilton, V. (1990), *The Book of Genesis: Chapters 1–17*, NICOT, Grand Rapids: Eerdmans.

—— (1995), *The Book of Genesis: Chapters 18–50*, NICOT, Grand Rapids: Eerdmans.

Hart, I. (1995), 'Genesis 1:1–2:3 as a Prologue to the Book of Genesis', *TynBul* 46.2: 315–336.

Hartman, L. F. (1978), *The Book of Daniel*, AB, Garden City: Doubleday.

Harvey, J. E. (2010), 'Jehoiachin and Joseph: Hope at the Close of the Deuteronomistic History', in R. Heskett and B. Irwin (eds.), *The Bible as a Human Witness to Divine Revelation: Hearing the Word of God*

Through Historically Dissimilar Traditions, LHBOTS 469, New York: T&T Clark, 54–55.

Hasel, G. (1972), *The Remnant: The History and Theology of the Remnant Idea from Genesis to Isaiah*, Berrien Springs: Andrews University Press.

Hays, R. (1989), *Echoes of Scripture in the Letters of Paul*, New Haven: Yale University Press.

—— (2005), *Conversion of the Imagination*, Grand Rapids: Eerdmans.

—— (2006), 'The Canonical Matrix of the Gospels', in S. Barton (ed.), *The Cambridge Companion to the Gospels*, Cambridge: Cambridge University Press, 53–75.

—— (2014), *Reading Backwards: Figural Christology and the Fourfold Gospel Witness*, Waco: Baylor University Press.

—— (2016), *Echoes of Scripture in the Gospels*, Waco: Baylor University Press.

Hays, R., and J. Green (2010), 'The Use of the Old Testament by New Testament Writers', in J. Green (ed.), *Hearing the New Testament: Strategies for Interpretation*, Grand Rapids: Eerdmans, 122–139.

Heal, K. (2002), 'Joseph as a Type of Christ in Syriac Literature', *BYU Studies* 41.1: 29–49.

—— (2008), 'Tradition and Transformation: Genesis 37 and 39 in Early Syriac Sources', PhD diss., University of Birmingham.

Heaton, E. W. (1947), 'The Joseph Saga', *ExpTim* 59: 134–136.

Henry, M. (1935), *Matthew Henry's Commentary on the Whole Bible*, vol. 1, Genesis to Deuteronomy, New York: Fleming H. Revell.

Henze, M. (2012), 'The Use of Scripture in the Book of Daniel', in M. Henze (ed.), *A Companion to Biblical Interpretation in Early Judaism*, Grand Rapids: Eerdmans, 279–307.

Herzog, W. R. (1994), *Parables as Subversive Speech: Jesus as Pedagogue of the Oppressed*, Louisville: Westminster John Knox.

Hester, J. D. (1992), 'Socio-Rhetorical Criticism and the Parable of the Tenants', *JSNT* 45: 27–57.

Hildebrandt, T. (2010), 'A Song of Our Father Abraham: Psalm 105', in S. A. Hunt (ed.), *Perspectives on Our Father Abraham: Essays in Honor of Marvin R. Williamson*, Grand Rapids: Eerdmans, 44–67.

Hoffmeier, J. (1997), 'Joseph', *NIDOTTE* 4: 805–808.

Hollander, H. (1975), 'The Ethical Character of the Patriarch Joseph: A Study in the Ethics of the Testaments of the Twelve Patriarchs', in G. W. E. Nickelsburg Jr (ed.), *Studies on the Testament of Joseph*, SBLSCS 5, Missoula: Scholars Press, 47–104.

—— (1998), 'The Portrayal of Joseph in Hellenistic Jewish and Early Christian Literature', in M. E. Stone and T. A. Bergren (eds.), *Biblical Figures Outside the Bible*, Harrisburg: Trinity Press International, 237–263.

Hood, J. (2011), *The Messiah, His Brothers, and the Nations: Matthew 1:1–7*, LNTS 441, London: T&T Clark.

Hood, J. B., and M. Y. Emerson (2013), 'Summaries of Israel's Story: Reviewing a Compositional Category', *CBR* 11.3: 328–348.

Hoop, R. de (1998), *Genesis 49 in Its Literary and Historical Context*, Leiden: Brill.

Hoskins, P. M. (2006), *Jesus as the Fulfillment of the Temple in the Gospel of John*, PBM, Eugene: Wipf & Stock.

House, P. (2005), 'Examining the Narratives of Old Testament Narrative: An Exploration in Biblical Theology', *WTJ* 67: 229–245.

House, P. R. (1998), *Old Testament Theology*, Downers Grove: IVP Academic.

Huddleston, J. (2012), *Eschatology in Genesis*, FAT 2.57, Tübingen: Mohr Siebeck.

Huddlestun, J. (2002), 'Divestiture, Deception, and Demotion: The Garment Motif in Genesis 37–39', *JSOT* 98: 47–62.

Humphreys, W. L. (1973), 'A Life-Style for Diaspora: A Study of the Tales of Esther and Daniel', *JBL* 92.2: 211–223.

—— (1988), *Joseph and His Family: A Literary Study*, Studies on Personalities of the Old Testament, Columbia: University of South Carolina Press.

Jeska, J. (2001), *Die Geschichte Israels in der Sicht des Lukas. Apg 7,2b–53 und 13,17–25 im Kontext antik-jüdischer Summarien der Geschichte Israels*, FRLANT 195. Göttingen: Vandenhoeck & Ruprecht.

Johnson, L. T. (1992), *The Acts of the Apostles*, SP, Collegeville: Liturgical Press.

—— (2002), *Septuagintal Midrash in the Speeches of Acts*, The Pére Marquette Lecture in Theology 2002, Milwaukee: Marquette University.

Johnson, M. (1969), *The Purpose of Biblical Genealogies*, New York: Cambridge University Press.

Joüon, P., and T. Muraoka (2009), *A Grammar of Biblical Hebrew*, 2nd edn, SB 27, Rome: Gregorian & Biblical Press.

Kaminski, C. (2004), *From Noah to Israel: Realization of the Primaeval Blessing After the Flood*, JSOTSup 413, London: T&T Clark.

Keel, O. (1978), *The Symbolism of the Biblical World: Ancient Near Eastern Iconography and the Book of Psalms*, New York: Seabury.

Keener, C. (2013), *Acts: An Exegetical Commentary 3:1–14:28*, vol. 2, Grand Rapids: Baker.

Keil, C. F., and F. Delitzsch (1989), *The Pentateuch*, tr. J. Martin, Peabody: Hendrickson.

Kennedy, J. (2008), *The Recapitulation of Israel: Use of Israel's History in Matthew 1:1–4:11*, WUNT 2.257, Tübingen: Mohr Siebeck.

Kidner, D. (1967), *Genesis: An Introduction and Commentary*, TOTC 1, London: Tyndale; Downers Grove: InterVarsity Press.

Kilgallen, J. (1976), *The Stephen Speech: A Literary and Redactional Study of Acts 7, 2–53*, AnBib 67, Rome: Biblical Institute Press.

—— (1989), 'The Function of Stephen's Speech (Acts 7, 2–53)', *Bib* 70: 173–193.

Kim, J.-W. (2007), 'Explicit Quotations from Genesis Within the Context of Stephen's Speech in Acts', *Neot* 41.2: 341–360.

Kim, M. M. (2010), 'The Blessing of the Curse: Fulfilling Genesis 1:28 in a Context of Suffering', PhD diss., Wheaton College.

Kline, M. (1972), *The Structure of Biblical Authority*, Grand Rapids: Eerdmans.

—— (2000), *Kingdom Prologue: Genesis Foundations for a Covenantal Worldview*, Overland Park: Two Age.

Kline, M., D. Guthrie and J. A. Motyer (1970), 'Genesis', in D. Guthrie and J. A. Motyer (eds.), *The New Bible Commentary: Revised*, 3rd edn, Leicester: Inter-Varsity Press; Grand Rapids: Eerdmans, 79–114.

Kloppenborg, J. (2006), *The Tenants in the Vineyard: Ideology, Economics, and Agrarian Conflict in Jewish Palestine*, WUNT 195, Tübingen: Mohr Siebeck.

Koester, C. (2001), *Hebrews*, AB, New York: Doubleday.

Kugel, J. (1994), *In Potiphar's House: The Interpretive Life of Biblical Texts*, Cambridge: Harvard University Press.

Labonté, G. G. (1993), 'Genèse 41 et Daniel 2: Question d'origine', in A. S. van der Woude (ed.), *The Book of Daniel in Light of New Findings*, BETL 106, Louven: Leuven University Press, 271–284.

Labuschagne, C. J. (1989), 'The Life Span of the Patriarchs', in A. S. van der Woude (ed.), *New Avenues in the Study of the Old Testament: A Collection of Old Testament Studies Published on the Occasion of the Fiftieth Anniversary of the Oudtestamentisch Werkgezelschap and the Retirement of Prof. Dr. M. J. Mulder*, Leiden: Brill, 121–127.

Lambe, A. J. (1998), 'Genesis 38: Structure and Literary Design', in P. R. Davies and David Clines (eds.), *The World of Genesis: Persons, Places, Perspectives*, London: JSOT Press, 102–120.

Lampe, G. W. H. (1957), 'The Reasonableness of Typology', in G. W. H. Lampe and K. J. Woollcombe (eds.), *Essays on Typology*, SBT 22, Naperville: Alec R. Allenson, 9–38.

Lane, W. (1991), *Hebrews 9–13*, vol. 47b, WBC, Dallas: Word.

Lanier, G. (2013), 'The Rejected Stone in the Parable of the Wicked Tenants: Defending the Authenticity of Jesus' Quotation of Psalm 118:22', *JETS* 56.4: 733–751.

LaSor, W. S., D. A. Hubbard and F. W. Bush (1996), *Old Testament Survey: The Message, Form, and Background of the Old Testament*, Grand Rapids: Eerdmans.

Lee, C.-C. (2009), 'גּים in Genesis 35:11 and the Abrahamic Promise of Blessings for the Nations', *JETS* 52.3: 467–482.

Leeman, J. (2010), *The Church and the Surprising Offense of God's Love: Reintroducing the Doctrines of Church Membership and Discipline*, Wheaton: Crossway.

Leithart, P. (2003), *A Son to Me: An Exposition of 1 & 2 Samuel*, Moscow, Idaho: Canon.

—— (2006), *1 & 2 Kings*, Grand Rapids: Brazos.

—— (2009), *Deep Exegesis: The Mystery of Reading Scripture*, Waco: Baylor University Press.

Lerner, B. D. (1989), 'Joseph the Unrighteous', *Judaism* 38: 278–281.

Levenson, J. (1993), *The Death and Resurrection of the Beloved Son: The Transformation of Child Sacrifice in Judaism and Christianity*, New Haven: Yale University Press.

—— (1997), *Esther: A Commentary*, Louisville: Westminster John Knox, 1997.

—— (2006), *Resurrection and the Restoration of Israel: The Ultimate Victory of the God of Life*, New Haven: Yale University Press.

Link Jr, P. J., and M. Y. Emerson (2017), 'Searching for the Second Adam: Typological Connections Between Adam, Joseph, Mordecai, and Daniel', *SBJT* 21.1: 123–144.

Lints, R. (1993), *The Fabric of Theology: A Prolegomena to Evangelical Theology*, Grand Rapids: Eerdmans.

Loader, J. A. (1974), 'Chokma – Joseph – Hybris', in W. C. van Wyk (ed.), *Studies in the Pentateuch*, Ou Testamentiese Werkgemeenskap in Suid-Afrika 17: 18.

Lockwood, P. F. (1992), 'Tamar's Place in the Joseph Cycle', *Lutheran Theological Quarterly* 26: 35–43.

Lohfink, G. (1966), *Paulus vor Damaskus: Arbeitsweisen der neueren Bibelwissenschaft dargestellt an den Texten Apg 9:1–19, 22:3–21, 26:9–18*, SBS 4, Stuttgart: Katholisches Bibelwerk.

Longacre, R. E. (1989), *Joseph: A Story of Divine Providence: A Text Theoretical and Textlinguistic Analysis of Genesis 37 and 39–48*, Winona Lake: Eisenbrauns.

Longenecker, R. (1975), *Biblical Exegesis in the Apostolic Period*, Grand Rapids: Eerdmans.

Lowenthal, E. (1973), *The Joseph Narrative in Genesis*, New York: KTAV.

Lucas, E. C. (2002), *Daniel*, AOTC 20, Leicester: Apollos; Downers Grove: IVP Academic.

Lunn, N. (2008), 'The Last Words of Jacob and Joseph: A Rhetorico-Structural Analysis of Genesis 49:29–33 and 50:24–26', *TynBul* 59.2: 161–179.

—— (2012), 'Allusions to the Joseph Narrative in the Synoptic Gospels and Acts: Foundations of a Biblical Type', *JETS* 55.1: 27–41.

—— (2014), '"Raised on the Third Day According to the Scriptures": Resurrection Typology in the Genesis Narrative', *JETS* 57.3: 523–535.

Luz, U. (2005), *Matthew 21–28*, Hermeneia 3, Minneapolis: Fortress.

McKenzie, B. A. (1983), 'Jacob's Blessing on Pharaoh: An Interpretation of Gen 46:31–47:26', *WTJ* 45: 386–399.

McMillion, P. (2010), 'Psalm 105: History with a Purpose', *ResQ* 52.3: 167–179.

Mann, T. (1991), '"All the Families of the Earth:" The Theological Unity of Genesis', *Int* 45: 341–353.

Marcus, J. (2009), *Mark 8–16*, AB 27a, New Haven: Yale University Press.

Marshall, I. H. (1983), *Acts: An Introduction and Commentary*, TNTC, Leicester: Inter-Varsity Press.

—— (2007), 'Acts', in G. K. Beale and D. A. Carson (eds.), *Commentary on the New Testament Use of the Old Testament*, Grand Rapids: Baker, 513–606.

Martin, O. (2015), *Bound for the Promised Land: The Land in God's Redemptive Plan*, NSBT 34, Nottingham: Apollos; Downers Grove: InterVarsity Press.

Martín-Asensio, G. (1999), 'Participant Reference and Foregrounded Syntax in the Stephen Episode', in S. Porter and J. T. Reed (eds.), *Discourse Analysis and the New Testament*, JSNTSup 170, London: Sheffield Academic Press, 235–257.

Mathews, D. (2012), *Royal Motifs in the Pentateuchal Portrayal of Moses*, New York: T&T Clark.

Mathews, K. (1996), *Genesis 1–11:26*, NAC 1A, Nashville: B&H.

—— (2000), 'Genesis', *NDBT*, 140–146.

—— (2005), *Genesis 11:27–50:26*, NAC 1B, Nashville: B&H.

Mathews, V. (1995), 'The Anthropology of Clothing in the Joseph Narrative', *JSOT* 65: 25–36.

Mathewson, S. D. (1986), 'The Relationship of Genesis 38 to the Joseph Story', MA thesis, Western Conservative Baptist Seminary.

—— (1989), 'An Exegetical Study of Genesis 38', *BSac* 146: 373–392.

Meek, R. (2014), 'Intertextuality, Inner-Biblical Exegesis, and Inner-Biblical Allusion: The Ethics of a Methodology', *Bib* 95.1: 280–291.

Meinhold, A. (1975), 'Die Gattung der Josephsgeschichte und des Estherbuches: Diasporanovelle, Part I', *ZAW* 87: 306–324.

—— (1976), 'Die Gattung der Josephsgeschichte und des Estherbuches: Diasporanovelle, Part II', *ZAW* 88: 72–93.

Meyer, B. F. (1964), '"But Mary Kept All These Things . . ." (Lk 2:19, 51)', *CBQ* 26.1: 31–49.

Milán, F. (2013), '¿Un Daniel polifónico? El libro de Daniel y la tradición del Antiguo Testamento', *ScrTh* 45: 335–362.

Millar, J. G. (2000), 'Land', *NDBT*, 623–627.

Miller, C. L. (1995), 'Discourse Functions of Quotative Frames in Biblical Hebrew', in W. R. Bodine (ed.), *Discourse Analysis of Biblical Literature: What It Is and What It Offers*, SBLSS, Atlanta: Scholars Press, 155–182.

—— (1996), *The Representation of Speech in Biblical Hebrew Narrative: A Linguistic Analysis*, HSMM, 55, Atlanta: Scholars Press, 51–52, 186, 192–194.

Miscall, P. D. (1978), 'The Jacob and Joseph Story as Analogies', *JSOT* 6: 28–40.

Mitchel, T. C. (1993), 'Shared Vocabulary in the Pentateuch and the Book of Daniel', in R. S. Hess, P. E. Satterthwaite and G. J. Wenham (eds.), *He Swore an Oath: Biblical Themes from Genesis 12–50*, Cambridge: Tyndale House, 131–141.

Mitchell, C. W. (1987), *The Meaning of BRK 'To Bless' in the Old Testament*, SBLDS 95, Atlanta: Scholars Press.

Mitchell, D. C. (2005a), 'The Fourth Deliverer: A Josephite Messiah in 4Q175', *Bib* 86.4: 545–553.

—— (2005b), 'Rabbi Dosa and the Rabbis Differ: Messiah Ben Joseph in the Babylonian Talmud', *RBJ* 8: 77–90.

—— (2006a), 'Firstborn Shor and Rem: A Sacrificial Josephite Messiah in 1 Enoch 90:37–38 and Deuteronomy 33:17', *JSP* 15.3: 211–228.

—— (2006b), 'Messiah Bar Ephraim in the Targums', *AS* 4.2: 221–241.

—— (2007), 'Messiah Ben Joseph: A Sacrifice of Atonement for Israel', *RBJ* 10.1: 77–94.

—— (2009), 'A Josephite Messiah in 4Q372', *JSP* 18.3: 181–205.

—— (2010), 'Messiah Ben Joseph in the Book of Psalms', paper presented at the Inter-Collegiate Senior Old Testament Seminar, University of Oxford.

Moberly, R. W. L. (2007), 'Christ in All the Scriptures? The Challenge of Reading the Old Testament as Christian Scripture', *JTI* 1: 79–100.

Moberly, W. (2009), *The Theology of the Book of Genesis*, Cambridge: Cambridge University Press.

Moessner, D. (1986), '"The Christ Must Suffer": New Light on the Jesus–Peter, Stephen, Paul Parallels in Luke–Acts', *NovT* 28.3: 220–256.

Moo, D. J. (1986), 'The Problem of Sensus Plenior', in D. A. Carson and J. D. Woodbridge (eds.), *Hermeneutics, Authority, and Canon*, Grand Rapids: Acadamie, 179–211.

—— (2007), 'Paul's Universalizing Hermeneutic in Romans', *SBJT* 11.3: 62–90.

—— (2013), Review by The Gospel Coalition of N. T. Wright, *Paul and the Faithfulness of God* <www.thegospelcoalition.org/reviews/paul-faithfulness-god>, accessed 1 February 2022.

Morris, G. (1994), 'Convention and Character in the Joseph Narrative', in T. Callan (ed.), *Proceedings, Eastern Great Lakes and Midwest Biblical Societies* 14, Buffalo: Canisius College, 69–85.

Müller, H. P. (1976), 'Märchen, Legende und Enderwartung: Zum Verständnis des Buches Daniel', *VT* 26: 338–350.

Murmelstein, B. (1932), '*Die Gestalt Josefs in der Agada und die Evangeliengeschichte* [Matt 27:3; John 19:23]', *Angelos* 4: 51–55.

Naselli, A. (2012), *From Typology to Doxology: Paul's Use of Isaiah and Job in Romans 11:34–35*, Eugene: Wipf & Stock.

Nel, M. (2002), 'Daniel 1 as Wysheidsliteratuur: Bevestiging van die Vergeldingsleer', *OTE* 15.3: 780–798.

Neudorfer, H.-W. (1998), 'The Speech of Stephen', in I. Howard Marshall and David Peterson (eds.), *Witness to the Gospel*, Grand Rapids: Eerdmans, 275–294.

Neufeld, E. (1994), 'The Anatomy of the Joseph Cycle', *JBQ* 22.1: 38–46.

Niditch, S., and R. Doran (1977), 'The Success Story of the Wise Courtier: A Formal Approach', *JBL* 96.2: 179–193.

Niehoff, M. (1992), *The Figure of Joseph in Post-Biblical Jewish Literature*, Leiden: Brill.

Nolan, B. (1979), *The Royal Son of God: The Christology of Matthew 1–2 in the Setting of the Gospel*, OBO 23, Göttingen: Vandenhoeck & Ruprecht.

O'Brien, M. (1997), 'The Contribution of Judah's Speech, Genesis 44:18–34, to the Characterization of Joseph', *CBQ* 59: 429–447.

—— (2010), *The Letter to the Hebrews*, PNTC, Grand Rapids: Eerdmans.

O'Brien, P. (2012), *The Letter to the Hebrews*, PNTC, Grand Rapids: Eerdmans.

O'Keefe, J., and R. R. Reno (2005), *Sanctified Vision: An Introduction to Early Christian Interpretation of the Bible*, Baltimore: Johns Hopkins University Press.

Olojede, F. (2012), 'Sapiential Elements in the Joseph and Daniel Narratives vis-à-vis Woman Wisdom – Conjunctions and Disjunctions', *OTE* 25.2: 351–368.

Owen, J. (1965), *The Works of John Owen*, vol. 2: *Communion with God*, Edinburgh: Banner of Truth.

—— (1994), *Biblical Theology or the Nature, Origin, Development, and Study of Theological Truth in Six Books*, Pittsburgh: Soli Deo Gloria.

Paap, C. (1995), Die Josephsgeschichte, Genesis 37–50: *Bestimmungen ihrer literarischen Gattung in der zweiten Hälfte des 20. Jahrhunderts*, Europäische Hochschulschriften, 23, Theologie, 534, Frankfurt am Main: P. Lang.

Pao, D. (2000), *Acts and the Isaianic New Exodus*, Grand Rapids: Baker Academic.

Parker, B. E. (2011), 'The Nature of Typology and Its Relationship to Competing Views of Scripture', paper presented at the annual meeting of the Evangelical Theological Society, San Francisco, California.

—— (2017), 'The Israel–Christ–Church Typological Pattern: A Theological Critique of Covenant and Dispensational Theologies', PhD diss., The Southern Baptist Theological Seminary.

Parsons, M. (2008), *Acts*, PCNT, Grand Rapids: Baker.

Patterson, R. (1993), 'Holding on to Daniel's Court Tales', *JETS* 36.4: 445–454.

—— (2007), 'Joseph in Pharaoh's Court', *BSac* 164: 148–164.

Patterson, T. (2003), 'The Righteousness and Survival of the Seed: The Role of Plot in the Exegesis and Theology of Genesis', PhD diss., Trinity International University.

Patton, M. (2014), 'Hope for a Tender Sprig: Jehoiachin in Biblical Theology', PhD diss., Wheaton College.

Payne, B. (2008), 'The Summing up of All Things in Christ and the Restoration of Human Viceregency: Implications for Ecclesiology', PhD diss., The Southern Baptist Theological Seminary.

Penner, T. (2004), *In Praise of Christian Origins: Stephen and the Hellenists in Lukan Apologetic Historiography*, ESEC 10, New York: T&T Clark.

Pennington, J. (2012), *Reading the Gospels Wisely: A Narrative and Theological Introduction*, Grand Rapids: Baker.

Pervo, R. (2009), *Acts*, Hermeneia, Minneapolis: Fortress.

Pesch, R. (1976), *Das Markusevangelium*, HTKNT 2, Freiburg: Herder.

Peterson, B. (2014), 'Stephen's Speech as a Modified Prophetic RÎB Formula', *JETS* 57.2: 351–369.

Peterson, D. G. (2009), *The Acts of the Apostles*, PNTC, Grand Rapids: Eerdmans.

Philpot, J. (2018), 'Was Joseph a Type of Daniel? Typological Correspondence in Genesis 37–50 and Daniel 1–6', *JETS* 61.4: 681–696.

Pink, A. W. (1922), *Gleanings in Genesis*, Chicago: Moody.

Pirson, R. (2001), 'The Sun, the Moon and Eleven Stars: An Interpretation of Joseph's Second Dream', in A. Wénin (ed.), *Studies in the Book of Genesis: Literature, Redaction and History*, BETL 155, Leuven: Leuven University Press, 561–568.

—— (2002), *The Lord of the Dreams: A Semantic and Literary Analysis of Genesis 37–50*, JSOTSup 355, Sheffield: Sheffield Academic Press.

Polhill, J. (1992), *Acts*, NAC, Nashville: B&H.

Rad, G. von, (1953), 'Josephsgeschichte und ältere Chokma', VTSup 1, G. W. Anderson et al. (eds.), Leiden: Brill, 120–127.

—— (1963), *Old Testament Theology*, vol. 2, New York: Harper & Row.

—— (1966), 'The Joseph Narrative and Ancient Wisdom', in E. W. Trueman Dicken (tr.), *The Problem of the Hexateuch and Other Essays*, New York: McGraw-Hill, 292–300.

—— (1972), *Genesis: A Commentary*, tr. J. H. Marks, OTL, Philadelphia: Westminster Press.

Redford, D. B. (1970), *A Study of the Biblical Story of Joseph*, VTSup 20, Leiden: Brill.

Reese, R. A. (2015), 'Joseph Remembered the Exodus: Memory, Narrative, and Remembering the Future', *JTI* 9.2: 267–286.

Reno, R. R. (2010), *Genesis*, BTCB, Grand Rapids: Brazos.

Ribbens, B. (2011), 'A Typology of Types: Typology in Dialogue', *JTI* 5: 81–96.

Richard, E. (1979), 'The Polemical Character of the Joseph Episode in Acts 7', *JBL* 98.2: 255–267.

Richardson, C. A. (2012), *Pioneer and Perfecter of Faith*, WUNT 2.338, Tübingen: Mohr Siebeck.

Rindge, M. (2010), 'Jewish Identity Under Foreign Rule: Daniel 2 as a Reconfiguration of Genesis 41', *JBL* 129.1: 85–104.

Robertson, O. P. (2000), *The Israel of God: Yesterday, Today, and Tomorrow*, Phillipsburg: P&R.

Römer, T. (1997), 'Transformations in Deuteronomistic and Biblical Historiography: On "Book-Finding" and Other Literary Strategies', *ZAW* 109: 1–12.

—— (2005), *The So-Called Deuteronomistic History: A Sociological, Historical, and Literary Introduction*, London: T&T Clark.

Römer, T., and J. Rückl (2009), 'Jesus, Son of Joseph and Son of David, in the Gospels', in M. Tait and P. Oakes (eds.), *Torah in the New Testament: Papers Delivered at the Manchester-Lausanne Seminar of June 2008*, LNTS 401, London: T&T Clark, 65–81.

Roncace, M. (2005), *Jeremiah, Zedekiah, and the Fall of Jerusalem*, New York: T&T Clark.

Ronning, J. L. (1997), 'The Curse on the Serpent (Genesis 3:15) in Biblical Theology and Hermeneutics', PhD diss., Westminster Theological Seminary.

Rosenthal, L. (1895), 'Die Josephgeschichte, mit den Büchern Ester und Daniel verglichen', *ZAW* 15: 278–284.

Rosner, B. (2000), 'Biblical Theology', *NDBT*, 3–11.

Ross, A. P. (1996), *Creation and Blessing: A Guide to the Study and Exposition of Genesis*, Grand Rapids: Baker.

Ruppert, L. (1965), *Die Josephserzählung der Genesis: Ein Beitrag zur Theologie der Pentateuchquellen*, SANT, München: Kösel-Verlag.

Ruprecht, E. (1979), 'Der traditionsgeschichtliche Hintergrund der einzelnen Elemente von Gen 12:2–3', *VT* 29: 444–464.

Sailhamer, J. (1992), *The Pentateuch as Narrative: A Biblical-Theological Commentary*, Grand Rapids: Zondervan.

Sarna, N. M. (1966), *Understanding Genesis*, New York: Schocken.

—— (1972), 'Bible: The Canon, Text, and Editions', EJ, Jerusalem: Encyclopaedia Judaica.

—— (2008), *New Testament Theology: Magnifying God in Christ*, Grand Rapids: Baker Academic.

Sasson, J. M. (1978), 'A Genealogical "Convention" in Biblical Chronography?', *ZAW* 90: 171–185.

Schlimm, M. R. (2011), *From Fratricide to Forgiveness: The Language and Ethics of Anger in Genesis*, Siphrut 7, Winona Lake: Eisenbrauns.

Schmid, K. (1999), *Erzväter und Exodus: Untersuchungen zur doppelten Begründung der Ursprünge Israels innerhalb der Geschichtsbücher des Alten Testaments*, WMANT 81, Neukirchen-Vluyn, Germany: Neukirchener Verlag.

Schnabel, E. (2012), *Acts*, ZECNT 5, Grand Rapids: Zondervan.

Schreiner, T. R. (1998), *Romans*, BECNT, Grand Rapids: Baker Academic.

—— (2013), *The King in His Beauty: A Biblical Theology of the Old and New Testaments*, Grand Rapids: Baker.

—— (2015), *Commentary on Hebrews*, BTCP, Nashville: B&H Academic.

Schrock, D. (2014), 'What Designates a Valid Type? A Christotelic, Covenantal Proposal', *STR* 5.1: 3–26.

Scullion, J. J. (1992), 'Genesis, the Narrative of', *ABD*, New York: Doubleday.

Segal, M. (2009), 'From Joseph to Daniel: The Literary Development of the Narrative in Daniel 2', *VT* 59: 123–149.

Seitz, C. (2001), *Figured Out: Typology and Providence in Christian Scripture*, Louisville: Westminster John Knox.

Sequeira, A., and S. Emadi (2017), 'Biblical Theological Exegesis and the Nature of Typology', *SBJT* 21.1: 11–34.

Seybold, D. (1974), 'Paradox and Symmetry in the Joseph Narrative', in K. R. R. Gros Louis, J. S. Ackerman and T. Warshaw (eds.), *Literary Interpretations of Biblical Narratives*, Nashville: Abingdon, 57–93.

Shepherd, M. (2009), *Daniel in the Context of the Hebrew Bible*, Studies in Biblical Literature 123, New York: Peter Lang.

Sigmon, B. (2011), 'Shadowing Jacob's Journey: Gen 47:13–26 as a Sideshow', *BibInt* 19: 454–470.

—— (2013), 'Between Eden and Egypt: Echoes of the Garden Narrative in the Story of Joseph and His Brothers', PhD diss., Marquette University.

Sleeman, M. (2009), *Geography and the Ascension Narrative in Acts*, SNTSMS 146, Cambridge: Cambridge University Press.

Smith, B. (2002), 'The Presentation of Judah in Genesis 37–50 and Its Implications for the Narrative's Structural and Thematic Unity', PhD diss., Bob Jones University.

—— (2005), 'The Central Role of Judah in Genesis 37–50', *BSac* 162: 158–174.

Smith, G. (1977), 'Structure and Purpose of Genesis 1–11', *JETS* 20.4: 307–319.

Smothers, T. G. (1964), 'The Joseph Narrative and Wisdom', PhD diss., The Southern Baptist Theological Seminary.

Snodgrass, K. (1983), *The Parable of the Wicked Tenants: An Inquiry into Parable Interpretation*, WUNT 2.27, Tübingen: Mohr Siebeck.

—— (1998), 'Recent Research on the Parable of the Wicked Tenants: An Assessment', *BBR* 8: 187–216.

—— (2008), *Stories with Intent: A Comprehensive Guide to the Parables of Jesus*, Grand Rapids: Eerdmans.

Sparks, K. L. (2008), *God's Word in Human Words: An Evangelical Appropriation of Critical Biblical Scholarship*, Grand Rapids: Baker.

Speiser, E. A. (1964), *Genesis*, vol. 1, AB, Garden City: Doubleday.

Sprinkle, P. (2007), 'The Use of Gen 42:18 (Not Leviticus 18:5) in Luke 10:28: Joseph and the Good Samaritan', *BBR* 17.2: 193–205.

Spurgeon, C. (1899), *Christ in the Old Testament: Sermons on the Foreshadowing of Our Lord in Old Testament History*, London: Passmore & Alabaster.

Squires, J. T. (1993), *The Plan of God in Luke-Acts*, SNTSMS 76, Cambridge: Cambridge University Press.

Steinmann, A. (2008), *Daniel*, Concordia Commentary, St Louis: Concordia.

Sternberg, M. (1985), *The Poetics of Biblical Narrative: Ideological Literature and the Drama of Reading*, Bloomington: Indiana University Press.

Stevenson, K., and M. Glerup (eds.) (2008), *Ezekiel, Daniel*, ACCS 13, Downers Grove: InterVarsity Press.

Stone, T. J. (2012), 'Joseph in the Likeness of Adam: Narrative Echoes of the Fall', in N. MacDonald, M. Elliot and G. Macaskill (eds.), *Genesis and Christian Theology*, Grand Rapids: Eerdmans, 62–73.

Stott, J. R. W. (1990), *The Message of Acts*, BST, Leicester: Inter-Varsity Press; Downers Grove: InterVarsity Press.

Sweeney, J. P. (2002), 'Stephen's Speech (Acts 7:2–53): Is It as "Anti-Temple" as Is Frequently Alleged?', *TJ* 23: 185–210.

Talmon, S. (1963), '"Wisdom" In the Book of Esther', *VT* 13.4: 419–455.

Thomas, M. (2011), *These Are the Generations: Identity, Covenant, and the Toledot Formula*, LHBOTS, New York: T&T Clark.

Thompson, A. (2011), *The Acts of the Risen Lord Jesus: Luke's Account of God's Unfolding Plan*, NSBT 27, Nottingham: Apollos; Downers Grove: InterVarsity Press.

Treat, J. (2014), *The Crucified King: Atonement and Kingdom in Biblical and Systematic Theology*, Grand Rapids: Zondervan.

Treier, D. (2008), *Introducing Theological Interpretation of Scripture: Recovering a Christian Practice*, Grand Rapids: Baker Academic.

Turner, L. A. (1990), *Announcements of Plot in Genesis*, JSOTSup 96, London: JSOT Press.

Van Groningen, G. (1990), *Messianic Revelation in the Old Testament*, Grand Rapids: Baker, 1990.

Vanhoozer, K. J. (2005), 'Introduction: What Is the Theological Interpretation of the Bible?', in K. J. Vanhoozer (ed.), *Dictionary for Theological Interpretation of the Bible*, Grand Rapids: Baker, 2005.

Van Seters, A. (1965), 'The Use of the Story of Joseph in Scripture', PhD diss., Union Theological Seminary.

Vos, G. (1975), *Biblical Theology of the Old and New Testaments*, Edinburgh: Banner of Truth.

Wahl, H. M. (1999), 'Die Sprache des hebräischen Esterbuches. Anmerkungen zu seinem historischen und traditionsgeschichtlichen Referenzrahmen', *ZAH* 12.1: 21–47.

—— (2000), 'Das Motiv des "Aufstiegs" in der Hofgeschichte: Am Beispiel von Joseph, Esther und Daniel', *ZAW* 112: 59–74.

Walsh, J. T. (2001), *Style and Structure in Biblical Hebrew Narrative*, Collegeville: Liturgical Press.

Waltke, B. K. (2001), *Genesis: A Commentary*, Grand Rapids: Zondervan.

—— (2007), *An Old Testament Theology*, Grand Rapids: Zondervan.

Walton, J. (2003), 'Eden, Garden of', *DOTP*, 202–207.

Warning, W. (2000), 'Terminological Patterns and Genesis 38', *AUSS* 38.2: 293–305.

—— (2001), 'Terminological Patterns and Genesis 39', *JETS* 44.3: 409–419.

Watt, T. (1995), 'Joseph's Dreams', in D. L. Miller (ed.), *Jung and the Interpretation of the Bible*, New York: Continuum, 55–70.

Weihs, A. (2000), 'Die Eifersucht der Winzer: Zur Anspielung auf LXX Gen. 37,20 in der Parabel von der Tötung des Sohnes (Mk. 12, 1–12)', *ETL* 76.1: 5–29.

Weimar, P. (1974), 'Die Toledot-Formel in der priesterschriftlichen Geschichtsdarstellung', *BZ* 18.1: 65–93.

Wenham, G. J. (1987), *Genesis 1–15*, WBC, Dallas: Word.

—— (1994a), *Genesis 16–50*, WBC, Dallas: Word.

—— (1994b), 'Sanctuary Symbolism in the Garden of Eden Story', in R. Hess and D. T. Tsumura (eds.), *I Studied Inscriptions from Before the Flood: Ancient Near Eastern, Literary, and Linguistic Approaches to Genesis 1–11*, Sources for Biblical and Theological Study, Winona Lake: Eisenbrauns, 399–404.

—— (1999), 'Pondering the Pentateuch: The Search for a New Paradigm', in D. W. Baker and B. T. Arnold (eds.), *The Face of Old Testament Studies: A Survey of Contemporary Approaches*, Grand Rapids: Baker, 116–144.

—— (2000), *Story as Torah: Reading the Old Testament Ethically*, Edinburgh: T&T Clark.

—— (2012), *Psalms as Torah: Reading Biblical Song Ethically*, Grand Rapids: Baker.

Wénin, A. (2000), 'Promise and Fulfillment: The Territorial Inheritance', in P. Johnston and P. W. L. Walker (eds.), *The Land of Promise: Biblical, Theological, and Contemporary Perspectives*, Downers Grove: IVP Academic, 15–34.

Weren, W. J. C. (1998), 'The Use of Isaiah 5, 1–7 in the Parable of the Tenants (Mark 12, 1–2; Matthew 21:33–46)', *Bib* 79: 1–26.

Wesselius, J.-W. (1999), 'Discontinuity, Congruence and the Making of the Hebrew Bible', *SJOT* 13.1: 24–77.

—— (2005), 'The Literary Nature of the Book of Daniel and the Linguistic Character of Its Aramaic', *AS* 3.2: 241–283.

Wessels, J. P. H. (1984), 'The Joseph Story as a Wisdom Novelette', *OTE* 2: 39–60.

Westermann, C. (1982), *Genesis 37–50*, tr. J. J. Scullion, Minneapolis: Augsburg.

Wheaton, B. (2008), 'As It Is Written: Old Testament Foundations for Jesus' Expectation of Resurrection', *WTJ* 70: 245–253.

White, H. C. (1991), *Narration and Discourse in the Book of Genesis*, Cambridge: Cambridge University Press.

Whitenton, M. R. (2012), 'Rewriting Abraham and Joseph: Stephen's Speech (Acts 7:2–16) and Jewish Exegetical Traditions', *NovT* 54: 149–167.

Widder, W. (2014), 'The Court Stories of Joseph (Gen 41) and Daniel (Dan 2) in Canonical Context: A Theological Paradigm for God's Work Among the Nations', *OTE* 27.3: 1112–1128.

Wiens, D. (1995), *Stephen's Sermon and the Structure of Luke-Acts*, North Richland Hills: Bibal.

Wifall, W. (1974), 'Gen 3:15 – a Protoevangelium?', *CBQ* 36.3: 361–365.

Wilcox, M. (1987), 'The Bones of Joseph: Hebrews 11:22', in B. Thompson (ed.), *Scripture: Meaning and Method, Essays Presented to Anthony Tyrrell Hanson for His Seventieth Birthday*, Hull: Hull University Press, 114–130.

Wildavsky, A. (1993), *Assimilation Versus Separation: Joseph the Administrator and the Politics of Religion in Biblical Israel*, New Brunswick: Transaction.

Wilder, W. N. (2006), 'Illumination and Investiture: The Royal Significance of the Tree of Wisdom in Genesis 3', *WTJ* 68: 51–69.

Wilken, R. L. (1998), 'In Defense of Allegory', *MTh* 14.2: 197–212.

Williams, P. J. (1998), 'The LXX of 1 Chronicles 5:1–2 as an Exposition of Genesis 48–49', *TynBul* 49.2: 369–371.

Williamson, P. R. (2000a), *Abraham, Israel, and the Nations: The Patriarchal Promise and Its Covenantal Development in Genesis*, JSOTSup, Sheffield: Sheffield Academic Press.

—— (2000b), 'Promise and Fulfillment: The Territorial Inheritance', in P. Johnston and P. W. L. Walker (eds.), *The Land of Promise: Biblical, Theological, and Contemporary Perspectives*, Downers Grove: IVP Academic, 15–34.

Wills, L. (1990), *The Jew in the Court of the Foreign King: Ancient Jewish Court Legends*, HDR 26, Minneapolis: Fortress.

Wilson, L. (2004), *Joseph Wise and Otherwise: The Intersection of Wisdom and Covenant in Genesis 37–50*, Carlisle: Paternoster Press.

—— (2010), 'On Psalms 103–106 as a Closure to Book IV of the Psalter', in E. Zenger (ed.), *Composition of the Book of Psalms*, Walpole: Peeters, 755–766.

Wilson, R. R. (1975), 'The Old Testament Genealogies in Recent Research', *JBL* 94: 169–189.

Winslow, O. (1863), *The Fulness of Christ as Unfolded in the Typical History of the Patriarch Joseph*, London: John F. Shaw.

Wiseman, P. J. (1985), *Ancient Records and the Structure of Genesis*, Nashville: Nelson.

Witherington III, B. (1998), *The Acts of the Apostles: A Socio-Rhetorical Commentary*, Grand Rapids: Eerdmans.

Wolff, H. W. (1974), 'The Kerygma of the Yahwist', in W. Brueggemann and H. W. Wolff (eds.), *The Vitality of Old Testament Traditions*, 2nd edn, Atlanta: John Knox, 41–66.

Woudstra, M. (1970), 'The Toledot of the Book of Genesis and Their Redemptive-Historical Significance', *CTJ* 5: 185–189.

Wright, C. J. H. (1997), 'אב', *NIDOTTE* 1: 219–223.

Wright, G. R. H. (1982), 'The Positioning of Genesis 38', *ZAW* 94: 523–529.

Wright, N. T. (1997), *Jesus and the Victory of God*, vol. 2: *Christian Origins and the Question of God*, Minneapolis: Fortress.

Young, F. (1997), *Biblical Exegesis and the Formation of Christian Culture*, Cambridge: Cambridge University Press.

Youngho, K. (1991), 'Judah's Role in Joseph's (?) Story', ThM thesis, Covenant Theological Seminary.

Index of authors

Ahearne-Kroll, S. P., 142
Albright, W. F., 3, 7
Alexander, T. D., 8, 10, 16, 44–47,
    54–56, 62, 63, 68, 78, 96
Allison Jr, D. C., 142
Alter, R., 3, 12, 57, 71, 72, 130
Anderson, G. A., 14
Argyle, A. W., 2, 6
Arnold, B. T., 8, 9, 34, 35, 39, 40, 42,
    48, 90
Astruc, J., 7

Bailey, N. A., 40
Baker, D. W., 53
Barber, M., 104
Beale, G. K., 20, 24, 26, 27, 29, 45–47,
    64–66, 71, 83, 93, 119, 125
Beckerleg, C., 45
Beetham, C., 45
Berg, S. B., 13, 116, 117
Berkhof, L., 26
Bezalel, N., 13, 108
Blomberg, C. L., 142
Bock, D., 131, 134, 135, 136
Braun, H., 130, 131
Breck, J., 85
Brodie, T., 79
Bronn, W., 140
Brown, R., 140
Brueggemann, W., 8, 9, 42, 43, 52, 72
Bruno, C., 124
Burns, D. G., 130

Calvin, J., 6, 43
Carrol, R., 35
Carson, D. A., xii, 21, 29

Cassuto, U., 32, 43, 57
Chan, M., 12, 116, 117, 119
Chase, M., 97, 103, 136
Childs, B. S., 1, 8, 9, 38, 44, 147
Christensen, D. L., 54
Ciampa, R. E., 98
Clark, W. M., 94
Coats, G. W., 1, 9, 41, 43, 106
Collins, J. J., 13, 108, 117
Conzelmann, H., 122, 134
Coxe, N., 148
Currid, J. D., 29, 69
Curtis, E., 43

Dahlberg, B. T., 10, 11, 79, 94
Davidson, R., 21
Davies, P. R., 13, 108, 142
Delitzsch, F., 16
Dempster, S. G., 11, 25, 35, 42, 45–47,
    62, 64, 65, 72, 74, 83, 84, 89, 92, 97,
    116
DeRouchie, J., 31–33, 36, 65
Diffey, D. S., 49, 50, 51
Dillard, R. B., 41
Donahue, J. R., 143
Doran, R., 117
Dorsey, D. A., x, 85
Dumbrell, W. J., 35, 45, 68

Edwards, J., 6
Ellingworth, P., 138
Emadi, M. H., 49
Emadi, S., vii, xii, 19, 39,
Emerson, M. Y., 116, 123
Emerton, J. A., 43
Evans, C., 142

Fairbairn, P., 21
Fishbane, M., 39
Fitzmyer, J. A., 133, 134
Fokkelman, J. P., 39, 43
Fortner, J. L., 2
France, R. T., 24, 141
Frei, H., 21
Fretheim, T. E., 54
Frieden, K., 13, 108
Fuller, A., 6, 45
Fung, Y., 42, 67

Gan, M., 13, 108, 116
Garrett, D., 7, 31, 41, 92
Gathercole, S., 98, 99
Gentry, P. J., ix, 23, 28, 29, 45–48, 72, 88, 115, 148
Gignilliat, M., 22
Glerup, M., 108
Gnilka, J., 142
Gnuse, R., 13, 108, 109
Goldin, J., 43
Goldingay, J., 108, 110, 115
Goligher, L., 42
Gonzales Jr, R. R., 42, 47, 53, 79
Goodwin, T., 6
Goppelt, L., 21
Granowski, J., 12, 116, 119
Grant, J., 104
Green, B., 53
Greidanus, S., 15, 108
Gubler, M., 141
Gundersen, D. A., 104
Gunkel, H., 7, 9

Haenchen, E., 122
Hahn, S. W., 47, 49
Hamilton, J. M., ix, 12–15, 19, 20, 35, 47, 49, 62, 66, 78, 89, 103, 104, 108, 109, 113–115, 118, 135, 140, 142, 144
Hamilton, V., 2, 32, 48, 53, 54, 56, 68, 70, 84, 85
Harrington, D. J., 143

Hartman, L. F., 108
Hasel, G., 70
Harvey, J. E., 12, 116, 117
Hays, R., 21, 22, 142, 144, 145
Heaton, E. W., 69
Henry, M., 6
Henze, M., 108
Hoffmeier, J., 41
Hollander, H., 121
Hood, J. B., 123, 124
Hoop, R. de, 7
House, P. R., 41, 104
Huddleston, J., 81
Humphreys, W.L., 43, 117

Johnson, L. T., 33, 137

Kaminski, C, 37, 40, 76, 77
Keel, O., 80, 97
Keil, C. F., 16
Kennedy, J., 141
Kidner, D., 16, 41
Kim, M. M., 66
Kline, M., 45, 92, 96
Kloppenborg, J., 142, 144
Koester, C., 138
Kugel, J. L., 1, 43

Labonté, G. G., 13, 108, 109
Labuschagne, C. J., 56
Lambe, A. J., 43
Lampe, G. W. H., 2
Lane, W., 138
Lanier, G., 142
LaSor, W. S., 41
Lee, C. C., 68
Leeman, J., 45
Leithart, P., 12, 85
Lerner, B. D., 42
Levenson, J., 3, 13, 14, 96, 97, 99, 116
Link Jr, P. J., 116
Lints, R., 26
Loader, J. A., 41

Index of authors

Lockwood, P. F., 43
Longacre, R. E., 1
Longman, T., 41
Lowenthal, E., 53, 54
Lucas, E. C., 113
Lunn, N., 15, 85–87, 97, 131, 140, 142, 143
Luz, U., 142

McKenzie, B. A., 42, 91, 92
Marshall, I. H., 2, 134, 136
Martin, O., 83
Martín-Asensio, G., 132
Mathews, D., 12
Mathews, K., 2, 68, 70, 78
Mathews, V., 53, 79, 81
Mathewson, S. D., 43
Meinhold, A., 13, 108
Meyer, B. F., 140
Milán, F., 13, 108
Millar, J. G., 84
Miller, C. L., 65
Miscall, P. D., 41, 67
Mitchell, C. W., 80, 121
Moberly, R. W. L., 22
Moo, D. J., 20, 95
Morris, G., 13, 108, 117
Müller, H. P., 117
Murmelstein, B., 140

Naselli, A., 29
Nel, M., 13, 108
Niditch, S., 117
Niehoff, M., 5

O'Brien, M., 138
O'Keefe, J., 5
Olojede, F., 13, 108
Owen, J., 6, 148

Paap, C., 7
Pao, D., 127
Parker, B. E., 21, 25

Parsons, M., 130
Patterson, R., 11, 16, 117
Patton, M., 12, 116
Payne, B., 45
Pennington, J., 142
Pervo, R., 130
Pesch, R., 142
Peterson, B., 131
Philpot, J., 108, 109, 115
Pink, A. W., 6
Pirson, R., 41, 42, 53, 54–56, 61, 67, 80

Rad, G. von, 7–9, 13, 35, 41, 43, 119
Redford, D. B., 7, 8, 44, 57, 108
Reno, R. R., 5, 16
Richardson, C. A., 139
Rindge, M., 13, 108, 109, 112, 115
Robertson, O. P., 84
Römer, T., 12, 116, 140
Roncace, M., 12
Ronning, J. L., 47, 79
Rosenthal, L., 13, 108, 116, 117
Rosner, B., 19
Ross, A. P., 85
Rückl, J., 140
Ruppert, L., 12
Ruprecht, E., 48

Sailhamer, J., 11, 61, 62, 74, 87, 90
Sarna, N. M., 43, 116
Sasson, J. M., 40
Schmid, K., 116
Schnabel, E., 127, 131, 134, 136
Schreiner, T. R., ix, 25, 41, 134, 138
Schrock, D., x, 14, 15, 21, 27–29
Scullion, J. J., 41, 172
Segal, M., 13, 108
Sequeira, A., x, 19, 54
Shepherd, M., 13, 61, 62, 108
Sigmon, B., 11, 76, 78–80, 94, 130
Sleeman, M., 127
Smith, B., 7, 41–43, 47, 57–60, 70, 71, 73

Smothers, T. G., 41
Snodgrass, K., 142
Sparks, K. L., 23
Speiser, E. A., 3
Sprinkle, P., 140
Spurgeon, C., 6
Steinmann, A., 113
Sternberg, M., 42
Stevenson, K., 108
Stone, T. J., 10, 11, 15, 62, 76, 79, 90, 94

Talmon, S., 13
Thomas, M., 31–33, 37, 74
Thompson, A., 121, 125, 127, 128, 136, 137
Treat, J., 19, 25, 45–47, 96, 97
Treier, D., 21
Turner, L. A., 66

Van Groningen, G., 16
Vanhoozer, K. J., 21
Van Seters, A., 2, 12, 14, 116

Wahl, H. M., 13, 108
Walsh, J. T., 85
Waltke, B. K., 16, 42, 52, 87, 89
Walton, J., 45
Watt, T., 42, 92
Weihs, A., 142, 144

Weimar, P., 32
Wellum, S., ix, 23, 29, 45–48, 88, 148
Wenham, G. J., 7, 16, 39, 41, 42, 45, 48, 49, 56, 62, 69–71, 73, 86, 92, 104
Wénin, A., 41
Wesselius, J. W., 13, 108, 109
Wessels, J. P. H., 41
Westermann, C., 2, 3, 5, 9, 11–14, 42, 52, 53, 62, 69, 72, 101
Wheaton, B., 97
White, H. C., 72
Whitenton, M. R., 130
Widder, W., 13, 108, 115
Wifall, W., 47
Wildavsky, A., 42
Wilder, W. N., 52
Wilken, R. L., 22
Williamson, P. R., 68, 84
Wills, L., 117
Wilson, L., 10, 41–43, 53, 70–72, 74, 75, 79, 85, 130
Wilson, R. R., 80
Winslow, O., 6
Wolff, H. W., 35, 89
Wright, C. J. H., 141
Wright, G. R. H., 43
Wright, N. T., 68, 124

Young, F., 5

Index of Scripture references

OLD TESTAMENT

Genesis
1 45, 56
1 - 2 24, 45, 46, 93
1 - 3 84
1 - 11 10, 85, 89
1 - 36 99
1:1 73
1:1 - 2:3 32, 65
1:1 - 11:9 34
1:2 84
1:22 76
1:26–28 45, 46, 65
1:28 33, 34, 47, 51, 65, 66, 76, 77, 88, 93, 96, 102
2 46
2 - 3 94
2 - 4 11
2:3 88
2:4 31, 32, 34, 36
2:4 - 4:26 32
2:9, 17 94
2:15 46
3 5, 11, 46, 65, 76, 78, 89, 94
3 - 11 35, 45, 55
3:1–7 32
3:4 94
3:5, 22 94
3:14 88, 89
3:14, 17 35

3:14–19 35, 88
3:15 10, 32–34, 46, 47, 63, 64, 66, 78, 79, 96, 97
3:16 66, 88
3.17 89, 94
3:17–19 69, 84, 88
3:21 94
3:24 84
4 78–80
4:1–16 32
4:1–26 69
4:4–5 79
4:8 79, 80
4:11 35, 80, 88, 89
4:12–16 84
4:26 32
5:1 31, 32, 34
5:1–3 45
5:1 - 6:8 32
5:21–24 40
5:29 35, 47, 84, 89
6 - 8 97
6:1–7 32
6:9 31, 32, 34
6:9 - 9:29 69
6:19–20 70
7:3 70
7:6 87
8:17 76
9:1 47, 51, 66, 76, 77
9:4–6 80
9:7 47, 51, 66, 76, 77, 102

9:16–17 47
9:25 35, 88, 89
10 74
10:1 31, 34
10:1 - 11:9 32
10:5 35, 89
10:18, 20, 31 35
10:32 31, 35
11 35
11:4 35
11:10 31, 32, 34
11:10–26 32
11:27 31, 34
11:27 - 25:11 32
12 48, 50, 66, 84, 106
12 - 36 9, 10, 55, 85
12:1–2 48
12:1–3 35, 47, 48, 55, 89
12:2 35, 48, 49, 66, 72, 89
12:2–3 28, 48, 90, 102
12:3 34, 48, 89, 91, 92
12:4 72
12:7–8 106
12:10 70
12:10–20 69, 84, 87, 114
12:15, 16 87
12:17 106
12:38 87
13:1, 2, 7, 18 87

14 48
15 49, 50
15:1–21 70
15:7, 18–21 84
15:13–16 138
16 94
16:2 66
16:10 76, 77
17 49, 50, 51
17:1 50
17:1–21 70
17:2 49, 66, 76, 77
17:3 87
17:4 68
17:5 50
17:6 48–50, 56, 66, 76, 77, 106
17:7 50
17:8 49, 50, 66, 87
17:16 48–50, 56, 66, 68
17:18 84
17:19 50
17:20 50, 76
17:21 50
18 89
18:16–33 89
20 49, 89, 106
20:6, 7 106
20:14, 17 89
21 53
21:2, 7 53
21:16 79
21:22–34 49
21:32–33 71
22 93, 96, 97, 114

183

Genesis (cont.)
22:1–18 70
22:1–19 69
22:2 143
22:11 71
22:17 49, 76, 77, 96
22:17b–18 34, 49
22:18 66
22:19 71
23:2 79
23:6 49
24 66
25 – 26 93
25:12–18 32
25:12, 19 31, 34
25:13 31
25:19 31
25:19 – 35:29 32
25:21 66
25:21–23 78
26 106
26:1 70
26:1–5 71
26:3–4 66
26:3–5, 24 89
26:4, 24 76, 77
26:11, 29 106
26:23–25, 32–33 71
26:26–31 49
27:29 61
28 71
28:3 50, 77
28:3–4, 14 66
28:13–15 71
29:1–14 40
29:15–30 40
29:31 66
29:31 – 30:24 40, 66
30:25–43 40

30:27 90
30 – 36 39
31 89
31:1–55 40
31:3 89
32 89
32:1 87
32:9 69
33:1 87
33:2, 7 40
34:29 73
35 50, 51, 71
35:9–15 85
35:10 51
35:11 49, 50, 71, 76, 77
35:11–12 51, 66
35:22–26 40
35:22b 40
35:22b–26 37, 71
35:23–26 102
36 31, 78
36:1 31, 34
36:1–8 31, 32
36:9 31, 34
36:9–43 31
36:9 – 37:1 32
37 1, 41, 42, 52, 55, 57–59, 61, 79, 80, 140, 143, 144
37 – 45 9, 75
37 – 50 1, 4–9, 22, 36, 39, 40, 42–44, 57, 58, 92, 95, 98, 99, 116, 117, 121, 128, 130, 132, 133
37:1 34
37:1–17 57
37:2 31, 32, 38, 52, 54

37:2–4 54
37:2 – 50:26 32, 37
37:3 52, 53, 81, 94
37:3–4 143
37:4 60, 79, 81
37:5 79
37:7 55, 60–62
37:7–8 61
37:8 52, 54, 56, 79
37:9 52, 55, 60–62
37:10 52, 55, 60, 61
37:11 79, 128, 140
37:12 54, 61
37:12–14 52
37:13 143
37:14 60
37:15–17 80
37:18–19 143
37:18–20 79
37:19 52
37:20 2, 52, 80, 143
37:21 80
37:21–22 57, 61
37:21–28 79
37:22 80
37:23–24 81
37:24 143
37:26 80
37:26–27 57, 61, 140
37:27 108
37:28 108, 140
37:29–30 61
37:29–31 57
37:31, 32 58
37:31–33 80
37:33 58, 61, 97
37:34 79, 97
37:35 79
37:36 79, 129

37:50 85, 92, 105, 111, 116
38 41, 43, 57–59, 61, 79, 90
38 – 39 58
38:1 58
38:7, 10 41, 59
38:9 59
38:12–25 59
38:17, 25 58
38:26 58, 59
38:27–30 58
39 11, 41, 58, 59, 61, 94, 103, 129
39 – 41 9, 57, 58
39 – 47 1
39:1 55, 58
39:1–36 41
39:2 41, 59, 89, 99, 129
39:3 41, 59, 89, 129
39:3–4 116
39:4–5 28, 90
39:5 41, 59
39:6 94, 109, 116
39:9 94, 109
39:10 58, 94, 116
39:12 81, 94
39:20 55, 61
39:21 41, 59, 90, 109, 129, 130
39:23 41, 59, 90, 99, 129
40 – 41 112
40:1, 4 55
40:2 116
40:3, 5 61
40:9, 10 61
40:13 117
40:20 116
41 109–112
41:1 110

41:8 *110–112*
41:10–12 *110*
41:12 *110*
41:14 *80, 110, 116, 117*
41:15 *110*
41:25–37 *112*
41:33 *130*
41:34–37 *116*
41:38 *112*
41:38–57 *61*
41:39 *109, 130*
41:40 *90, 115*
41:41 *67*
41:42 *81, 112, 116*
41:43 *115, 116, 140*
41:45 *109*
41:46 *116, 140*
41:50–52 *58*
41:51–52 *79*
41:56, 57 *90*
42 – 44 *42*
42 – 45 *61, 80, 131*
42:1–2 *70*
42:4 *55, 60*
42:6 *62*
42:9 *61*
42:13, 32 *79*
42:15–16 *80*
42:21 *57, 97*
42:22 *80, 97*
42:24 *61*
42:36, 38 *79*
42:37 *61*
43 *72*
43:3–4 *61*
43:8 *72*
43:8–10 *59, 61*
43:14 *116*
43:26 *55, 60–62*
43:28 *55, 60, 62*

43:31 *116*
44:16–34 *61*
44:18–34 *60, 80*
44:20 *53*
44:24 *116*
44:28 *61*
44:34 *116*
45 *67, 69, 75, 85, 98, 105, 131, 140*
45:1 *116*
45:1–7 *74*
45:1–8 *104*
45:3–4 *68*
45:3a, 3b–4a *68*
45:4 *129*
45:4b *68*
45:4–8 *77, 105*
45:4–9 *41*
45:5 *68–70*
45:5–6 *68*
45:5–7 *74*
45:5, 7, 8 *69, 98*
45:5–8 *11, 68, 69, 74, 81*
45:5–11 *41*
45:6–7 *74*
45:7 *68–70, 104, 105*
45:8 *56, 67–69, 105*
45:8b *67*
45:8–9 *140*
45:8–27 *74*
45:9 *56, 68*
45:9–10 *70*
45:9–13 *68*
45:10–13a *68*
45:11 *70*
45:13b *68*
45:21 *70*
45:22 *81*
45:26 *56, 97*

45:28 *75*
46 *70, 72–74, 131*
46 – 47 *70*
46 – 50 *75*
46:1, 2–4 *71*
46:1–4 *41, 72*
46:1–27 *75*
46:2 *71*
46:3 *71, 73, 89, 114*
46:4 *85, 89*
46:5 *72, 73*
46:5–7 *72*
46:6, 7 *73*
46:8 *73, 102*
46:8–27 *72, 73*
46:26 *102*
46:27 *74, 102*
46:28 *60*
46:29 *61*
46:33–34 *72*
47:6 *90*
47:7–10 *90–92*
47:12 *73*
47:13 *75*
47:13–26 *42, 76, 92*
47:24 *73*
47:25 *42, 76, 92*
47:27 *74–76, 77, 102, 114*
48 *90*
48:3 *50*
48:4 *76, 77, 85, 87*
49 *60, 61, 90*
49:1 *57, 62*
49:8 *60, 61, 63, 97, 99*
49:8–12 *61, 63*
49:9 *61*
49:10 *57*
49:11 *61*
49:18 *41, 58*

49:22 *93*
49:22–26 *61, 93*
49:25 *50*
49:27 *61*
49:29 *85, 88*
49:29 – 50:3 *86*
49:29 – 50:26 *85*
49:30 *85*
50 *86, 87, 94*
50:1 *79*
50:2 *86*
50:3 *116*
50:4–6, 5 *86*
50:7–14 *86, 87, 113*
50:7 *87*
50:8 *73, 87*
50:9, 11, 12, 13, 14 *87*
50:15 *81*
50:15–21 *80, 86*
50:16, 17 *86*
50:19–21 *41, 81*
50:20 *11, 67, 70, 94, 98, 104, 105*
50:21 *73*
50:22–26 *86*
50:24 *37, 38, 86, 113*
50:24–25 *113, 114, 116, 119*
50:24b, 25b *88*
50:24–26 *102, 103, 138*
50:25 *86, 88, 113*
50:26 *86*

Exodus
1:1–6 *102*
1:5, 6 *1*
1:7 *76, 102*
1:8 *1, 77, 102*
3:12 *125*

Exodus (*cont.*)
7:11, 22 *112*
8.3, 14, 15 *112*
8:24 *87*
9:11 *112*
10:24, 26 *87*
12:29 *80*
12:32, 37, 38 *87*
13:18 *87*
13:19 *1, 102, 113, 138*
14:9, 17, 18, 20, 23, 26, 28 *87*
15:19 *87*
21:16 *79*
33:3, 5 *127*

Leviticus
4:3, 5, 16 *106*
6:15 *106*
14:34 *87*
25:24 *87*
26:1–30 *127*

Numbers
3:7–8 *46*
8:26 *46*
18:5–6 *46*
20:14–21 *78*
24 *47, 63*
24:5–9 *64*
24:9 *63*
24:14 *63*
24:17 *63*
24:18 *78*

Deuteronomy
18:15–18 *24*
23:7 *78*
24:7 *79*
30:1–10 *24*
32:49 *87*
34:10–12 *24*

Joshua
21:12 *87*
24:32 *1, 102, 103, 113, 138*

Judges
9:2, 6, 8 *52*

1 Samuel
2:10, 35 *106*
12:3, 5 *106*
16:6 *106*
16:11 *54*
16:12, 18 *109, 116*
17:34 *54*
24:7, 11 *106*
26:9, 11, 16, 23 *106*

2 Samuel
1:14, 16, 21 *106*
5:2 *54*
7 *127*
7:7 *54*
7:9 *48*
7:14 *143*
9 – 20 *8*
12:16–18, 22 *79*
13:18 *53*
19:22 *106*
22:51 *106*
23:1 *106*

1 Kings
8:10–13 *125*

2 Kings
8:10–13 *125*
19:31 *68*
25:27 *117*
25:27–30 *119*
25:28–30 *116*

1 Chronicles
2:2 *1, 102*
5:1 *1*
5:1–2 *12, 102*
6:42 *106*
16:22 *106*

2 Chronicles
9:26, 30 *52*
36:23 *116*

Ezra
1:1–11 *113*

Nehemiah
9:16–17 *127*

Esther
1:3 *116*
1:21 *116*
2:3–4 *116*
2:7 *109, 116*
2:12, 17, 18, 21 *116*
3:4 *116*
3:10 *116*
4:16 *116*
5:10 *116*
6:11 *116*
8:2, 6, 15 *116*
10:3 *116*

Psalms
2:2 *106*
2:7 *143*
8 *45*
18:51 *106*
20:7 *106*
22 – 23 *142*
28:1 *80*
28:8 *106*
30:3b, 4b *80*
47:10 *105*

72 *47*
81 *1*
84:10 *106*
88:5, 7 *80*
89 *47, 104*
89:39, 52 *106*
104 – 106 *103, 104*
104:22 *130*
105 *1, 5, 12, 77, 95, 102–105, 120, 123*
105:1–8 *106*
105:6 *105, 107*
105:8–11 *105*
105:9 *105*
105:13 *107*
105:14–15 *105, 106*
105:15 *106, 107*
105:16, 20–22 *77*
105:17 *1, 77, 105, 107, 113*
105:17–19 *95*
105:17–24 *67*
105:21 *105*
105:22 *130*
105:23–24 *77*
105:26, 43 *107*
105:42 *105, 106*
107 *104*
110 *104*
118 *142, 144, 145*
118:22–23 *142, 145*
132:10, 17 *106*

Proverbs
1:12 *80*
28:17 *80*

Ecclesiastes
8:1 *112*

Isaiah
5 *144, 145*
5:1–2, 5–6 *141*
6:1–3 *125*
10:11 *127*
10:20 *68, 69*
14:15, 19 *80*
16:12 *127*
19:1 *127*
21:9 *127*
24:22 *80*
31:7 *127*
37:32 *69*
38:11, 17–19 *79*
38:18 *80*
40:3–5 *115*
45:1 *106*
46:6 *127*
52:13 – 53:12
  25
63:10 *127*

Jeremiah
6:10 *127*
9:26 *127*
33:21, 26 *52*
37:16 *80*
52:31 *117*

Lamentations
4:20 *106*

Ezekiel
1:4–28 *125*
8:1–4 *125*
10:1–22 *125*
14:14, 20 *113*
26:20 *80*
28:3 *113*
28:13 *83*
31:16 *80*
32:18, 23–25,
  29–30 *80*

37:1–14 *114*
37:11–14 *103*

Daniel
1 – 2 *115*
1:3–6, 17–20
  108
1.4 *109, 116*
1.7, 8–16 *109*
1.9 *109, 116*
1.17 *109*
1:20 *112*
2 *108–111*
2 – 5 *112*
2:1 *110, 111*
2:1–11 *112*
2:2 *110, 112*
2:3 *110, 111*
2:4–11 *110*
2:12 *110, 112*
2:13 *115*
2:14, 16, 25, 26
  110
2.28–30 *111*
2.31–35 *111*
2.31–45 *112*
2.37–44 *111*
2:43 *65*
2:45 *111*
2:46, 48 *111*
2:46–49 *109*
4:8, 9, 18 *112*
5 *112*
5:11 *109, 112*
5.14 *112*
5:16, 29 *111, 112*
6:1–3 *113*
6:10 *109*
7:16 *112*
9:15 *115*
9:25 *106*
16–19 *115*
26:2 *106*

Hosea
2:14–15 *115*
11:1 *143*

Joel
2:32 *69*

Habakkuk
3:13 *106*

Zechariah
9:11 *80*
11:12–13 *140*

APOCRYPHA

1 Maccabees
2:50–61 *123*

NEW TESTAMENT

Matthew
1:17 *40*
1:1–17 *123*
1:22 *141*
2:15, 17, 23 *141*
2:18 *140*
3:17 *142*
4:3, 6 *142*
4:14 *141*
8:29 *142*
14:33 *142*
17 *141*
17:5 *142*
21:34–36 *142*
21:37 *142, 143*
21:38 *2, 143*
21:39 *143*
21:41, 43–44
  141
21:42 *141, 142*
21:45, 46 *141*
23 *141*

26:14–15 *140*
28:19 *142*

Mark
1:1, 11 *142*
3:11 *142*
5:7 *142*
9:7 *142*
10:45 *16*
12:1–12 *124*
12:6 *143, 145*
12:7, 8, 16 *143*
14:61 *142*
15:39 *142*

Luke
1:32, 35 *142*
2:40 *134, 136*
2:40–52 *130*
2:51 *140*
2:52 *136*
3:22 *142*
3:23 *140*
6:8 *136*
7:36 *136*
8:28 *142*
9:35 *142*
10:22 *142*
20:13 *143, 146*
20:14 *2, 143*
23:34, 46 *136*
24 *25*
24:46 *25*

John
5 *25*
5:46–47 *25*

Acts
2 *140*
2:23, 36 *134*
2:24, 36 *134*
2:36 *140*

Acts (*cont.*)
3:13–14 *136*
3:13–15 *134*
3:15 *134*
4:10–11 *134*
5:17, 30 *134*
5:31 *134, 136*
6 *124, 125*
6:3, 8, 10 *134*
6:8 *130, 136*
6:9 *124*
6:10 *130, 136*
6:11 *124, 125*
6:13, 14 *125*
6:13–14 *122, 124*
7 *2, 12, 17, 95, 121, 122, 124, 125, 134–136, 144, 146*
7:2 *124, 129*
7:2–16 *125, 126*
7:6–7 *126*
7.7 *125*
7.8 *128, 133*
7:9 *129, 131–133, 136*
7:9a *128, 129*
7:9b *129*
7:9–10 *95, 126*
7:9b–10 *129*

7:9–16 *121, 122, 128, 131, 132*
7:9–14 *1*
7:10 *129–132, 140*
7:11 *131–133*
7:11–13 *131*
7:12 *132*
7:13 *123, 131, 132*
7:14, 15 *132, 133*
7:14–16 *131*
7:17 *126*
7:17–45a *124, 126*
7:19, 20, 22, 35–36 *132*
7:22 *130, 136*
7:24–25, 35 *132*
7:25, 27–28, 35, 39 *132*
7:30–33, 35, 38, 44 *132*
7:35, 37 *136*
7:39 *132*
7:41 *127*
7:45b, 47, 48 *127*
7:45b–50 *124*
7:51 *127, 128, 130, 132, 135*
7:51b, 52–53 *127*
7:51–53 *127, 133*
7:51–53, 56 *127*
7:52 *127, 130, 133*

7:52–53 *127*
7:55 *127*
7:55–56 *127, 133*
7:56 *127*
7:59, 60 *136*
8 *125, 128*
9 *126, 128*
9:22 *25*
10 *129*
10:38 *130, 131, 134, 136*
13:16–41 *124*
13:45 *134*
17:15 *134*
18 *25*
18:28 *25*
23 *126*
27 *126*
28:23 *25*
30, 35, 36, 39, 44, 45 *126*
46 *127*

Romans
1:2 *26*
3:21 *26*
5 *24*
5:12–21 *135*
5:14 *24*
15:8 *26*
16:25–27 *26*

1 Corinthians
10 *24*
15:1–3 *25*

Galatians
3:8 *26*

Hebrews
11 *12, 17, 121, 123, 138, 139*
11:1 *138*
11:8–16 *138*
11:21–22 *1*
11:22 *88, 102, 121, 137*
12:1–3 *139*

1 Peter
3 *24*

Revelation
12 *124*

ADDITIONAL

1 Clement
3–6, 9–12; 17.1–19.2; 31.1–32.4 *123*

1QS
1.21–2.6 *123*

Titles in this series:

1 *Possessed by God*, David Peterson
2 *God's Unfaithful Wife*, Raymond C. Ortlund Jr
3 *Jesus and the Logic of History*, Paul W. Barnett
4 *Hear, My Son*, Daniel J. Estes
5 *Original Sin*, Henri Blocher
6 *Now Choose Life*, J. Gary Millar
7 *Neither Poverty Nor Riches*, Craig L. Blomberg
8 *Slave of Christ*, Murray J. Harris
9 *Christ, Our Righteousness*, Mark A. Seifrid
10 *Five Festal Garments*, Barry G. Webb
12 *Now My Eyes Have Seen You*, Robert S. Fyall
13 *Thanksgiving*, David W. Pao
14 *From Every People and Nation*, J. Daniel Hays
15 *Dominion and Dynasty*, Stephen G. Dempster
16 *Hearing God's Words*, Peter Adam
17 *The Temple and the Church's Mission*, G. K. Beale
18 *The Cross from a Distance*, Peter G. Bolt
19 *Contagious Holiness*, Craig L. Blomberg
20 *Shepherds After My Own Heart*, Timothy S. Laniak
21 *A Clear and Present Word*, Mark D. Thompson
22 *Adopted into God's Family*, Trevor J. Burke
23 *Sealed with an Oath*, Paul R. Williamson
24 *Father, Son and Spirit*, Andreas J. Köstenberger and Scott R. Swain
25 *God the Peacemaker*, Graham A. Cole
26 *A Gracious and Compassionate God*, Daniel C. Timmer
27 *The Acts of the Risen Lord Jesus*, Alan J. Thompson
28 *The God Who Makes Himself Known*, W. Ross Blackburn
29 *A Mouth Full of Fire*, Andrew G. Shead
30 *The God Who Became Human*, Graham A. Cole
31 *Paul and the Law*, Brian S. Rosner
32 *With the Clouds of Heaven*, James M. Hamilton Jr
33 *Covenant and Commandment*, Bradley G. Green

34 *Bound for the Promised Land*, Oren R. Martin

35 *'Return to Me'*, Mark J. Boda

36 *Identity and Idolatry*, Richard Lints

37 *Who Shall Ascend the Mountain of the Lord?*, L. Michael Morales

38 *Calling on the Name of the Lord*, J. Gary Millar

40 *The Book of Isaiah and God's Kingdom*, Andrew T. Abernethy

41 *Unceasing Kindness*, Peter H. W. Lau and Gregory Goswell

42 *Preaching in the New Testament*, Jonathan I. Griffiths

43 *God's Mediators*, Andrew S. Malone

44 *Death and the Afterlife*, Paul R. Williamson

45 *Righteous by Promise*, Karl Deenick

46 *Finding Favour in the Sight of God*, Richard P. Belcher Jr

47 *Exalted Above the Heavens*, Peter C. Orr

48 *All Things New*, Brian J. Tabb

49 *The Feasts of Repentance*, Michael J. Ovey

50 *Including the Stranger*, David G. Firth

51 *Canon, Covenant and Christology*, Matthew Barrett

52 *Biblical Theology According to the Apostles*, Chris Bruno, Jared Compton and Kevin McFadden

53 *Salvation to the Ends of the Earth* (2nd edn), Andreas J. Köstenberger with T. Desmond Alexander

54 *The Servant of the Lord and His Servant People*, Matthew S. Harmon

55 *Changed into His Likeness*, J. Gary Millar

56 *Piercing Leviathan*, Eric Ortlund

57 *Now and Not Yet*, Dean R. Ulrich

58 *The Glory of God and Paul*, Christopher W. Morgan and Robert A. Peterson

59 *From Prisoner to Prince*, Samuel Emadi

An index of Scripture references for all the volumes may be found at http://www.thegospelcoalition.org/resources/nsbt.